*Microsoft*

# Step by Step

## Microsoft®
# Word
## Version 2002

 Microsoft® Office XP Application

D1404380

Perspection, Inc.

1 Creating Documents

2 Changing Text

3 Changing Document Appearance

4 Proofreading and Printing

5 Tables and Columns

6 Graphics and Drawings

7 Charts

8 Collaborating with Others

9 Web Documents

10 Customizing Word

11 Form Letters and Labels

12 Forms

13 Footnotes and Bookmarks

14 Contents and Indexes

PUBLISHED BY
Microsoft Press
A Division of Microsoft Corporation
One Microsoft Way
Redmond, Washington 98052-6399

Library of Congress Cataloging-in-Publication Data
Microsoft Word Version 2002 Step by Step / Perspection, Inc.
      p. cm.
   Includes index.
   ISBN 0-7356-1295-1
   1. Microsoft Word.  2. Word processing.  I. Perspection, Inc.

  Z52.5.M52 M535  2001
  652.5'5369--dc21                            2001030474

Printed and bound in the United States of America.

4 5 6 7 8 9   QWT   7 6 5 4 3 2

Distributed in Canada by H.B. Fenn and Company Ltd.

A CIP catalogue record for this book is available from the British Library.

Microsoft Press books are available through booksellers and distributors worldwide. For further information about international editions, contact your local Microsoft Corporation office or contact Microsoft
Press International directly at fax (425) 936-7329. Visit our Web site at mspress.microsoft.com. Send
comments to *mspinput@microsoft.com*.

FrontPage, Microsoft, MS-DOS, NetMeeting, Outlook, PowerPoint, SharePoint, Visual Basic, Windows,
and Windows NT are either registered trademarks or trademarks of Microsoft Corporation in the United
States and/or other countries. Other product and company names mentioned herein may be the trademarks of
their respective owners.

The example companies, organizations, products, domain names, e-mail addresses, logos, people, places,
and events depicted herein are fictitious. No association with any real company, organization, product,
domain name, e-mail address, logo, person, place, or event is intended or should be inferred.

**For Perspection, Inc.**
**Managing Editors:** Marjorie Hunt and
  Steve Johnson
**Authors:** Jane Pedicini, Jill Batistack, and Ed Dille
**Developmental Editor:** Lisa Ruffolo
**Production Editors:** Tracy Teyler,
  Beth Teyler, and Virginia Felix-Simmons
**Copy Editor:** Lisa Ruffolo
**Technical Editors:** Kristy Thielen and
  Melinda Lankford
**Indexer:** Michael Brackney of Savage Indexing

**For Microsoft Press**
**Acquisitions Editor:** Kong Cheung

Body Part No. X08-06188

# Contents

## 1   Creating a Document    1

## 2   Changing the Look of Text in a Document    22

## 3   Changing the Look of a Document    44

Contents

# 9 Working with Documents on the Web 150

# 10 Customizing Word for the Way You Work 168

# 11 Creating Form Letters and Labels 186

# 12 Creating Forms 208

# 13 Working with Footnotes and Bookmarks 222

# 14 Working with Tables of Contents and Indexes 240

# What's New in Microsoft Word 2002

You'll notice some changes as soon as you start Microsoft Word 2002. The toolbars and menu bar have a new look, and there's a new task pane on the right side of your screen. But the features that are new or greatly improved in this version of Word go beyond just changes in appearance. Some changes won't be apparent to you until you start using the program.

new for
**Office**XP

To help you quickly identify features that are new or greatly enhanced with this version, this book uses the icon in the margin whenever those features are discussed or shown. If you want to learn about only the new features of the program, you can skim through the book, completing only those topics that show this icon.

The following table lists the new features that you might be interested in, as well as the chapters in which those features are discussed.

| To learn how to | Using this new feature | See |
| --- | --- | --- |
| Quickly access commonly grouped commands | Task pane | Chapter 1, page 3 |
| Quickly access Help by asking a question | Ask A Question box | Chapter 1, page 4 |
| Open and repair recovered documents | Document Recovery task pane | Chapter 1, page 9 |
| Display file format information about a document | Show document format | Chapter 1, page 10 |
| Select text in different places within a document | Select nonadjacent text | Chapter 1, page 14 |
| Quickly access multiple items on the Office Clipboard | Office Clipboard task pane | Chapter 1, page 15 |
| Have more than one user edit the same document | Multiuser editing | Chapter 1, page 16 |
| Show formatting for current text selection | Reveal Formatting task pane | Chapter 2, page 24 |
| Perform common tasks associated with information, such as inserting the date and time and recognizing names and e-mail recipients | Smart Tags | Chapter 2, page 29 |

*(continued)*

| To learn how to | Using this new feature | See |
|---|---|---|
| Show or hide the white space between pages | White space between pages | Chapter 2, page 36 |
| Define a style for a bulleted or numbered list | List styles | Chapter 2, page 42 |
| Quickly create and apply styles and formatting to text | Styles and Formatting task pane | Chapter 3, page 56 |
| Translate text into other languages | Translate text | Chapter 4, page 68 |
| Change AutoFit settings | Selection handle | Chapter 5, page 76 |
| Define a style for a table | Table styles | Chapter 5, page 82 |
| Create diagrams | Diagram | Chapter 6, page 94 |
| Create pictures or text for the background of a document | Watermarks | Chapter 6, page 97 |
| Draw shapes and objects in a document | Drawing canvas | Chapter 6, page 107 |
| Insert and change comments | Revision balloons | Chapter 8, page 130 |
| Display changes in a document by reviewer | Display for Review and Show lists | Chapter 8, page 131 |
| Merge comments and revisions from multiple reviewers | Compare and merge documents | Chapter 8, page 136 |
| Track changes in a document | Reviewing toolbar | Chapter 8, page 139 |
| Password-protect a document | Password protection | Chapter 8, page 144 |
| Send a document for review using e-mail | Send for review | Chapter 8, page 147 |
| Create an optimized Web page | Filtered Web page | Chapter 9, page 152 |
| Save all the elements of a Web site as a single document | Web archive | Chapter 9, page 152 |
| Add a collection of hyperlinks to pages in your Web site | Link bar | Chapter 9, page 160 |
| Add an electronic secure stamp of authentication to a document | Digital signature | Chapter 9, page 163 |
| Create a form letter using mail merge | Mail Merge task pane | Chapter 11, page 190 |
| Display the number of characters, words, paragraphs, or pages in a document | Word count | Chapter 13, page 239 |

For more information about the Word product, see *http://www.microsoft.com/office/xp*.

# Getting Help

Every effort has been made to ensure the accuracy of this book and the contents of its CD-ROM. If you do run into problems, please contact the appropriate source for help and assistance.

## Getting Help with This Book and Its CD-ROM

If your question or issue concerns the content of this book or its companion CD-ROM, please first search the online Microsoft Knowledge Base, which provides support information for known errors in or corrections to this book, at the following Web site:

*http://mspress.microsoft.com/support/search.htm*

If you do not find your answer at the online Knowledge Base, send your comments or questions to Microsoft Press Technical Support at:

*mspinput@microsoft.com*

## Getting Help with Microsoft Word 2002

If your question is about a Microsoft software product, including Word, and not about the content of this Microsoft Press book, please search the Microsoft Knowledge Base at:

*http://support.microsoft.com/directory*

In the United States, Microsoft software product support issues not covered by the Microsoft Knowledge Base are addressed by Microsoft Product Support Services. The Microsoft software support options available from Microsoft Product Support Services are listed at:

*http://support.microsoft.com/directory*

Outside the United States, for support information specific to your location, please refer to the Worldwide Support menu on the Microsoft Product Support Services Web site for the site specific to your country:

*http://support.microsoft.com/directory*

# Using the Book's CD-ROM

The CD-ROM inside the back cover of this book contains all the practice files you'll use as you work through the exercises in this book. By using practice files, you won't waste time creating samples and typing document information—instead, you can jump right in and concentrate on learning how to use Microsoft Word 2002.

**Important**

This book does not contain the Word 2002 software. You should purchase and install that program before using this book.

## System Requirements

To use this book, you will need:

- **Computer/Processor**

  Computer with a Pentium 133-megahertz (MHz) or higher processor

- **Memory**

  RAM requirements depend on the operating system used:

  - **Windows 98, or Windows 98 Second Edition**

    24 MB of RAM plus an additional 8 MB of RAM for each Office program (such as Microsoft Word) running simultaneously

  - **Windows Me, or Microsoft Windows NT**

    32 MB of RAM plus an additional 8 MB of RAM for each Office program (such as Microsoft Word) running simultaneously

  - **Windows 2000 Professional**

    64 MB of RAM plus an additional 8 MB of RAM for each Office program (such as Microsoft Word) running simultaneously

- **Hard Disk**

  Hard disk space requirements will vary depending on configuration; custom installation choices may require more or less hard disk space.

  - 245 MB of available hard disk space with 115 MB on the hard disk where the operating system is installed. (Users without Windows 2000, Windows Me, or Office 2000 Service Release 1 [SR-1] require an extra 50 MB of hard disk space for System Files Update.)

■ An additional 6 MB of hard drive space is required for installing the practice files.

■ **Operating System**

Windows 98, Windows 98 Second Edition, Windows Millennium Edition (Windows Me), Windows NT 4.0 with Service Pack 6 (SP6) or later, or Windows 2000 or later. (On systems running Windows NT 4.0 with SP6, Microsoft Internet Explorer must be upgraded to at least version 4.01 with SP1.)

■ **Drive**

CD-ROM drive

■ **Display**

Super VGA (800 × 600) or higher-resolution monitor with 256 colors

■ **Peripherals**

Microsoft Mouse, Microsoft IntelliMouse, or compatible pointing device

■ **Software**

Microsoft Word 2002, Microsoft Excel 2002, Microsoft Outlook 2002, and Microsoft Internet Explorer 5 or later

# Installing the Practice Files

You need to install the practice files on your hard disk before you use them in the chapters' exercises. Follow these steps to prepare the CD's files for your use:

1    Insert the CD-ROM into the CD-ROM drive of your computer.

A menu screen appears.

**Important**

If the menu screen does not appear, start Windows Explorer. In the left pane, locate the icon for your CD-ROM and click this icon. In the right pane, double-click the **StartCD** file.

2    Click **Install Practice Files**.

3    Click **OK** in the initial message box.

4    If you want to install the practice files to a location other than the default folder (C:\SBS\Word), click the **Change Folder** button, select the new drive and path, and then click **OK**.

5    Click the **Continue** button to install the selected practice files.

6    After the practice files have been installed, click **OK**.

Within the installation folder are subfolders for each chapter in the book.

7    Remove the CD-ROM from the CD-ROM drive, and return it to the envelope at the back of the book.

# Using the Practice Files

Each chapter's introduction lists the files that are needed for that chapter and explains any file preparation that you need to take care of before you start working through the chapter.

Each topic in the chapter explains how and when to use any practice files. The file or files that you'll need are indicated in the margin at the beginning of the procedure above the CD icon:

OpenDoc

The following table lists each chapter's practice files.

| Chapter | Folder | Files |
|---------|--------|-------|
| 1 | CreatingDoc | ExistDoc, OpenDoc, EditDoc, and ReplaceText |
| 2 | FormattingText | FormatText, FormatAuto, FormatPara, and CreateList |
| 3 | FormattingDoc | FormatPage, FormatStyle, and FormatTheme |
| 4 | ProofingPrint | SpellCheck and PreviewPrint |
| 5 | AddingTables | CreateTable, FormatTable, DataTable, InsertTable, and CreateColumn |
| 6 | Drawing | OrgChart, InsertPics, Gardenco, AlignPics, WordArt, and DrawShape |
| 7 | Charting | AddChart, ModChart, ImportData, and FileImport |
| 8 | Collaborating | TrackChange, CompareMerge, Merge1, Merge2, RevComment, ProtectDoc, Send, Attach1, and Attach2 |
| 9 | WorkingWeb | CreateWeb, OtherLogos, ModWebDoc, AddSignature, WebSignature |
| 10 | Customizing | CustomMenu, CustomToolbar, RecordMacro, ModifyMacro |
| 11 | MergingData | FormLetter, Data, NewFormLtr, Data2, FinalFormLtr, MergeLtr, and Data3 |
| 12 | CreatingForms | CreateForm and UseForm |

*(continued)*

| Chapter | Folder | Files |
|---------|--------|-------|
| 13 | CreatingNotes | Footnote, ReviseNotes, SepLine, Bookmark, and Master |
| 14 | CreatingTOC | TabContents, MarkEntry, and CreateIndex |

# Uninstalling the Practice Files

After you finish working through this book, you should uninstall the practice files to free up hard disk space.

**1** On the Windows taskbar, click the **Start** button, point to **Settings**, and then click **Control Panel**.

**2** Double-click the **Add/Remove Programs** icon.

**3** In the list of installed programs, click **Microsoft Word 2002 SBS Files**, and then click **Add/Remove**. (If you're using Windows 2000 Professional, click the **Remove** or **Change/Remove** button.)

**4** Click **Yes** when the confirmation dialog box appears.

**Important**

If you need additional help installing or uninstalling the practice files, please see the section "Getting Help" earlier in this book. Microsoft's product support does not provide support for this book or its CD-ROM.

# Conventions and Features

You can save time when you use this book by understanding how the Step by Step series shows special instructions, keys to press, buttons to click, and so on.

| Convention | Meaning |
|---|---|
| **1**<br>**2** | Numbered steps guide you through hands-on exercises in each topic. |
| ● | A round bullet indicates an exercise that has only one step. |
| (CD icon) | This icon at the beginning of a chapter lists the files that the lesson will use and explains any file preparation that needs to take place before starting the lesson. |
| FileName<br>(CD icon) | Practice files that you'll need to use in a topic's procedure are shown above the CD icon. |
| W2002-3-1<br>(MOUS icon) | This icon indicates a section that covers a MOUS exam objective. The numbers above the icon refer to the specific MOUS objective. |
| new for<br>**Office**XP | This icon indicates a new or greatly improved feature in this version of Microsoft Word. |
| **Tip** | This section provides a helpful hint or shortcut that makes working through a task easier. |
| Important | This section points out information that you need to know to complete the procedure. |
| **Troubleshooting** | This section shows you how to fix a common problem. |
| Save<br>(button icon) | When a button is referenced in a topic, a picture of the button appears in the margin area with a label. |
| Alt + Tab | A plus sign (+) between two key names means that you must hold down the first key while you press the other key. For example, "Press Alt + Tab" means that you hold down the Alt key while you press Tab. |

*(continued)*

| Convention | Meaning |
|---|---|
| **Black Boldface type** | Program features that you click or press are shown in black boldface type. |
| **Blue Boldface type** | Terms that are explained in the glossary at the end of the book are shown in blue boldface type within the chapter. |
| **Red Boldface type** | Text that you are supposed to type appears in red boldface type in the procedures. |

# MOUS Objectives

Each Microsoft Office User Specialist (MOUS) certification level has a set of objectives, which are organized into broader skill sets. To prepare for the MOUS certification exam, you should confirm that you can meet its respective objectives.

This book will prepare you fully for the MOUS exam at either the core or the expert level because it addresses all the objectives for both exams. Throughout this book, content that pertains to a MOUS objective is identified with the MOUS logo and objective number in the margin:

W2002-3-2

## Core MOUS Objectives

| Objective | Skill | Page |
|-----------|-------|------|
| **W2002-1** | **Inserting and Modifying Text** | |
| W2002-1-1 | Insert, modify, and move text and symbols | 6–9, 14–18, 19–21, 28–33, 63–68 |
| W2002-1-2 | Apply and modify text formats | 23–27, 28–33 |
| W2002-1-3 | Correct spelling and grammar usage | 63–68 |
| W2002-1-4 | Apply font and text effects | 23–27 |
| W2002-1-5 | Enter and format date and time | 28–33 |
| W2002-1-6 | Apply character styles | 23–27 |
| **W2002-2** | **Creating and Modifying Paragraphs** | |
| W2002-2-1 | Modify paragraph formats | 33–40 |
| W2002-2-2 | Set and modify tabs | 33–40 |
| W2002-2-3 | Apply bullet, outline, and numbering format to paragraphs | 41–43 |
| W2002-2-4 | Apply paragraph styles | 56–59 |
| **W2002-3** | **Formatting Documents** | |
| W2002-3-1 | Create and modify a header and footer | 50–55 |
| W2002-3-2 | Apply and modify columns settings | 89–91 |

*(continued)*

**xvii**

| Objective | Skill | Page |
|---|---|---|
| W2002-3-3 | Modify document layout and Page Setup options | 50–55 |
| W2002-3-4 | Create and modify tables | 76–81, 82–85 |
| W2002-3-5 | Preview and print documents, envelopes, and labels | 69–73 |
| **W2002-4** | **Managing Documents** | |
| W2002-4-1 | Manage files and folders for documents | 6–9 |
| W2002-4-2 | Create documents using templates | 46–49 |
| W2002-4-3 | Save documents using different names and file formats | 6–9, 10 |
| **W2002-5** | **Working with Graphics** | |
| W2002-5-1 | Insert images and graphics | 96–101, 104–106 |
| W2002-5-2 | Create and modify diagrams and charts | 93–96, 113–117, 118–124 |
| **W2002-6** | **Workgroup Collaboration** | |
| W2002-6-1 | Compare and merge documents | 136–139 |
| W2002-6-2 | Insert, view, and edit comments | 139–143 |
| W2002-6-3 | Convert documents into Web pages | 152–159 |

# Expert MOUS Objectives

| Objective | Skill | Page |
|---|---|---|
| **W2002e-1** | **Customizing Paragraphs** | |
| W2002e-1-1 | Control pagination | 50–55 |
| W2002e-1-2 | Sort paragraphs in list and tables | 41–43, 76–81 |
| **W2002e-2** | **Formatting Documents** | |
| W2002e-2-1 | Create and format document sections | 50–55 |
| W2002e-2-2 | Create and apply character and paragraph styles | 56–59 |
| W2002e-2-3 | Create and update document indexes and tables of contents, figures, and authorities | 242–246, 246–250, 251–254 |
| W2002e-2-4 | Create cross-references | 246–250 |
| W2002e-2-5 | Add and revise endnotes and footnotes | 224–227, 227–232 |
| W2002e-2-6 | Create and manage master documents and subdocuments | 236–239 |
| W2002e-2-7 | Move within documents | 234–236 |
| W2002e-2-8 | Create and modify forms using various form controls | 210–216, 216–221 |
| W2002e-2-9 | Create forms and prepare forms for distribution | 216–221 |

*(continued)*

# Taking a MOUS Exam

As desktop computing technology advances, more employers rely on the objectivity and consistency of technology certification when screening, hiring, and training employees to ensure the competence of these professionals. As an employee, you can use technology certification to prove that you meet the standards set by your current or potential employer. The Microsoft Office User Specialist (MOUS) program is the only Microsoft-approved certification program designed to assist employees in validating their competence using Microsoft Office applications.

## About the MOUS program

A Microsoft Office User Specialist is an individual who has certified his or her skills in one or more of the Microsoft Office desktop applications of Microsoft Word, Microsoft Excel, Microsoft PowerPoint, Microsoft Outlook, Microsoft Access, Microsoft FrontPage, or Microsoft Project. The MOUS program typically offers certification exams at the "core" and "expert" skill levels. (The availability of Microsoft Office User Specialist certification exams varies by application, application version, and language. Visit *http://www.mous.net* for exam availability.) The Microsoft Office User Specialist Program is the only Microsoft-approved program in the world for certifying proficiency in Microsoft Office desktop applications and Microsoft Project. This certification can be a valuable asset in any job search or career advancement.

### What Does This Logo Mean?

APPROVED COURSEWARE

It means this courseware has been approved by the Microsoft Office User Specialist Program to be among the finest available for learning Word 2002. It also means that upon completion of this courseware, you may be prepared to become a Microsoft Office User Specialist.

## Selecting a MOUS Certification Level

In selecting the MOUS certification(s) level that you would like to pursue, you should assess the following:

- The Office application and version(s) of the application with which you are familiar
- The length of time you have used the application
- Whether you have had formal or informal training

Candidates for the core-level MOUS certification exams are expected to successfully complete a wide range of standard business tasks, such as formatting a document. Successful candidates generally have six or more months of experience with the application, including either formal instructor-led training with a MOUS Authorized Instructor or self-study using MOUS-approved books, guides, or interactive computer-based materials.

Candidates for expert-level certification, by comparison, are expected to complete more complex business-oriented assignments utilizing the application's advanced functionality, such as importing data and recording macros. Successful candidates generally have two or more years of experience with the application, again including formal instructor-led training with a MOUS Authorized Instructor or self-study using MOUS-approved materials.

# MOUS Exam Objectives

Every MOUS certification exam is developed from a list of exam objectives, which are derived from studies of how the Office application is actually used in the workplace. Because these objectives dictate the scope of each exam, they provide you with critical information on how to prepare for MOUS certification.

MOUS Approved Courseware, including the Microsoft Press Step by Step series, is reviewed and approved on the basis of its coverage of the MOUS exam objectives.

# The Exam Experience

The MOUS certification exams are unique in that they are performance-based examinations that allow you to interact with a "live" version of the Office application as you complete a series of assigned tasks. All the standard menus, toolbars, and keyboard shortcuts are available—even the Help menu. MOUS exams for Office XP applications consist of 25 to 35 questions, each of which requires you to complete one or more tasks using the Office application for which you are seeking certification. For example:

Prepare the document for publication as a Web page by completing the following three tasks:

1   Convert the memo to a Web page.
2   Title the page **Revised Company Policy**.
3   Name the memo **Policy Memo.htm**.

The duration of MOUS exams ranges from 45 to 60 minutes, depending on the application. Passing percentages range from 70 to 80 percent correct.

## The Exam Interface and Controls

After you fill out a series of information screens, the testing software starts the exam and the respective Office application. You will see the exam interface and controls, including the test question, in the dialog box in the lower right corner of the screen.

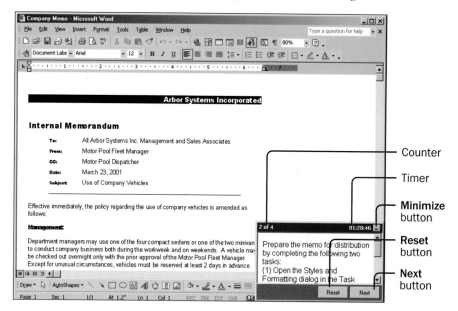

- If the exam dialog box gets in the way of your work, you can hide it by clicking the **Minimize** button in the upper right corner, or you can drag it to another position on the screen.

- The timer starts when the first question appears on your screen and displays the remaining exam time. The timer will not count the time required for the exam to be loaded between questions. It keeps track of only the time you spend answering questions. If the timer and the counter are distracting, click the timer to remove the display.

- The counter tracks how many questions you have completed and how many remain.

- The **Reset** button allows you to restart work on a question if you think you have made an error. The **Reset** button will *not* restart the entire exam or extend the exam time limit.

- When you complete a question, click the **Next** button to move to the next question.

## Important

It is not possible to move back to a previous question on the exam.

# Test-Taking Tips

- Follow all instructions provided in each question completely and accurately.

- Enter requested information as it appears in the instructions but without duplicating the formatting. For example, all text and values that you will be asked to enter will appear in the instructions as **bold** and **underlined**; however, you should enter the information without applying this formatting unless you are specifically instructed to do otherwise.

- Close all dialog boxes before proceeding to the next exam question unless you are specifically instructed otherwise.

- There is no need to save your work before moving on to the next question unless you are specifically instructed otherwise.

- Do not cut and paste information from the exam interface into the application.

- For questions that ask you to print a document, spreadsheet, chart, report, slide, and so forth, nothing will actually be printed.

- Responses are scored based on the result of your work, not the method you use to achieve that result (unless a specific method is explicitly required), and not the time you take to complete the question. Extra keystrokes or mouse clicks do not count against your score.

- If your computer becomes unstable during the exam (for example, if the application's toolbars or the mouse no longer functions) or if a power outage occurs, contact a testing center administrator immediately. The administrator will then restart the computer, and the exam will return to the point before the interruption occurred.

## Certification

At the conclusion of the exam, you will receive a score report, which you can print with the assistance of the testing center administrator. If your score meets or exceeds the minimum required score, you will also be mailed a printed certificate within approximately 14 days.

# For More Information

To learn more about becoming a Microsoft Office User Specialist, visit *http://www.mous.net*

To purchase a Microsoft Office User Specialist certification exam, visit *http://www.DesktopIQ.com*

To learn about other Microsoft Office User Specialist approved courseware from Microsoft Press, visit *http://mspress.microsoft.com/certification/mous/*

**Create a document,**
page 6

**Work with an existing document,**
page 10

**Edit a document,**
page 14

**Replace text in a document,**
page 19

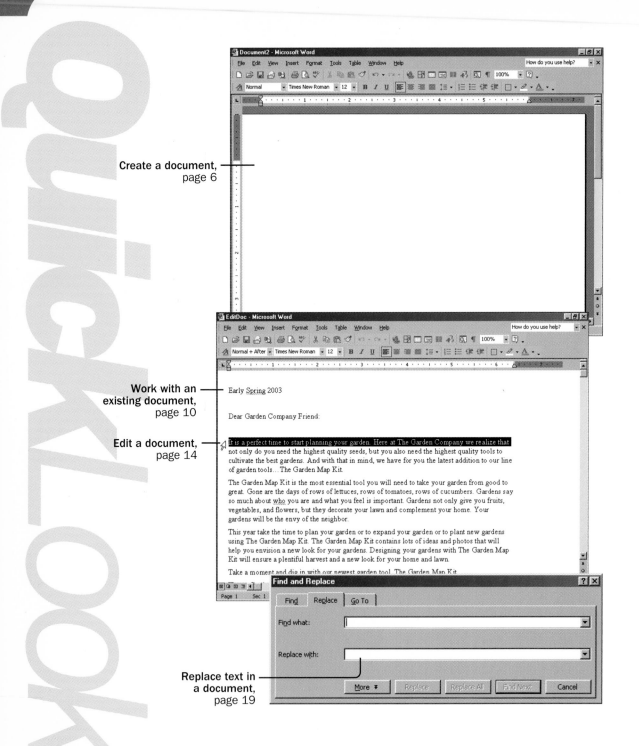

# Chapter 1
# Creating a Document

**After completing this chapter, you will be able to:**

✔   Get started with Word.

✔   Create a document.

✔   Work with an existing document.

✔   Edit a document.

✔   Replace text in a document.

**Word processing** is using a computer program to create, edit, and produce text documents. Word-processing programs help you create professional-quality documents because they let you type and format text, correct errors, and preview your work before you print or distribute a document.

Microsoft Word is a word-processing program that you can use to compose and update a wide range of business and personal documents. In addition, Word offers many **desktop-publishing** features that let you enhance the appearance of documents so that they are appealing and easy to read. Whether you need to create a letter, memo, fax, annual report, newsletter, or book, Word has the power and flexibility to produce professional documents quickly and easily.

In this chapter, you'll create and edit documents for The Garden Company, a business that provides supplies to gardeners. You'll start by entering text to create a document, and then you'll save the document as a file. You'll open other documents to navigate and switch between them. As you save a document with a new file name, you'll also create a folder for the file. Finally, you'll edit a document by inserting and deleting text, moving and copying text, and finding and replacing text.

This chapter uses the practice files ExistDoc, EditDoc, OpenDoc, and ReplaceText that you installed from this book's CD-ROM. For details about installing the practice files, see "Using the Book's CD-ROM" at the beginning of this book.

**Important**

If you haven't done so yet, you should install the book's practice files so that you can work through the exercises in this chapter. You can find instructions for installing the practice files in the "Using the Book's CD-ROM" section at the beginning of the book.

# Getting Started with Word

When you start Word, the Word program window opens. This window contains many of the same menus, tools, and other features that every Microsoft Office XP program has and some that are unique to Word. You enter and edit text in the Word document window, which is part of the Word program window. The insertion point, the blinking vertical line that appears in the document window, indicates where the text will appear when you type.

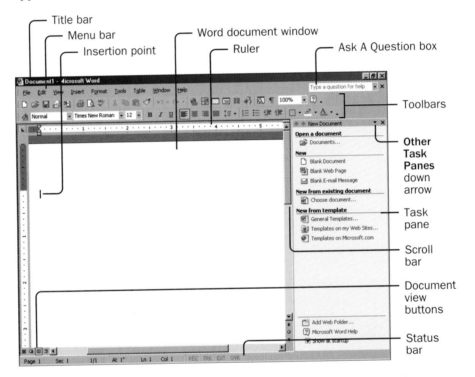

## Tip

Word uses personalized menus and toolbars to reduce the number of menu commands and toolbar buttons that you see on the screen and to display the ones that you use most often. When you click a menu name, a short menu appears, containing the commands that you use most often. To make the complete long menu appear, you can leave the pointer over the menu name for several seconds, double-click the menu name, or click the menu name and then click the small double arrow at the bottom of the short menu. When the long menu is open, the commands that did not appear on the short menu are light gray.

## Important

The default setting for the Standard and Formatting toolbars is for them to share one row, which prevents you from seeing all the buttons. The **Toolbar Options** down arrow at the end of the toolbar gives you access to the other buttons. If a button mentioned in this book doesn't appear on a toolbar, click the **Toolbar Options** down arrow on that toolbar to display the rest of its buttons. To make it easier for you to find buttons, the Standard and Formatting toolbars in this book appear on two rows. To change your settings to match the screens in this book, click **Customize** on the **Tools** menu, select the **Show Standard and Formatting toolbars on two rows** check box on the **Options** tab, and then click **Close**.

At the bottom of the document window are view buttons that allow you to look at a document in different ways. **Normal view** is the default editing view, which you use to write and edit your documents. **Web Layout view** shows your document as it appears as a Web page. This view is useful for viewing and editing text and graphics designed for use in a Web browser. **Print Layout view** shows your document as it appears on the printed page. This view is useful for changing page and column boundaries, editing headers and footers, and working with drawing objects. **Outline view** shows the structure of the document, which consists of headings and body text. This view is useful for viewing, moving, copying, and reorganizing text.

Task pane
new for
**Office**XP

Word organizes commands for common tasks in the **task pane**, a small window next to your document that opens when you need it. For example, when you start Word, you see the **New Document** task pane, which includes commands for opening and creating documents. Use the **New Document** task pane to open a saved or blank document, to create a document based on an existing one, or to create a document from a **template**, a file containing structure and style settings that help you create a specific type of document, such as a memo or resumé. You also can show or hide any task pane when you like. If you want to use a task pane and the one that you want does not appear, you can manually show the task pane and then select the specific task pane that you want from the **Other Task Panes** menu on the task pane. If you no longer need the task pane, you can hide it to free up valuable screen space in the program window. On the **View** menu, click **Task Pane**; clicking the command hides the task pane if it is currently displayed or shows it if it is currently hidden.

## Tip

The task pane opens each time you start Word and closes when you open a document. If you do not want the task pane to appear each time you start Word, clear the **Show at Startup** check box in the task pane.

When you have a question about using Word, you can save time by using the Ask A Question box rather than searching the table of contents or index in online Help. After you type a question or keyword and press the ⌷Enter⌷ key, Word lists Help topics so that you can choose the one that answers your question. Another way to get help is to use the **Office Assistant**. The Office Assistant offers tips for completing your task, such as creating and formatting a letter. For complete access to Help topics, you can open the Help window and use its table of contents, index, and Answer Wizard, or you can visit the Microsoft Web site to find Help information.

In this exercise, you start Word, close the **New Document** task pane, and ask a question about online Help.

**1** On the taskbar, click **Start**, point to **Programs**, and then click **Microsoft Word**.

The Word window opens with a blank document and the **New Document** task pane in the document window.

## Tip

Another way to start Word and create a new document is to click the **New Office Document** command at the top of the **Start** menu. When the **New Office Document** dialog box appears, double-click the **Blank Document** icon.

**2** In the title bar of the **New Document** task pane, click the **Other Task Panes** down arrow.

The **Other Task Panes** menu opens.

**3** Press the ⌷Esc⌷ key, or click an empty place in the document.

Word closes the **Other Task Panes** menu.

Close

❌

**4** Click the **Close** button in the **New Document** task pane.

The **New Document** task pane closes.

**5** On the **View** menu, click **Task Pane**.

The **New Document** task pane opens.

**6** On the right side of the menu bar, click in the Ask A Question box.

**7** Type **How do you use help?**, and then press ⌷Enter⌷.

A menu appears with Help topics that relate to the question that you typed.

**8** Click **About getting help while you work**.

The Microsoft Word Help window opens.

**9** Click the topic **Ask a Question box**.

The Microsoft Word Help window displays more information about the Ask A Question box.

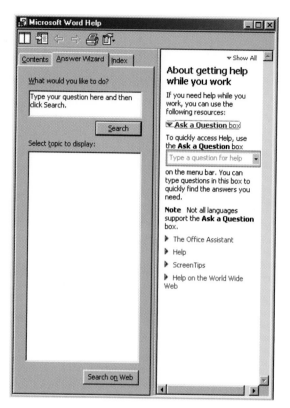

Close

**10** Click the **Close** button to close the Microsoft Word Help window.

**11** On the **Help** menu, click **Show the Office Assistant**.

The animated paper clip Office Assistant appears.

**12** Click the **Office Assistant**.

A yellow help box appears, as shown in the following illustration:

You can type a question in the box, and then click **Search** or click a Help topic provided.

**13** Right-click the Office Assistant, and then click **Hide** on the shortcut menu to hide the Office Assistant.

## Tip

To turn off the Office Assistant and use the Microsoft Help window or the Ask A Question box, right-click the **Office Assistant**, click **Options**, clear the **Use the Office Assistant** check box, and then click **OK**. On the **Help** menu, click **Microsoft Word Help**. To turn on the Office Assistant again, click **Show the Office Assistant** on the **Help** menu.

# Creating a Document

W2002-1-1
W2002-4-1
W2002-4-3

Creating a Word document is as simple as typing text. The insertion point indicates where the text will appear in the document. When the text you're typing goes beyond the right margin, Word "wraps" the text to the next line. **Word wrap,** a common feature of word processing and desktop publishing programs, means that pressing [Enter] starts a new paragraph, not a new line.

The text that you type appears in the document window and is stored by the computer, but only temporarily. If you want to keep a copy of the text, you must save the document to a **file**. You specify a name and location for the file. You can then retrieve the file later to continue working on the document.

Create New
Folder

To save a new document in Word, you click the **Save** button on the Standard toolbar. The first time that you save a document, you use the **Save As** dialog box to enter a file name and indicate where you want to save the file. To keep your documents organized and easily accessible, you can store them in folders that you create. You can store related documents in a single folder. To create a new folder, you click the **Create New Folder** button in the **Save As** dialog box.

Save

After you save a document once using the **Save As** dialog box, you can save changes that you make by clicking the **Save** button on the Standard toolbar. In other words, the newer version overwrites the original version. If you want to keep both the original file and the version with your recent changes, you click the **Save As** command on the **File** menu to save the new version with a new name. You can save the document with the new name in the same folder as the original or in a new folder, but you cannot store two documents in the same folder if the documents have the same name.

The Garden Company is preparing a new garden supply catalog. The inside cover of the catalog will need some text that describes the new catalog's theme, which is planning a garden.

In this exercise, you enter text in a document and then save your new document.

New Blank
Document

**1** On the Standard toolbar, click the **New Blank Document** button.

A new document window opens.

**2** With the insertion point at the top of the new document, type **Gardeners, Get Your Garden Tools Ready!**, and then press `Enter`.

The text appears in the new document.

**3** Press `Enter` again to insert a blank line below the heading.

**4** Type **With spring just around the corner, let's start thinking flowers and vegetables. Let's start planning for this year's garden. Let's start celebrating blue-ribbon zinnias and zucchini. Let's get your garden tools ready.**

Notice that you did not need to press `Enter` when the insertion point reached the right margin because the text wrapped to the left margin.

**Important**

If a wavy red or green line appears under a word or phrase, Word is flagging text that it does not recognize as a possible spelling or grammar error. If a wavy blue line appears under a word or phrase, Word is detecting inconsistent formatting. If a purple dotted line appears under a word or phrase, Word is displaying a Smart Tag, which recognizes certain types of text as data that you can use with other programs. For example, Word tags a person's name as data that you can add to an electronic address book. For now, ignore any errors and Smart Tags.

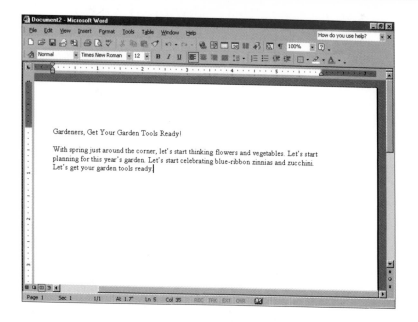

Save

**5**  On the Standard toolbar, click the **Save** button.

The **Save As** dialog box appears and displays the My Documents folder as the open folder.

## Tip

To help you locate the drive where you want to store a new folder and file, you can click the **Up One Level** button to move up a level in the hierarchy of folders, or you can use the Places Bar to move to another location on your computer. The **Places Bar** on the left side of the **Save As** and **Open** dialog boxes provides quick access to commonly used locations for storing and opening files. For instance, to save a file to a floppy disk, you click the **Desktop** icon on the **Places Bar**, double-click the **My Computer** icon, and then double-click **3½ Floppy (A:)**.

**6**  Click the **Save in** down arrow, and then click your hard disk, typically drive C.

**7**  In the list of file and folder names, double-click the **SBS** folder, and then double-click the **Word** folder.

The contents of the Word folder appear in the **Save As** dialog box.

**8**  Double-click the **CreatingDoc** folder.

The contents of the CreatingDoc folder appear in the **Save As** dialog box. You can see that the word *Gardeners*, the first word in the document, appears in the **File name** box.

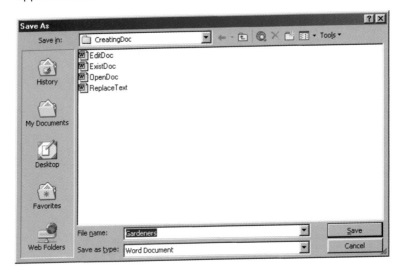

## Tip

Word uses the first few characters (or words) in the document to suggest a file name. You can accept this suggested name or type a new one. Depending on your Windows setup, file names might appear with an extension, which is a dot followed by a three-letter program identifier. For Word, the extension is .doc.

Create New
Folder

**9** Click the **Create New Folder** button.

The **New Folder** dialog box appears. The folder that you are creating is a sub-folder within the CreatingDoc folder.

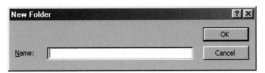

**10** Type **NewFolder**, and then click **OK**.

NewFolder becomes the current folder.

**11** In the **File name** box, double-click **Gardeners**, type **FirstSave**, and then click the **Save** button.

The **Save As** dialog box closes, and the file name *FirstSave* appears in the title bar.

## Tip

Document
Recovery
task pane
new for
**Office**XP

Word saves documents for recovery in case the program stops responding or you lose power. The **Document Recovery** task pane lists all recovered documents and allows you to open the documents, view the repairs, and compare the recovered versions. Word saves the changes in a recovery file based on the amount of time indicated in the AutoRecover option. To turn on the AutoRecover option and specify a time interval in which to save, on the **Tools** menu, click **Options**, click the **Save** tab, select the **Save AutoRecover info every** check box, specify the period of time, and then click **OK**.

Close Window

**12** Click the **Close Window** button in the document window.

The FirstSave document closes.

# Saving a File for Use in Another Program

W2002-4-3

Word allows you to save a document in a file format other than the Word document format. A **file format** is the way that a program stores a file so that the program can open up the file later. Saving a document in another format is important if you share documents with others who use programs or previous versions of Word that have a different file format, such as Word 6.0/95 or WordPerfect. For example, if you use Word 6.0 on the computer that you have at home, you can create a document in Word 2002, save it in the Word 6.0 format, and then open and edit the document on your home computer.

Show document format

new for **Office**XP

If you are not sure of the version of a document, you can use the **Properties** dialog box to display file format information about the document, which includes the version, type, and creator of the file. On the **File** menu, click **Properties**, and then click the **General** tab to display the document format information.

To save a file in another file format:

1   On the **File** menu, click **Save As**.

The **Save As** dialog box appears.

2   In the **File name** box, type a new name for the document.

3   Click the **Save as type** down arrow, and then select the file format that you want to use.

4   Click **Save**.

# Working with an Existing Document

Once you save a document to a file, you can open that document again. To open an existing document, you use the **Open** button on the Standard toolbar or an option on the **New Document** task pane. Using the **New Document** task pane, you can create a document based on an existing one. This is useful when you want to start a new document with existing text without changing the original document.

To enter or revise text, you start by positioning the insertion point. You can click to place the insertion point at a particular location, or you can press keys on the keyboard to move the insertion point in a document. When you use a **key combination**, you press two keys at the same time to perform an action. For example, pressing the ⌧ key moves the insertion point to the end of a line of text, whereas pressing the ⌧ and ⌧ keys at the same time moves the insertion point to the beginning of the document. To use a key combination, you hold down the first key (for example, ⌧) and then press the second key (for example, ⌧). Once the action takes place, you release both keys.

The following table shows the keys and key combinations that you can use to move the insertion point quickly.

| Pressing this key | Moves the insertion point |
| --- | --- |
| ← | Left one character at a time |
| → | Right one character at a time |
| ↓ | Down one line at a time |
| ↑ | Up one line at a time |
| Ctrl + ← | Left one word at a time |
| Ctrl + → | Right one word at a time |
| Home | To the beginning of the current line of text |
| End | To the end of the current line of text |
| Ctrl + Home | To the start of the document |
| Ctrl + End | To the end of the document |
| Ctrl + Page Up | To the beginning of the previous page |
| Ctrl + Page Down | To the beginning of the next page |
| Page Up | Up one screen |
| Page Down | Down one screen |

You can also use the vertical and horizontal scroll bars to move around in a document. However, using the scroll bars does not move the insertion point—it changes only your view of the document in the window. For example, if you drag the vertical scroll box down to the bottom of the scroll bar, the end of the document comes into view, but the insertion point does not move. The status bar shows the location of the insertion point (by page, section, inch, line, and column). Click the up or down scroll arrow on the vertical scroll bar to move the document window up or down one line of text. Click the left or right scroll arrow on the horizontal scroll bar to move the document window to the left or right several characters at a time.

**Select Browse Object**

As you create longer documents, you can use the **Select Browse Object** menu at the bottom of the vertical scroll bar to move quickly through a document. When you click the **Select Browse Object** button, a menu appears with browsing options, such as **Browse by Page**, **Browse by Comment**, and **Browse by Graphic**.

When you open a document, a program button with the Word program icon and document name appears on the taskbar. You can have many documents open at the same time, but only one is the current or active document. The program button of the current document appears pressed in. To move between open documents, click the program button on the taskbar, or use the **Window** menu, which lists all open documents. The check mark to the left of the document name in the **Window** menu indicates the current document.

The Garden Company sends marketing letters to its customers during the spring to promote new products. Before the letter is updated, the copy editor wants to review last year's letter to see what needs to be changed.

ExistDoc
OpenDoc

In this exercise, you move around a document and then switch between open documents. First, you open the document called ExistDoc, and then you move around the document to review the text.

**1**    On the Standard toolbar, click the **Open** button.

Open

The **Open** dialog box appears.

**2**    Navigate to the **SBS** folder on your hard disk, double-click the **Word** folder, and then double-click the **CreatingDoc** folder.

**3**    Double-click the **ExistDoc** file to open the document in the Word window.

The ExistDoc document opens.

## Tip

If a document doesn't open when you try to open it through the **Open** dialog box, you can repair it. On the Standard toolbar, click the **Open** button, select the file you want to open, click the **Open** down arrow, and then click **Open and Repair**.

**4**    In the greeting, click after the colon (:) to position the insertion point.

**5**    Press the Home key to move the insertion point to the beginning of the line.

**6**    Press the → key five times to move the insertion point to the beginning of the word *Garden* in the greeting.

**7**    Press ↓ two times to move the insertion point to the first paragraph.

**8**    Press the End key to move the insertion point to the end of the line of text.

**9**    Press Ctrl+End to move the insertion point to the end of the document.

**10**   Press Ctrl+Home to move the insertion point to the beginning of the document.

**11**   Drag the vertical scroll box to the bottom of the vertical scroll bar.

The insertion point is still at the beginning of the document, but the end of the document now comes into view.

**12**   In the vertical scroll bar, click the scroll up arrow five times.

The document changes to show five more lines of text.

**13**   Click above the vertical scroll box to change the view of the document by one screen.

**14** In the horizontal scroll bar, click the right scroll arrow twice so that the right side of the document comes into view by a few characters.

**15** Drag the horizontal scroll box all the way to the left.

The document is repositioned. Note that the location of the insertion point has not changed—just the view of the document.

**16** Press [Ctrl]+[Home] to move the insertion point to the beginning of the document.

Select Browse
Object

**17** Click the **Select Browse Object** button on the right side of the window.

When you click the button, a palette of objects appears.

**18** Move the pointer over the palette of objects.

The name of each object in the palette appears as you point to an object.

Browse by
Page

**19** Click the **Browse by Page** button.

The insertion point moves from page 1 to the beginning of page 2.

**20** On the Standard toolbar, click the **Open** button.

The **Open** dialog box appears.

**21** Navigate to the **SBS** folder on your hard disk, double-click the **Word** folder, double-click the **CreatingDoc** folder, and then double-click the **OpenDoc** file.

The OpenDoc document opens.

**22** On the taskbar, click the **ExistDoc** program button to make it the current document.

The ExistDoc document becomes the top window. The taskbar shows two program buttons, each with the name of an open document. The button that is pressed in indicates the active document, which is currently the ExistDoc document.

## Tip

You can set Word to show only one program button. On the **Tools** menu, click **Options**, click the **View** tab, clear the **Windows in Taskbar**, and then click **OK**.

**23** On the menu bar, click **Window**.

The two open files are listed at the bottom of the Window menu.

**24** On the **Window** menu, click **Arrange All**.

The two document windows are resized and stacked one on top of the other.

Close Window

**25** Click the **Close Window** button in the ExistDoc document window, and then click the **Close Window** button in the OpenDoc document window.

Maximize

**26** Click the **Maximize** button in the Word window to return the Word window to its original size.

# Editing a Document

W2002-1-1

When you edit a document, you revise its text. Editing encompasses many tasks, such as inserting and deleting words and phrases, correcting errors, and moving and copying text to different places in the document. Editing also includes searching for words, phrases, or even formatting, and replacing that text with different text.

Inserting text is as easy as positioning the insertion point and typing. When you insert text, existing text moves to the right to accommodate the text that you are inserting, and the text that reaches the right margin wraps to the next line, if necessary.

Before you can edit or work with text, you first need to select it. Selected text appears highlighted on the screen. To select a block of text quickly, you can use the selection area. The **selection area** is a blank area to the left of the document's left margin. When the pointer is in the selection area, it changes from an I-beam to a right-pointing arrow. To deselect text, click anywhere outside of the selected text.

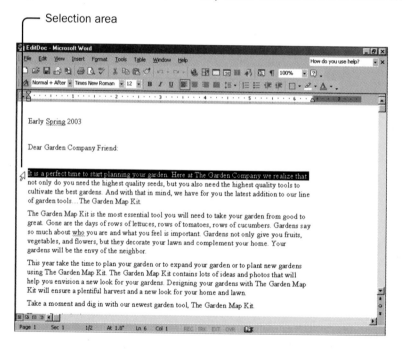

Selection area

Select nonadjacent text
new for **Office**XP

To select blocks of text that are not adjacent in a document, you select the first block of text, hold down Ctrl, and then select the next block of text. You can also use the Shift key and the arrow keys to select adjacent words, lines, or paragraphs. You position the insertion point in the text that you want to select, hold down the Shift key, and then press an arrow key or click at the end of the text that you want to select.

The following table describes methods that you can use to select text in a document.

| Selection | Action |
|---|---|
| A word | Double-click the word. |
| A line | Click the selection area to the left of the line. |
| A sentence | Click anywhere in the sentence while holding down the Ctrl key. The first character in the sentence through the space following the ending punctuation mark are selected. |
| A paragraph | Double-click the selection area to the left of the paragraph, or triple-click anywhere in the paragraph. |
| An entire document | Click anywhere in the selection area while holding down the Ctrl key, or triple-click in the selection area. |

Deleting text in a document is also an easy task. To delete a few characters, you can use the Backspace or Del key. Pressing Backspace deletes the character to the left of the insertion point. Pressing Del deletes the character to the right of the insertion point. Using these keys is a quick way to correct small errors. However, if you need to delete an entire sentence or a large block of text, first select the text, and then press Backspace or Del.

**Undo**

As you edit a document, Word keeps track of the changes that you make so that you can easily remove a change and restore your original text. This is useful when you make a mistake, as when you inadvertently delete a word. To undo the last action that you performed, click the **Undo** button on the Standard toolbar. To display the last five or six actions that you have performed, click the down arrow on the **Undo** button. Click the action in the list that you want to undo, and that action and all subsequent actions in the list are undone.

**Redo**

If you undo an action, you can restore, or redo, the action by clicking the **Redo** button. You can click the down arrow on the **Redo** button to restore multiple undone actions.

**Office Clipboard task pane**
new for **Office**XP

You can move selected text by cutting it and then pasting it in another place in the document. Text that you move, or cut, no longer appears in the document but is temporarily stored in an area of the computer memory called the **Office Clipboard**. Copying text is similar to moving text. However, when you copy selected text, the selected text remains in its original location, and you paste a copy of the selected text in another location. When you paste the selection, the text appears at the location of the insertion point.

**Clipboard icon**

You can use the Office Clipboard to store multiple items of information from several different sources in one storage area shared by all Office programs. The Office Clipboard appears as a task pane and shows all the items that you stored there. You can paste these items of information into any Office program, either individually or all at once. The Office Clipboard appears when you copy multiple items, unless the Office Clipboard option is turned off. To manually open the Office Clipboard, you click **Office Clipboard** on the **Edit** menu or double-click the **Clipboard** icon in the status area of the taskbar. The Clipboard icon appears on the taskbar when the Office Clipboard contains items. The Office Clipboard is useful for moving and copying information between pages and documents. If you need to move or copy text within a paragraph or line, you can drag the text instead of using the Office Clipboard. To move text, you select the text and drag it to another place. To copy or select text, you hold down [Ctrl] and drag it to another place.

**Multiuser editing**
**new for OfficeXP**

If you work on a network, more than one person at a time can edit the same document. When you open a document already open, choose to create a local copy and merge your changes later. When you finish editing and close the document, other users who have the document open can see your changes and merge them into the document.

Now that the marketing letter from last year has been reviewed, an assistant at The Garden Company can use it to create a new letter for this year's marketing campaign. The most efficient way to create the new letter is to edit last year's letter.

**EditDoc**

In this exercise, you edit text in the existing document. You insert and delete text, undo the deletion, copy and paste a phrase, and move a paragraph.

**1** On the Standard toolbar, click the **Open** button.

**Open**

The **Open** dialog box appears.

**2** Navigate to the **SBS** folder on your hard disk, double-click the **Word** folder, double-click the **CreatingDoc** folder, and then double-click the **EditDoc** file.

The EditDoc document opens.

**3** Double-click the word *Early* at the top of the document to select it, and then press [Enter] to delete the word and create a paragraph.

**4** Press [End] to move the insertion point to the end of the line, press [Space], and then type **Has Arrived!**

The text appears at the end of the line.

**5** Press [↓] four times, hold down [Ctrl], and then click anywhere in the sentence to select it.

**6** Press [Del] to delete the sentence.

**Undo**

**7** On the Standard toolbar, click the **Undo** button to restore the deleted text.

**8** Click the down scroll arrow until the phrase *Happy Gardening!* appears, position the mouse pointer in the selection area to the left of the text *Happy Gardening!*, and then click to select the entire line of text.

Copy

**9** On the Standard toolbar, click the **Copy** button to copy the text to the Clipboard.

**10** On the **Edit** menu, click **Office Clipboard**.

The **Clipboard** task pane appears, displaying the current items in the Office Clipboard.

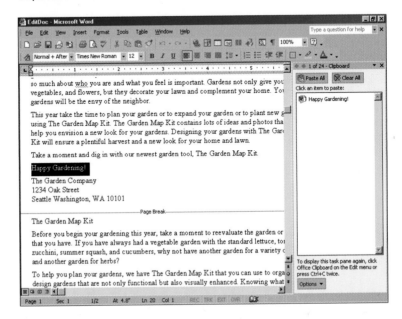

## Troubleshooting

You can turn on and off Office Clipboard options in the task pane. You can choose either to display the Office Clipboard when you are copying items or to copy items to the Office Clipboard without displaying the Office Clipboard. You can also choose to display the **Clipboard** icon on the taskbar when the Office Clipboard is turned on. To access these options, click **Options** at the bottom of the **Clipboard** task pane.

**11** Press `Ctrl`+`End` to move the insertion point to the end of the document, and then press `Enter` to insert a blank line.

**12** In the **Clipboard** task pane, click the *Happy Gardening!* box to place the text from the Clipboard into the document.

# Troubleshooting

If a **Paste Options** button appears next to the selection that you pasted, you can ignore it for now. The **Paste Options** button provides a list of options that allows you to determine how the information is pasted into your document.

Close

[X]

**13** In the **Clipboard** task pane, click the **Close** button to close the task pane.

**14** If necessary, scroll up to the paragraph that begins *The Garden Company welcomes your comments*, and then triple-click in the paragraph to select the paragraph.

**15** Drag the paragraph text down to above the text *Happy Gardening!*.

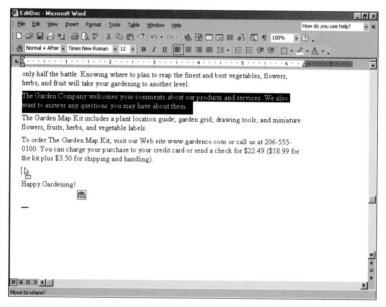

When you release the mouse, the text appears in its new location.

**16** On the Standard toolbar, click the **Save** button to save the document.

Close Window

[X]

**17** Click the **Close Window** button in the document window.

The EditDoc document closes.

# Replacing Text in a Document

W2002-1-1

Word corrects commonly misspelled words as you type so that you don't have to correct them yourself. For example, if you type *teh*, Word changes it to *the* as soon as you press [Space]. Changing the text like this is called **AutoCorrect**. Besides correcting misspelled words, AutoCorrect can also insert a long phrase when you type an abbreviation. For example, if you type the abbreviation *gc* to represent the company name, you can have AutoCorrect insert the full phrase *The Garden Company*. To add your own AutoCorrect entry, you enter the abbreviation and the full phrase in the AutoCorrect dialog box and then add the entry to the list of corrections.

AutoCorrect
Options

If you don't want Word to automatically change text, you can undo the change or turn off AutoCorrect options by clicking the **AutoCorrect Options** button that appears after the change. The **AutoCorrect Options** button first appears as a small blue box near the changed text and then changes to a button icon. If you are uncertain about AutoCorrect options or if you want to change or modify an AutoCorrect setting, you can open the **AutoCorrect** dialog box. You also use this dialog box to add your own AutoCorrect entry.

Besides replacing misspellings and abbreviations, you can also find and replace other text. If you know that you want to substitute one word or phrase for another, you can use the **Find and Replace** dialog box to find each occurrence of the word that you want to change and replace it with another. On the **Replace** tab of the **Find and Replace** dialog box, use the **Find Next** button to locate the next occurrence of the text that you enter in the **Find what** box, and then use the **Replace** button to replace the text that you found with the text in the **Replace with** box. You can use the **Replace** button to continue to replace each occurrence individually, the **Replace All** button to replace all of the occurrences, or the **Find Next** button to locate the next occurrence. If you want to only find text and not replace it, you can use the **Find** tab in the **Find and Replace** dialog box and use the **Find Next** button. You can access the **Find and Replace** commands on the **Edit** menu.

ReplaceText

In this exercise, you change an AutoCorrect setting, add an AutoCorrect entry, and change text as you type. You also find a phrase and replace it with another one throughout the entire document.

**1** On the Standard toolbar, click the **Open** button.

Open

The **Open** dialog box appears.

**2** Navigate to the **SBS** folder on your hard disk, double-click the **Word** folder, double-click the **CreatingDoc** folder, and then double-click the **ReplaceText** file.

The ReplaceText document opens.

**3**   On the **Tools** menu, click **AutoCorrect Options**.

The **AutoCorrect** dialog box appears, displaying the **AutoCorrect** tab.

**4**   Clear the **Capitalize first letter of sentences** check box so that Word will not capitalize a letter or word that follows a period.

**5**   Click in the **Replace** box, and then type **gc**.

**6**   Press the ⌷Tab⌷ key to move the insertion point in the **With** box.

**7**   Type **The Garden Company**.

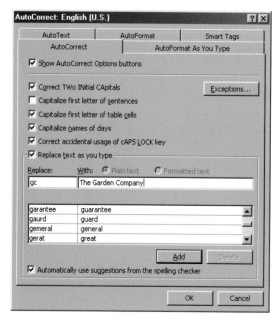

**8**   Click **Add** to add the entry to the correction list.

The text for the new AutoCorrect entry will be displayed each time you type its abbreviation and press ⌷Space⌷.

**9**   Click **OK** to close the **AutoCorrect** dialog box.

**10**   Press ⌷Ctrl⌷+⌷End⌷ to place the insertion point at the end of the document.

**11**   Type **gc**, and then press ⌷Space⌷.

The text *gc* changes to *The Garden Company*.

**12**   Press ⌷Ctrl⌷+⌷Home⌷ to move the insertion point to the beginning of the document.

**13**   On the **Edit** menu, click **Replace**.

The **Find and Replace** dialog box appears.

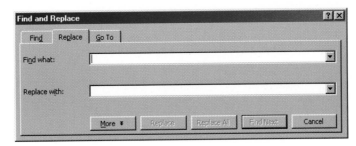

**14** In the **Find what** box, type Garden Map Kit, and then press ⌨ to move the insertion point in the **Replace with** box.

**15** In the **Replace with** box, type Interactive Garden, and then click **Find Next**.

Word finds and selects the first mention of *Garden Map Kit*.

**16** Click **Replace**.

The selection is replaced with the text *Interactive Garden*, and the next occurrence is selected.

**17** Click **Replace All**.

The Word message box that appears indicates that nine replacements were made.

**18** Click **OK**, and then click **Close** to close the **Find and Replace** dialog box.

**19** On the Standard toolbar, click the **Save** button to save the document.

Close Window

❎

**20** Click the **Close Window** button in the document window.

The ReplaceText document closes.

## Chapter Wrap-Up

To finish this chapter:

Close

❎

● On the **File** menu, click **Exit**, or click the **Close** button in the Word window.

Word closes.

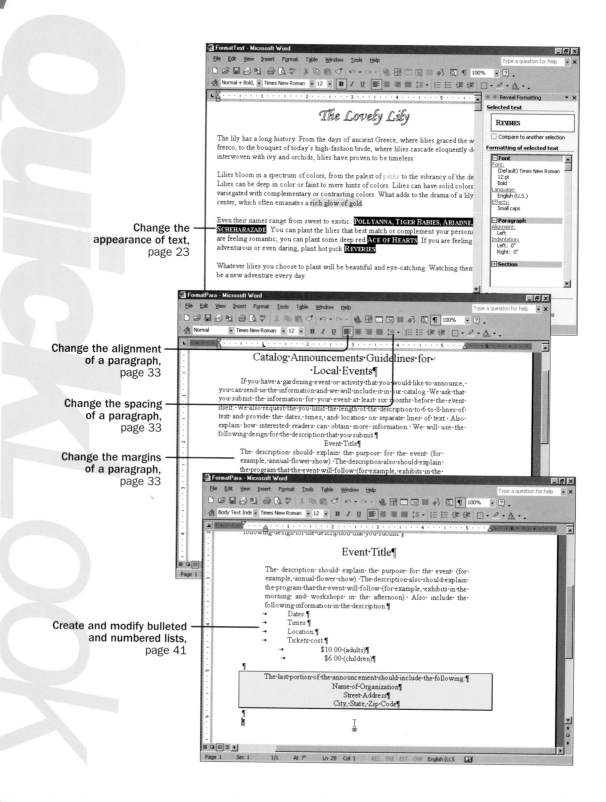

Change the
appearance of text,
page 23

**Change the alignment
of a paragraph,**
page 33

**Change the spacing
of a paragraph,**
page 33

**Change the margins
of a paragraph,**
page 33

**Create and modify bulleted
and numbered lists,**
page 41

# Chapter 2
# Changing the Look of Text in a Document

**After completing this chapter, you will be able to:**

✔ Change the appearance of text.

✔ Format text as you type.

✔ Change the appearance of a paragraph.

✔ Create and modify a list.

You want your documents to look professional—well designed and polished. The appearance of your text should reflect the content of your message. The format of your paragraphs and pages influences the appeal of your documents and helps draw the reader's attention to important information. To enhance the appearance of your documents, you can format the text to make your words stand out and arrange paragraphs to make them easy to read.

In this chapter, you'll improve the appearance of the text in a document by changing text characteristics, or **attributes**. You can change the text by making it bold, italic, or colored. You'll also change the appearance of the paragraphs in a document by indenting and changing the alignment and by setting tab stops for lines within paragraphs. Finally, you'll create and modify bulleted and numbered lists.

This chapter uses the practice files FormatText, FormatAuto, FormatPara, and Create-List that you installed from this book's CD-ROM. For details about installing the practice files, see "Using the Book's CD-ROM" at the beginning of this book.

## Changing the Appearance of Text

W2002-1-2
W2002-1-4
W2002-1-6

The text that you type in a document appears in a font typeface. A **font typeface**, or simply **font**, is a complete set of characters that uses the same design. Depending on your printer, the fonts available on your computer may vary. Some fonts are more common than others, such as Times New Roman, Courier, and Arial. In addition to the design, the size of each character is also part of the font. The **font size** of text is measured in **points**. A point is equal to about 1/72 of an inch.

You can emphasize text using special **font effects**, such as bold type, italics, all capital letters, or shadows. For example, to make a heading stand out, you could make it bold. To draw attention to a warning, you could make it italic. You can also add emphasis by changing the color of the text in your document. For example, you could use white text on a black or gray background. If you plan to print your documents on a color printer or send them electronically, you can apply other colors to the text and its background.

Reveal Formatting task pane

new for **Office**XP

When you are formatting a document, you can open the **Reveal Formatting** task pane to display the format of selected text, such as its font and font effects. The **Reveal Formatting** task pane allows you to display, change, or clear the formatting for the selected text. You also can use the **Reveal Formatting** task pane to select text based on formatting so that you can compare the formatting used in the selected text with formatting used in other parts of the document.

The Garden Company catalog will include an article on lilies in its upcoming spring catalog. The text in the document will be formatted to visually communicate the beauty of this type of flower.

FormatText

In this exercise, you change the font typeface, font size, and font color to format text in a document.

**1** Start Word, if necessary.

Open

**2** On the Standard toolbar, click the **Open** button.

The **Open** dialog box appears.

**3** Navigate to the **SBS** folder on your hard disk, double-click the **Word** folder, double-click the **FormattingText** folder and then double-click the **FormatText** file.

The FormatText document opens.

**4** Select the title *The Lovely Lily* at the top of the document.

**5** On the Formatting toolbar, click the **Font** down arrow, scroll down in the list of available fonts, and then click **Monotype Corsiva**.

## Troubleshooting

If Monotype Corsiva is not available, select a similar font, such as Brush Script MT.

The title at the top of the document now appears in a new font.

Font Size

26

**6** On the Formatting toolbar, click the **Font Size** down arrow, and then click **26** in the list.

The size of the title text is increased to 26 points.

**7** On the **Format** menu, click **Reveal Formatting**.

The **Reveal Formatting** task pane appears, displaying the formatting of the selected text.

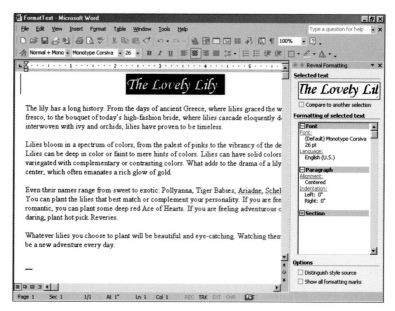

**8** In the **Reveal Formatting** task pane, click the **Font** link in the **Font** section. The **Font** dialog box appears.

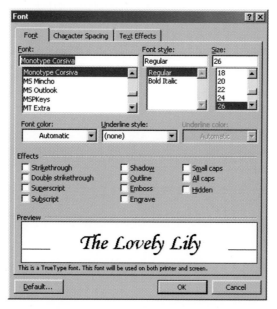

**9** In the **Effects** area, select the **Outline** check box, and then click **OK**.

The selected text appears with an outline effect, and that effect is now listed in the **Reveal Formatting** task pane in the **Font** section.

**10** In the **Reveal Formatting** task pane, point to the **Selected text** box at the top of the task pane.

A down arrow appears on the right side of the **Selected text** box.

**11** In the **Selected text** box, click the down arrow, and then click **Clear Formatting**.

The formatting for the selected text is removed.

Undo

**12** On the Standard toolbar, click the **Undo** button.

The formatting for the selected text is restored.

**13** Select the word *pinks* in the first sentence of the second paragraph.

Font Color

**14** On the Formatting toolbar, click the **Font Color** down arrow, and then click the **Pink** color box (first column, fourth row) on the color palette.

The color of the selected word is now pink, and the formatting is listed in the **Font** section of the **Reveal Formatting** task pane.

## Tip

To apply the most recently selected color to other text, select the word or phrase, and then click the **Font Color** button (not the down arrow). The color that appears on the **Font Color** button is applied to the selected text.

Highlight

**15** Select the phrase *rich glow of gold* at the end of the second paragraph, click the **Highlight** down arrow on the Formatting toolbar, and then click the **Yellow** color box (first column, first row).

The highlighted phrase now stands out from the rest of the text.

## Tip

Highlighting pointer

You do not have to select the text first before choosing a highlighting color. You can select a highlighting color from the color palette and then use the highlighting pointer to highlight the text.

**16** Scroll to the right and then select the text *Pollyanna, Tiger Babies, Ariadne, Scheharazade* in the third paragraph.

## Troubleshooting

If the **Reveal Formatting** task pane overlays some of the text in the document, you can resize the task pane. Position the pointer over the left edge of the task pane, and when the pointer changes to the double arrow pointer, drag the edge to the right so that the text of the document is visible.

**17** On the **Format** menu, click **Font** to open the **Font** dialog box, select the **Small caps** check box, and then click **OK**.

The lowercase letters in the names of the lilies now appear in small caps, making those names easier to find in the text.

**18** In the same paragraph, select the text *Ace of Hearts*, and then hold down the [Ctrl] key and double-click the text *Reveries* in the last line of the paragraph to select the nonadjacent text.

**19** Press the [F4] key.

The other lily names appear in small caps. When you press [F4], the change that you just made is applied to the selected text.

**20** In the **Reveal Formatting** task pane, point to the **Selected text** box, click the down arrow, and then click **Select All Text With Similar Formatting**.

All the flower names that have been formatted in small caps are selected.

Bold

**B**

**21** On the Formatting toolbar, click the **Bold** button.

The flower names are now bold.

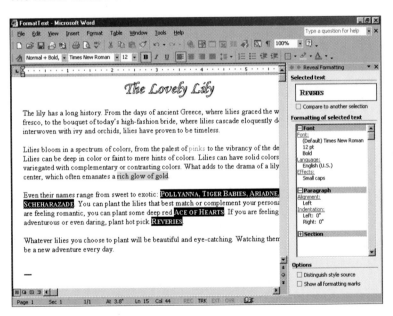

Close

**×**

**22** In the **Reveal Formatting** task pane, click the **Close** button.

The **Reveal Formatting** task pane closes.

**23** On the Standard toolbar, click the **Save** button to save the document.

Close Window

**×**

**24** Click the **Close Window** button in the document window.

The FormatText document closes.

# Adding Animation to Text

If someone using a computer will be reading your document, you can add effects that will make the text in your document vibrant and visually alive. You can apply sparkling and flashing lights or a marquee that will draw your reader's attention to specific words and phrases in the document. To add these special effects, you can apply an animation to selected text in your document.

To add animation to selected text:

**1**   Select the text that you want to animate.

**2**   On the **Format** menu, click **Font**.

The **Font** dialog box appears.

**3**   Click the **Text Effects** tab.

**4**   In the **Animations** box, select the animation effect that you want to add to the selected text.

**5**   Click **OK**.

# Formatting Text as You Type

W2002-1-2
W2002-1-5
W2002-1-1

Word provides automated formatting tools that let you enter and format text as you type. Word's **AutoText** feature can save you time and create consistency in your documents by providing standardized text for commonly used items, such as attention line entries, closings, and mailing instructions, that you want to insert in your document and by allowing you to create AutoText entries for words and phrases that you use repeatedly, such as your name, address, company, and job title. To insert one of the built-in AutoText entries, such as the closing of a letter, you click the **Insert** menu, point to **AutoText**, point to a category, such as **Closing**, and then select the closing (for example, *Respectfully yours,*) that you want to insert in your document. You can also create your own AutoText entries using the **AutoText** tab in the **Auto-Correct** dialog box. For example, you can create an AutoText entry for *Catherine Turner*, the owner of The Garden Company. Once the AutoText entry is stored, you can type the first four letters of the name *Catherine*, and a ScreenTip will display *Catherine Turner (Press ENTER to Insert)*. Then to insert the AutoText entry in the document, you press `Enter` and continue typing. If you don't want to insert the Auto-Text entry (that is, if you are inserting someone else's name), you just press `Space` and continue typing.

In addition to automating text entry, Word can also automate formatting as you type with a tool called **AutoFormat**. For example, instead of manually creating a line by typing underscores ( _ ) across the length of a page, you can type just a few equal signs (=) or dashes (-). When you type three consecutive equal signs and press ⎡Enter⎤, Word creates a double-line border; when you type three consecutive dashes and press ⎡Enter⎤, Word creates a single-line border.

Besides commonly used words and phrases, you can also insert symbols, special characters, and the date and the time. Certain kinds of documents require special characters or symbols, such as a degree symbol (°) or a copyright symbol (©). If the documents that you create are time sensitive, you can insert the current date and time. You can even choose to have Word update the date and time when you open the document. Word uses your computer's internal calendar and clock as its source.

Smart Tags
new for
**Office**XP

When you type certain information, such as the date and time, personal names, places, telephone numbers, or recent Microsoft Outlook e-mail recipients, Word recognizes the information and displays a **Smart Tag**, a dotted line under the text. A Smart Tag provides options for commonly performed tasks associated with the information. For example, you can add a name and address that you just typed in a Word document to your Contacts list in Microsoft Outlook. To do this, you point to the name in the document, click the **Smart Tag Actions** button, and then click **Add to Contacts** from the list of available Smart Tag options.

FormatAuto

In this exercise, you insert decorative design symbols in a document, insert one of the standard closings provided by Word, create an AutoText entry and insert it in the document, and add a double border using an AutoFormat shortcut. You also insert the date and examine actions that you can take using Smart Tags.

Open

**1** On the Standard toolbar, click the **Open** button.

The **Open** dialog box appears.

**2** Navigate to the **SBS** folder on your hard disk, double-click the **Word** folder, double-click the **FormattingText** folder, and then double-click **FormatAuto**.

The FormatAuto document opens.

**3** Press the ⎡End⎤ key to place the insertion point at the end of the first line of text, and then press ⎡Enter⎤ to insert a blank new line.

**4** On the **Insert** menu, click **Symbol**.

The **Symbol** dialog box appears.

**5** Click the **Font** down arrow, scroll to the bottom of the list, and then click **Wingdings 2**.

## Tip

The Wingdings fonts are sets of specials characters, shapes, symbols, and thumb-print-sized pictures that you can insert in the text of your documents to draw attention to the message that you are trying to convey. The following are examples of the Wingdings character set: ▱ ☿ ⑧ ☺.

**6** Scroll to the fifth row, and then click the decorative design symbol located in the sixth column and in the fifth row with a character code of *101*, as shown in the following illustration.

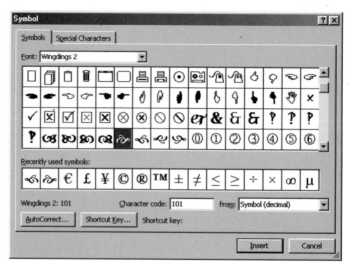

**7** Click **Insert**.

The decorative design symbol is inserted below the title of the document.

**8** Click the decorative design symbol located in the seventh column in the fifth row with a character code of *102*, click **Insert**, and then click **Close**.

The second decorative symbol appears in the document.

## Tip

You can automatically format a document as you type using the options in the **Auto-Format As You Type** tab in the **AutoCorrect** dialog box or you can format a document after you type using the **AutoFormat** command on the **Format** menu. In the **AutoFormat** dialog box, click the **AutoFormat now** option or the **AutoFormat and review each change** option, and then click **OK**.

**9** Press Ctrl+End to move the insertion point to the end of the document.

**10** On the **Insert** menu, point to **AutoText**, point to **Closing**, and then click **Respectfully,** to insert this standard closing text at the location of the insertion point.

**11** Press Enter four times to leave space for a signature.

**12** On the **Insert** menu, point to **AutoText**, and then click **AutoText**.

The **AutoCorrect** dialog box appears.

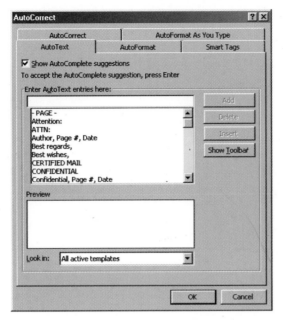

**13** In the **Enter AutoText entries here** box, type Catherine Turner, click **Add**, and then click **OK**.

The **AutoCorrect** dialog box closes, and the AutoText entry is stored.

**14** Type Cath.

The ScreenTip displays *Catherine Turner (Press ENTER to Insert)*.

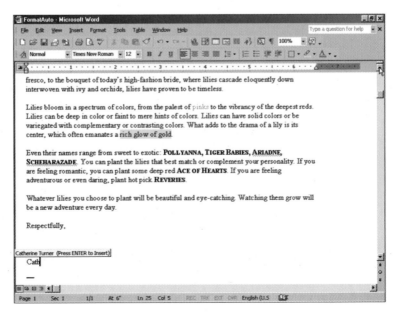

**15** Press ⏎ to insert the full name, and then press ⏎ twice to insert two blank lines.

**16** Press ⁝ three times, and then press ⏎.

A double border appears. The **AutoCorrect Options** button appears just above the double border. No modifications are needed.

## Tip

The **AutoCorrect Options** button provides options related to the AutoCorrect border that you have just inserted. You can choose to remove the border, disable (or turn off) the AutoCorrect border lines options, or open the **AutoCorrect** dialog box, in which you can make further modifications to this feature.

**17** On the **Insert** menu, click **Date and Time**.

The **Date and Time** dialog box appears.

**18** Click today's date with the **dd month yyyy** format, such as 15 March 2003.

**19** Click **OK** to enter the current date in the document, and then press ⏎ to insert a blank line.

Smart Tag
Actions

**20** Point to the date to display the **Smart Tag Actions** button, and then click the **Smart Tag Actions** button.

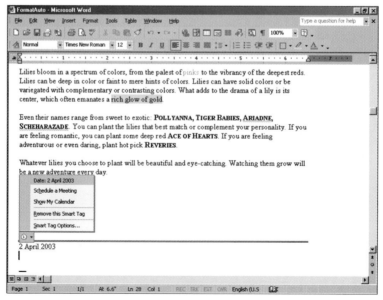

**21** On the menu, click **Smart Tag Options**.

The **AutoCorrect** dialog box appears, displaying the **Smart Tags** tab.

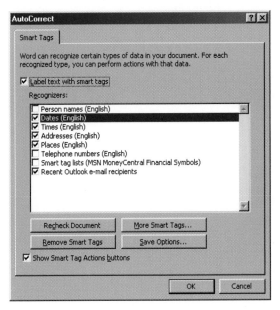

You can use this dialog box to turn on and off the Smart Tags feature. Do not turn off the feature at this time.

**22** Click **OK** to close the **AutoCorrect** dialog box.

**23** On the Standard toolbar, click the **Save** button to save the document.

Close Window

**24** Click the **Close Window** button in the document window.

The FormatAuto document closes.

# Changing the Appearance of a Paragraph

W2002-2-1
W2002-2-2

You can enhance the appearance of a paragraph by changing the way text is aligned, modifying the spacing between paragraphs, and adding borders and shading around text. In Word, a **paragraph** is any amount of text that ends when you press the `Enter` key. A paragraph can include several sentences or a single line of text consisting of one or more words.

You control the length of a line by setting the left and right margins and the length of a page by setting the top and bottom margins. The width of a margin controls the amount of white space that surrounds your text. You can use the options in the **Page Setup** dialog box to control the margins in the document.

After you've set up a document's margins, you can control the positioning of the text within the margins. In Word, you can align lines of text in different locations along the horizontal ruler using tab stops. You can also indent paragraphs. When you indent a paragraph, you control where the first line of text begins, where the second and subsequent lines begin, and where paragraph text wraps at the right margin.

You use the horizontal ruler, which you can display at the top of the Word document window, to set **tab stops**. Tab stops are locations along the ruler that you use to align text. By default, the tab stops in Word are set at every half-inch mark on the ruler. To set a tab using the ruler, you click the tab indicator, which is a button with a symbol on it, located at the left end of the ruler. Each time that you click the tab indicator, a different type of tab stop indicator appears. When the type of tab stop that you want to set appears, you click the ruler where you want to set the tab. To remove a tab stop, you drag it down and away from the ruler.

After you set a tab stop, you position the insertion point to the left of the text you want to align and then press the [Tab] key. The text is aligned along the next tab stop. For example, if you set a center tab, when you press [Tab], the text moves to the right and aligns itself using the center tab stop as the middle point. A decimal tab aligns numbers on their decimal points.

## Tip

In Word, you can display formatting marks to help you align and space the text in a document correctly. Formatting marks do not print with your document. They are displayed in your document just as an aid. To turn on formatting marks, click the **Show/ Hide ¶** button on the Standard toolbar. Examples of formatting marks include the paragraph mark ¶, which marks the end of a paragraph, and the tab stop (→), which marks the location of a tab stop. To turn off the display of formatting marks, click the **Show/Hide ¶** button again.

In addition to tab stops, the horizontal ruler also includes special markers that you can use to control how text wraps on the left or right side of a document. You use these markers if you want to **indent** the text toward the right or left. To indent text, you can use one of the indent markers located on the horizontal ruler. The following table describes each indent marker:

| Marker on Ruler | Icon | Description |
|---|---|---|
| First Line Indent | ▽ | Sets where the first line of text in a paragraph begins. |
| Hanging Indent | △ | Sets where the second and all subsequent lines of text wrap after reaching the right margin. |
| Left Indent | ▢ | Sets where the text indents when you press [Tab]. |

| Marker on Ruler | Icon | Description |
|---|---|---|
| **Right Indent** | △ | Sets where the text wraps as it reaches the right margin. By default, the right indent marker is set at the right margin, but you can change that setting. |

When you use the ruler to format paragraphs, you can use Print Layout view to see how far your page margins are from the borders of the page. Print Layout view also shows two rulers: the horizontal ruler at the top and the vertical ruler along the left side of the document window. The vertical ruler helps you adjust the top and bottom margins in the document.

You can also position text within the document's margin using the alignment buttons on the Formatting toolbar. Click the **Align Left** button to align text along the left margin, click the **Align Right** button to align the text along the right margin, click the **Center** button to align a paragraph between the left and right margins, and click the **Justify** button to align between the margins, creating a flush-right edge for the text.

To add space between paragraphs, you can press [Enter] to insert a blank line. For more precise control, you can adjust the spacing before and after paragraphs. For example, instead of indicating a new paragraph by indenting the first line, you could create a more professional appearance by adding twelve points of blank space before a new paragraph. You use the **Paragraph** dialog box to adjust the paragraph spacing.

To set off a paragraph from the rest of the document, you can add borders and shading. For example, if you are sending a long letter to a client, you can place a border around the paragraph that you want the client to pay the most attention to. You can also shade the background of a paragraph to create a subtler effect.

After you indent, align, space, border, or shade one paragraph, you can press [Enter] to apply these same effects to the next paragraph that you type. To apply the effects to an existing paragraph, you can use the **Format Painter** to quickly copy the format of one paragraph to another.

The Garden Company catalog includes an announcement, which needs to be formatted to fit the layout of the catalog and match its new color design.

FormatPara

In this exercise, you modify text alignment, insert and modify tab stops, modify line spacing, and add borders and shading around text to change the appearance of the paragraphs in the document.

**1** On the Standard toolbar, click the **Open** button.

Open

The **Open** dialog box appears.

**2** Navigate to the **SBS** folder on your hard disk, double-click the **Word** folder, double-click the **FormattingText** folder, and then double-click the **Format-Para** file.

The FormatPara document opens.

Print Layout
View

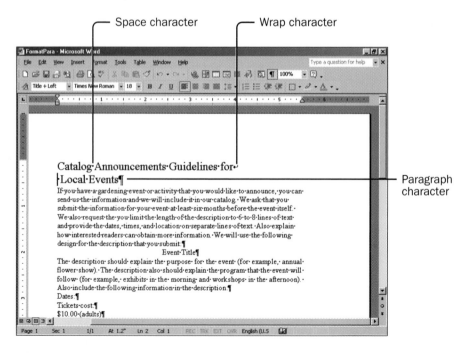

**3** Click the **Print Layout View** button.

The document view changes. You can see how the work area is aligned between the left and right margins. In addition to the horizontal ruler at the top of the document window, a vertical ruler also appears on the left side of the document window.

## Tip

White space
between pages

new for
**Office**XP

In Print Layout view, you can show or hide the white space between the pages. Position the pointer between the pages until the Show White Space pointer or Hide White Space pointer appears, and then click the page.

Show/Hide ¶

**4** On the Standard toolbar, click the **Show/Hide ¶** button to display the formatting marks.

**5** Click immediately to the left of the word *for* in the title, hold down the Shift key, and then press Enter.

Part of the title wraps to the second line of text.

Center

**6** On the Formatting toolbar, click the **Center** button to center the title to make it appear more balanced.

Justify

**7** Click anywhere in the first paragraph, and then click the **Justify** button on the Formatting toolbar.

The paragraph is now formatted with the text flush against both left and right margins.

First Line Indent

**8** Drag the **First Line Indent** marker to the 0.5-inch mark on the horizontal ruler.

The first line of text in the paragraph is indented a half inch from the left margin.

Left Indent

**9** Click anywhere in the paragraph that starts with the text *The description should explain*, and then drag the **Left Indent** marker to the 0.5-inch mark on the horizontal ruler.

The paragraph is indented on the left side.

Right Indent

**10** Drag the **Right Indent** marker to the 5-inch mark on the ruler.

The paragraph now appears indented on the right side as well.

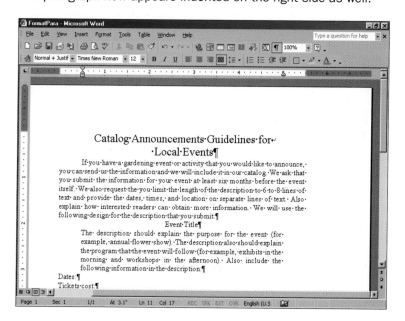

Left Tab icon

**11** Scroll down the page, select the two lines that include the text *Dates:* and *Tickets cost:*, make sure that the **Tab Indicator** button shows the **Left Tab** icon, and then click the ruler at the 1-inch mark to set a left tab.

**12** Click to the left of the word *Dates* to deselect all the text, and then press [Tab] to align the text at the new tab stop.

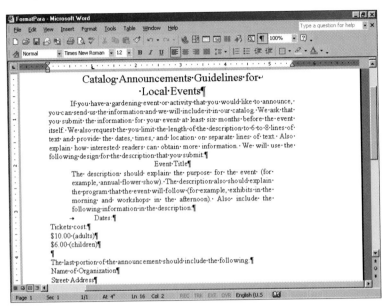

**13** Press [End] to move the insertion point to the end of the line, and then press [Enter] to create a new line. Press [Tab], and then type **Times:**.

**14** Press [Enter] to create a new line, press [Tab], type **Location:**, press the [→] key to move the insertion point to the beginning of the next line, and then press [Tab].

Decimal Tab icon

**15** Select the two lines that start with text *$10.00* and *$6.00*, click the **Tab Indicator** three times to see a **Decimal Tab** icon, and then click the ruler at the 2.5-inch mark to set a decimal tab.

**16** Click to the left of the text *$10.00* to deselect the text, press [Tab], click to the left of the text *$6.00*, and then press [Tab].

The dollar amounts are aligned along their decimal points.

**17** Select the two lines of text with the dollar amounts again, and drag the decimal tab from the 2.5-inch mark to the 2.0-inch mark to adjust the tab stop.

**18** Press [Ctrl]+[Home] to move the insertion point to the top of the document, and then on the **Format** menu, click **Paragraph**.

The **Paragraph** dialog box appears.

## Tip

You can also use the **Paragraph** dialog box to control the left and right indentation instead of using the ruler.

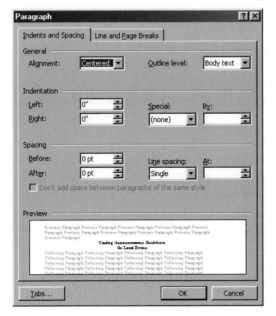

**19** In the **Spacing** area, click the **After** up arrow two times to display *12 pt*, and then click **OK**.

The paragraphs below the title move down. The added space helps to set the title off from the rest of the document.

Format Painter

**20** On the Standard toolbar, click the **Format Painter** button, move the mouse pointer to the paragraph that begins *Event Title*, and then click the text to copy the formatting from the title paragraph.

Additional spacing appears between the first paragraph and the *Event Title* text and the font size changes to 18 points.

**21** On the **Format** menu, click **Paragraph** to open the **Paragraph** dialog box. In the **Spacing** area, click the **Before** up arrow twice to display *12 pt*, and then click **OK**.

There is more spacing between the *Event Title* text and the paragraph before it.

Center

**22** Scroll down the page, select the last four lines of text in the document, which start with the line *The last portion of*, and then on the Formatting toolbar, click the **Center** button to center these lines of text.

**23** On the **Format** menu, click **Borders and Shading**.

The **Borders and Shading** dialog box appears, displaying the **Borders** tab.

**24** In the **Setting** area, click the **Shadow** icon to select that border style.

**25** Click the **Shading** tab, click the **Light Yellow** color box on the color palette (third column, last row), and then click **OK**.

A border with a shadow surrounds the text, and the background color is light yellow.

**26** Click a blank area two lines below the yellow shaded box, and then move the pointer to the center of the line until it changes shape.

Align center
pointer

The pointer shape changes to the Click and Type's Align center pointer to indicate that when you click and type, the text will be centered.

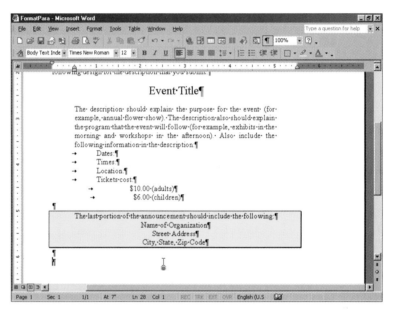

**27** When the pointer changes shape, double-click to position the insertion point, and then type **All announcements must be submitted 6 months in advance.**

The newly inserted text appears centered in the document

Show/Hide ¶

**28** On the Formatting toolbar, click the **Show/Hide ¶** button to hide the formatting marks.

**29** On the Standard toolbar, click the **Save** button to save the document.

Close Window

**30** Click the **Close Window** button in the document window.

The FormatPara document closes.

# Creating and Modifying a List

W2002-2-3
W2002e-1-2

To organize lists in your document, such as lists of events, names, numbers, or procedures, you can format the information in a bulleted or numbered list. A **bullet** is a small graphic, such as a large dot, that sets off an item in a list. Use numbers instead of bullets when you want to emphasize sequence, as in a series of steps. If you move, insert, or delete items in a numbered list, Word renumbers the list for you. If the items in a list are out of order, alphabetically or numerically, you can sort the items in ascending or descending order using the **Sort** command on the **Table** menu.

For emphasis, you can change any bullet or number style to one of Word's predefined formats. For example, you can switch round bullets to check boxes, or Roman numerals to lowercase letters. You can also customize the list style or insert a picture as a bullet. Use the **Bullets and Numbering** dialog box to modify, format, and customize your list.

Word makes it easy to start a bulleted or numbered list. For a bulleted list, you simply click at the beginning of a line, type * (an asterisk), and then press `Space` or `Tab`; for a numbered list, you type **1.**, press `Space` or `Tab`, type the first item in the list, and then press `Enter`. The next bullet or number in the list appears, and Word changes the formatting to a list. You can type the next item in the list or press `Enter` or `Backspace` to end the list.

You can change a bulleted or numbered list into an outline or create one of your own. Outlines are useful for organizing information, such as topics in an essay. An outline typically consists of main headings and subheadings. To start an outline, you click at the beginning of a line, type **I.**, press `Tab`, type a main heading, and then press `Enter`. You can type another main heading or press `Tab` to add a subheading under the main heading.

The Garden Company needs to complete the announcement that will be used on the back pages of the catalog.

CreateList

In this exercise, you create a bulleted and numbered list, modify it by adjusting its indents, and then apply outline numbering.

**1**    On the Standard toolbar, click the **Open** button.

Open

The **Open** dialog box appears.

**2**    Navigate to the **SBS** folder on your hard disk, double-click the **Word** folder, double-click the **FormattingText** folder, and then double-click the **CreateList** file.

The CreateList document opens.

**3**    Select the four lines that start with the word *Dates*.

Numbering

**4** On the Formatting toolbar, click the **Numbering** button.

The selected text appears as a numbered list.

**5** On the **Format** menu, click **Bullets and Numbering**.

The **Bullets and Numbering** dialog box appears, displaying the **Numbered** tab.

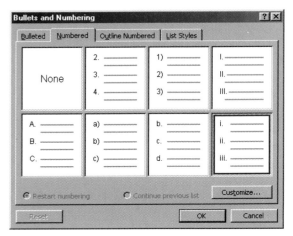

**6** Click the A, B, C box (first column, second row), and then click **OK**.

The numbered list changes from numbers to letters.

**7** Select the two lines that start with the text *$10.00* and *$6.00*.

Bullets

**8** On the Formatting toolbar, click the **Bullets** button.

The selected text appears as a bulleted list.

Decrease
Indent

**9** On the Formatting toolbar, click the **Decrease Indent** button.

The bulleted list is indented to the left and becomes part of the list.

## Tip

List styles
new for
**Office**XP

You can define a style for a bulleted or numbered list to make one list look like another. On the **Format** menu, click **Bullets and Numbering**, click the **Styles** tab, click **New**, define the style, and then click **OK**.

Increase Indent

**10** On the Formatting toolbar, click the **Increase Indent** button.

The bulleted list is indented to the right and becomes a bulleted list again under the text *Tickets cost*.

**11** On the **Format** menu, click **Bullets and Numbering**.

The **Bullets and Numbering** dialog box appears.

**12** Click the **Bulleted** tab, if necessary, click the color bullet box (first column, second row), and then click **OK**.

The bullet character changes from circles to colors.

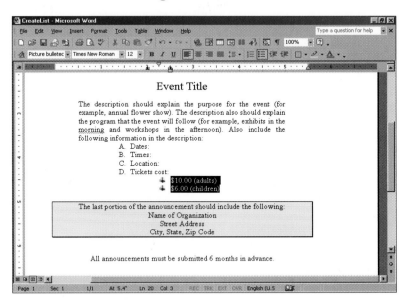

**13** Select the six lines that start with the word *Dates*.

**14** On the **Format** menu, click **Bullets and Numbering**.

The **Bullets and Numbering** dialog box appears.

**15** Click the **Outline Numbered** tab, if necessary, click the A Heading box (third column, second row), and then click **OK**.

The lettered list changes from letters to numbers and the bulleted list changes to letters.

**16** On the Standard toolbar, click the **Save** button to save the document.

Close Window

**17** Click the **Close Window** button in the document window.

The CreateList document closes.

# Chapter Wrap-Up

To finish this chapter:

Close

● On the **File** menu, click **Exit**, or click the **Close** button in the Word window.

Word closes.

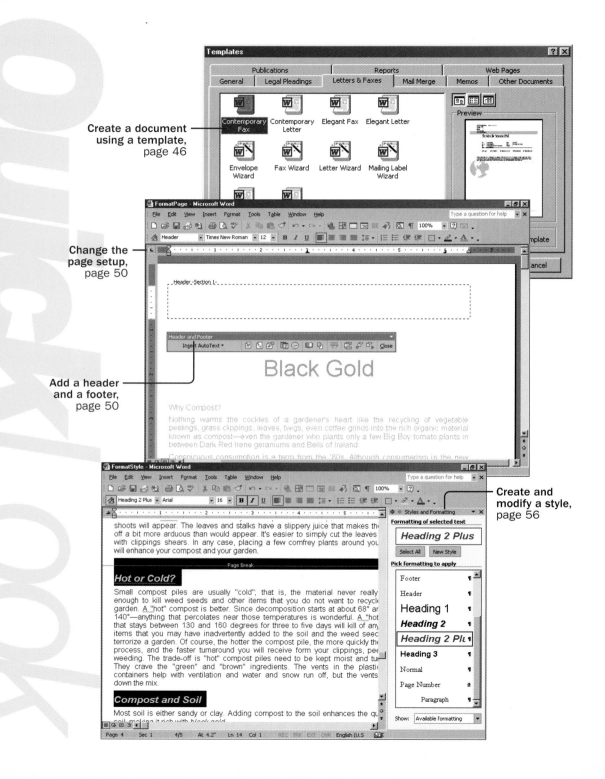

**Create a document using a template,** page 46

**Change the page setup,** page 50

**Add a header and a footer,** page 50

**Create and modify a style,** page 56

# Chapter 3
# Changing the Look of a Document

**After completing this chapter, you will be able to:**

✔ Change the design of a document with templates.

✔ Change the way each page appears in a document.

✔ Change the look of a document with styles.

✔ Change the look of a document with a theme.

To draw a reader's attention to important information in a document, you can format the text so that it is visually appealing. The way that paragraphs in your document look can help to convey its message.

Word comes with formatting tools, such as templates, styles, and themes, that you can use to enhance the appearance of your documents. You can change the characteristics, or attributes, of the text by applying bold formatting or italics to words and phrases or by changing the color of the text that you type. You can also apply these visually enhancing attributes to paragraphs. To ensure a consistent and polished look for your document, you can apply those same attributes throughout your document.

In this chapter, you'll create a new template by modifying one of Word's templates. Then you will use the new template to create a fax cover page. You will also insert page and section breaks in a multiple-page document and make sure that the page breaks do not leave single words or phrases at the top or bottom of a page. You will change the way that the text is laid out on a page, and you will add text that will appear at the top and bottom of every page in the document. Finally, you'll apply, modify, and delete a formatting style using the **Styles and Formatting** task pane and then apply a theme to an existing document.

This chapter uses the practice files FormatPage, FormatStyle, and FormatTheme that you installed from this book's CD-ROM. For details about installing the practice files, see "Using the Book's CD-ROM" at the beginning of this book.

# Changing the Design of a Document with Templates

W2002-4-2

The accuracy of the information in a document and the appearance of a document are both essential for effective communication. To help you create visually appealing documents, you can use one of Word's professionally designed templates.

A **template** is a special document that stores text, styles, formatting, macros, and page information for use in other documents. You can start with a predefined Word template or use one that you create. Word comes with templates for all types of documents, including publications, reports, letters, faxes, memos, and Web pages.

To create a document using one of Word's available templates, you click **Open** on the **File** menu to display the **Open** dialog box, which contains several tabs that provide a wide range of templates from which to choose. When you create a document using a template, the document that appears on the screen displays placeholders that you use to enter your own text, or if you do not need the placeholders, you can delete them. A placeholder is surrounded by brackets. For example, *[click here and type name]* is one of the placeholders that appear in the document when you choose the Contemporary Fax template. To modify a placeholder, you click the placeholder text to select it and then enter your own text. Once you have entered the text that you need for the document, you can save the document. The template is not changed in any way. It is available to you to use for other documents.

You can also modify the templates to address professional and personal needs. In other words, you can create a document based on a template, and then after entering your own text, such as your name and address, you can then save the modified document as another template. You can then use the template that you created instead of the ones provided by Word.

You can quickly try a new look by attaching a different template to your current document. The attached template's styles replace the styles in your document. To attach a template to an existing document, you click **Templates and Add-Ins** on the **Tools** menu, click **Attach**, and then navigate to and open the template.

The Garden Company needs to send a fax to a supplier for review and confirmation of delivery of an order. Each fax that the company sends includes a fax cover page. The Garden Company uses one of Word's built-in templates but would rather have a template that already contains the company-specific information in place.

In this exercise, you create a new template based on an existing Word template. Then you create a fax cover page document using the new template.

**1** Start Word, if necessary.

**2** On the **View** menu, click **Task Pane**, if necessary, to display the **New Document** task pane.

**3** In the **New Document** task pane, click **General Templates** in the **New from template** section to open the **Templates** dialog box.

**4** Click the **Letters & Faxes** tab.

**5** Click the **Contemporary Fax** icon.

The template appears in the preview window.

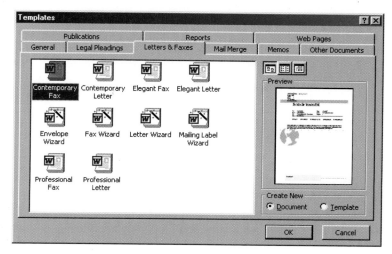

**6** Click **OK**.

A new document with the template placeholders appears.

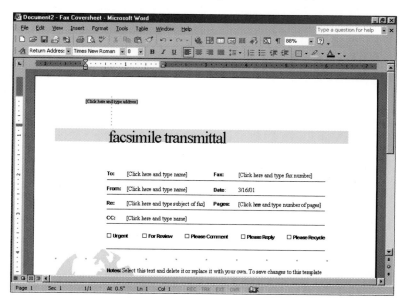

**7** Click the placeholder *[Click here and type address]*, type **The Garden Company,** and then press the Enter key.

**8** Type **1234 Oak Street**, press Enter, and then type **Seattle, WA 10101** to enter text in the placeholder.

**9** Click the *From* placeholder *[Click here and type name]*, and then type **The Garden Company** to replace the placeholder text with your own.

**10** On the **File** menu, click **Save As**.

The **Save As** dialog box appears.

**11** In the **File name** box, type **FaxTemplate**.

**12** Click the **Save as type** down arrow, and then click **Document Template**.

**13** Navigate to the **Windows** folder on your hard disk, double-click the **Application Data** folder, double-click the **Microsoft** folder, and then double-click the **Templates** folder.

**14** Click **Save**.

Word saves the template; it will appear as an icon on the **General** tab in the **Templates** dialog box along with the other Word templates.

Close Window
❌

**15** Click the **Close Window** button in the document window.

The FaxTemplate closes.

**16** On the **File** menu, click **New**.

The **New Document** task pane appears.

**17** In the **New Document** task pane, click **General Templates** in the **New from template** section.

The **Templates** dialog box appears.

**18** Click the **General** tab, click the **FaxTemplate** icon, and then click **OK**.

The company-specific template appears in the document window.

**19** Click the *To* placeholder *[Click here and type name]*, and then type **Flower Supplier**.

**20** Click the *Fax* placeholder *[Click here and type fax number]*, and then type **1-800-555-0190**.

**21** Click the *Re* placeholder *[Click here and type subject of fax]*, and then type **Order Confirmation**.

**22** Click the *Pages* placeholder *[Click here and type number of pages]*, and then type **2**.

**23** Click the *CC* placeholder *[Click here and type name]*, and then press the Del key.

**24** Select the paragraph that starts with *Select this text and delete*, and then press Del.

The instructional text is deleted.

**25** Type **Please review this order and confirm your availability for delivery.** and then press `Enter`.

The fax cover page is complete.

Save

**26** On the Standard toolbar, click the **Save** button.

The **Save As** dialog box appears.

**27** In the **File name** box, type **FaxCover**.

**28** If necessary, click the **Save as type** down arrow, and then click **Word Document**.

**29** Navigate to the **SBS** folder on your hard disk, double-click the **Word** folder, double-click the **FormattingDoc** folder, and then click **Save.**

The document based on the template is stored in the FormattingDoc folder.

Close Window

**30** Click the **Close Window** button in the document window.

The FaxCover document closes.

## Changing a Default File Location

W2002e-6-7

When you open and save a document or template, Word displays the **Open** or **Save As** dialog box with a default folder location. If you want to display a different default folder in the **Open** and **Save As** dialog boxes, you can change the location using the **File Locations** tab in the **Options** dialog box. The **File Locations** tab also defines where Word looks for files, such as clip art pictures files or Workgroup templates. **Workgroup templates** are templates shared over a network. If the **File Locations** tab doesn't display a file location for a file type, such as Workgroup templates, you can also define a location where you can easily find the documents and templates that you use most often.

To change the default file location of documents or templates:

**1** On the **Tools** menu, click **Options**.

The **Options** dialog box appears.

**2** Click the **File Locations** tab.

**3** In the **File types** box, click a file type, and then click **Modify**.

The **Modify Location** dialog box appears.

**4** Navigate to the new default folder location, and then click **OK**.

The **Modify Location** dialog box closes, and the new default folder location appears in the **File types** box.

**5** Click **OK** to close the **Options** dialog box.

# Changing the Way Each Page Appears in a Document

W2002-3-1
W2002-3-3
W2002e-1-1
W2002e-2-1

Using a template is a great way to begin your document. Many of the documents that you create (with or without a template) will be more than a page or two. When you create a document that contains more than one page, Word paginates your document for you. To paginate a document means to insert page breaks—the page breaks that Word inserts are called **soft page breaks**. A soft page break appears as a dotted line across the page. If you don't like where Word inserts a page break, you can insert one yourself. A page break that you insert is called a **manual page break**. A manual page break appears as a dotted line across the page with the words *Page Break* in the middle. You insert a manual page break when you want to begin a new page.

## Tip

Word repaginates a document as you make changes to it. In other words, as you insert, delete, and move text, Word changes where it inserts soft page breaks. Word does not change the location of manual page breaks; you must do that yourself.

Regardless of whether you keep Word's soft page breaks or insert your own manual page breaks, you should make sure that the page breaks do not leave widows and orphans. A **widow** is the last line of a paragraph printed by itself at the top of a page. An **orphan** is the first line of a paragraph printed by itself at the bottom of a page. Leaving a word or short phrase at the top or bottom of a page can interrupt the flow of long documents. To eliminate widows and orphans and to further control where Word inserts page breaks, you can use the options in the **Paragraph** dialog box. The following table explains the options in the **Paragraph** dialog box that you can use to specify how Word should treat situations that might cause paragraphs to break at undesirable places.

| Line and page break options | |
|---|---|
| Widow/Orphan control | Prevents Word from printing the last line of a paragraph by itself at the top of a page (widow) or the first line of a paragraph by itself at the bottom of a page (orphan). |
| Keep lines together | Prevents a page break within a paragraph. |
| Keep with next | Prevents a page break between the selected paragraph and the following paragraph. |
| Page break before | Inserts a page break before the selected paragraph. |

## Important

You have to apply the options in the dialog box on a paragraph-by-paragraph basis.

You can also insert a section break in your document. A **section break** identifies a portion of the document that you can format with unique page settings, such as different margins. A section break appears as a double-dotted line across the page with the words *Section Break* and the type of section break in the middle. There are several types of section breaks that you can insert. For example, if you want a section to begin on a new page, you insert a New page section break. You can also insert a Continuous section break or Even page or Odd page section breaks. Dividing a document into sections is especially helpful when you are creating long documents that cover a wide range of topics.

## Tip

As you make changes to your document, you might want to preview the way that it looks. Previewing your document helps you determine if and where you might need a manual page break or where you might want to insert a section break. To preview your document, click the **Print Preview** button on the Standard toolbar. Not only can you review the layout of your document in the Print Preview window, but you can also make changes to the layout from within the Print Preview window.

The way in which a page is laid out in a printed document is called the **page orientation**. The default page orientation in Word is portrait. When the page orientation is **portrait**, the page is taller than it is wide. **Landscape** orientation, on the other hand, is when the page is wider than it is tall. A document has only one page orientation unless you divide your document into sections. Then each section can have its own page orientation.

If you have a multiple-page document, you might want to insert page numbers. You can do this by using the **Page Numbers** command on the **Insert** menu. Page numbers appear in the lower-right corner of each page by default, but you can change their position and alignment by using the **Position and Alignment** options in the **Page Numbers** dialog box. You can change the position of the page numbers to the top and align them on the left or center them, depending on your personal preference.

You can also add information, such as the name of your company or the author of the document, that is printed on every page of your document. The **header** is text that is printed at the top of each page. The **footer** is text that is printed at the bottom of each page. To enter text for a header or footer, you select the **Header and Footer** command on the **View** menu. When you select the command, the document view changes to Print Layout view, the Header section appears at the top of the page, and the Footer section appears at the bottom of the page. The Header and Footer toolbar appears as well. You can use the Header and Footer toolbar to enter document-related text, such as the name of the file or the date the document was last printed. If your document contains section breaks, you can have different headers and footers for each section.

The Garden Company often sends articles to its customers. An article written on composting needs to be paginated, and the last page about the do's and don'ts of composting needs to be formatted differently from the rest of the article.

FormatPage

In this exercise, you insert page and section breaks, make sure that page breaks do not leave widows and orphans, change the page orientation, and add a header and a footer in the document.

**1** On the Standard toolbar, click the **Open** button.

Open

The **Open** dialog box appears.

**2** Navigate to the **SBS** folder on your hard disk, double-click the **Word** folder, double-click the **FormattingDoc** folder, and then double-click the **FormatPage** file.

The FormatPage document opens.

Print Preview

**3** On the Standard toolbar, click the **Print Preview** button.

The Print Preview window appears.

Multiple Pages

**4** Click the **Multiple Pages** button on the Print Preview toolbar, and then drag the pointer to select four pages (2 x 2 Pages).

The Print Preview window shows the four pages of the document with a widow at the top of the second page.

**5** On the **File** menu, click **Page Setup**.

The **Page Setup** dialog box appears, displaying the **Margins** tab.

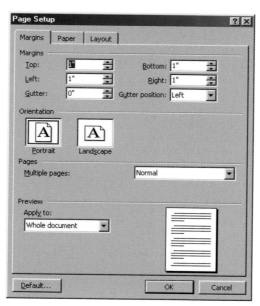

**6** In the **Margins** area, select the value in the **Top** box and type **1.25"**, select the value in the **Bottom** box and type **1.25"**, and then click **OK**.

The amount of blank space at the top and bottom of each page increases from 1 inch to 1.25 inches. The changes in the margins eliminated the widow at the top of page 2.

## Tip

The standard size of a page is 8.5 inches by 11 inches. With margins of 1.5 inches on each side, you are left with a work area that is 5.5 inches wide.

Close Preview

**7** On the Print Preview toolbar, click the **Close Preview** button to close the Print Preview window.

**8** Press the ⬇ key four times, and then click in the first line of text in the paragraph that begins with the text *If you take the time*.

The first two lines of the paragraph appear at the bottom of page 2. You can keep these lines of text with the rest of the paragraph.

**9** On the **Format** menu, click **Paragraph** to display the **Paragraph** dialog box, and then click the **Line and Page Breaks** tab, if necessary.

**10** If necessary, select the **Widow/Orphan control** check box, select the **Keep lines together** check box, and then click **OK**.

The page break moves up so that all the lines of text in the paragraph appear on the same page.

**11** Press ⬇ twice, and then click to the left of the text *Hot or Cold?*.

**12** On the **Insert** menu, click **Break** to display the **Break** dialog box.

**13** In the **Break types** area, verify that the **Page break** option is selected, and then click **OK**.

A dotted line with the words *Page Break* appears, indicating that you inserted a manual page break. There are now five pages in the document.

**14** Scroll down to the last paragraph, and then position the insertion point to the left of the title *COMPOSTING DO's AND DON'Ts*.

**15** On the **Insert** menu, click **Break** to open the **Break** dialog box, click the **Next page** option in the **Section break types** area, and then click **OK**.

A double dotted line with the text *Section Break (Next Page)* appears.

**16** Press Ctrl+Home to move the insertion point to the beginning of the document, and then on the **View** menu, click **Header and Footer**.

The document is now in Print Layout view. At the top of the document window, there is an empty box in which you can enter the text for the header for section 1 of the document.

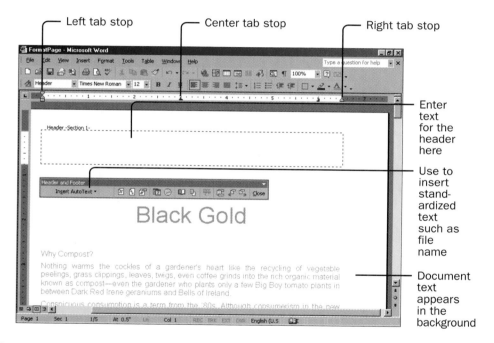

Left tab stop     Center tab stop     Right tab stop

Enter text for the header here

Use to insert standardized text such as file name

Document text appears in the background

Black Gold

**17** Type **The Garden Company**, and then click the **Show Next** button on the Header and Footer toolbar.

The insertion point is now in the **Header - Section 2** text box.

**18** On the Header and Footer toolbar, click the **Same As Previous** button, click the **Yes** button in the message box (if necessary), select the text *The Garden Company*, and then press Del.

The company is deleted from the header so that it doesn't appear as the previous header.

Switch
Between
Header and
Footer

**19** Click the **Switch Between Header and Footer** button to switch to the footer text box. You do not want the same footer for section 2 as you have for section 1.

Same as
Previous

**20** On the Header and Footer toolbar, click the **Same As Previous** button, and then click the **Show Previous** button on the Header and Footer toolbar.

The insertion point is now in the Footer - Section 1 text box.

Insert Page
Number

**21** Press the ⊞ key to move the insertion point to the center tab stop, click the **Insert Page Number** button on the Header and Footer toolbar, and then click the **Close Header and Footer** button.

The first four pages in the first section of the document are numbered.

Print Preview

**22** On the Standard toolbar, click the **Print Preview** button to display the print preview window.

Multiple Pages

**23** On the Print Preview toolbar, click the **Multiple Pages** button, click and drag the pointer to select six pages (2 x 3 Pages) so that all five pages in the document are displayed, and then click the last page in the document to enlarge the view of the page.

**24** On the **File** menu, click **Page Setup** to open the **Page Setup** dialog box, click the **Margins** tab, click the **Landscape** icon, make sure that **This section** in the **Apply to** section is selected, and then click **OK**.

**25** Click the page with the pointer so that all five pages are redisplayed in the Print Preview window.

Note that the company name appears at the top of the first four pages of the document and that there are page numbers on the bottom of the first four pages. Note also that the last page is wider than it is tall and does not have header or footer text.

Close Preview

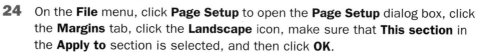

**26** On the Print Preview toolbar, click the **Close Preview** button to close the Print Preview window.

**27** On the Standard toolbar, click the **Save** button to save the document.

Close Window

**28** Click the **Close Window** button in the document window.

The FormatPage document closes.

# Changing the Look of a Document with Styles

W2002-2-4
W2002e-2-2

As you change the appearance of the text in your documents, you might find that you have created a look, or style, of your own. You may want to take advantage of the styles that Word provides. A **style** is a collection of text and paragraph formatting that you can apply to text throughout your document.

You can apply a set of formatting changes to your documents at the same time using styles. **Character styles** format selected words and lines of text within a paragraph, whereas **paragraph styles** format entire paragraphs, including their indents, alignment, and tabs. For example, a character style might be 18-point, bold, underlined, and centered text, whereas a paragraph style might include a border and hanging indent. Instead of applying each of these formatting effects or attributes individually, you can apply all of theses attributes using a style.

Unless you choose a template from the **Templates** dialog box, the documents that you create use the same default template, the Normal template. In the Normal template (as in all templates), there are styles that make up the formatting attributes of the template. For example, the Normal style includes the default font style, font size, and alignment. The default Normal style is 12-point Times New Roman text that is aligned on the left margin. The text that you type in your document uses the Normal style until you apply another style. For example, you might apply the Heading 1 style to text that you want to use as the title of your document.

Styles and
Formatting
task pane
new for
**Office**XP

To apply another style to the text in your document, you can use the **Style** down arrow on the Formatting toolbar or the **Styles and Formatting** task pane. You can also create a new style. You can modify an existing style or create a new style based on text that you have formatted. When you modify a style, the text in your document associated with that style is updated to reflect the changes.

To enhance the appearance of the article on composting, The Garden Company wants to format the main headings by using styles.

FormatStyle

Open

In this exercise, you apply, modify, and delete a style using the **Styles and Formatting** task pane.

1   On the Standard toolbar, click the **Open** button.

The **Open** dialog box appears.

2   Navigate to the **SBS** folder on your hard disk, double-click the **Word** folder, double-click the **FormattingDoc** folder, and then double-click the **Format-Style** file.

The FormatStyle document opens.

3   Select the line of text *Why Compost?*.

4   On the **Format** menu, click **Styles and Formatting**.

The **Styles and Formatting** task pane appears.

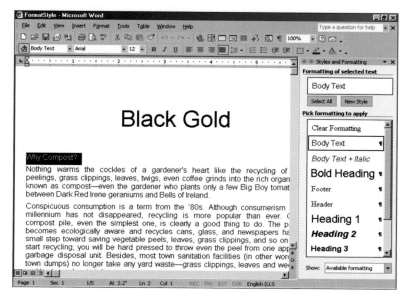

**5**  In the **Styles and Formatting** task pane, point to the preview box in the **Formatting of selected text** selection.

A ScreenTip appears, displaying the style and attributes of the selected text. In this case, the style is Body Text, and the attributes are Normal style plus the default font Arial with the text justified and the spacing before and after the paragraph at 6 points.

**6**  In the **Styles and Formatting** task pane, scroll down the list, and then click the **Heading 2** style in the **Pick formatting to apply section**.

The selected text changes to the Heading 2 style.

**7**  Click in the document, scroll down the document, hold down the ⌷Ctrl key, select the line of text *What Is a Compost Pile?,* scroll down the document, select the line of text *How Do You Make a Compost Pile?*, scroll down the document, select the line of text *Hot or Cold?*, and then select the line of text *Compost and Soil*.

**8**  In the **Styles and Formatting** task pane, click the **Heading 2** style to apply the style to the selected text.

**9**  Scroll to the top of the document, click in the line of text *Why Compost?*, and then click **Select All** in the **Styles and Formatting** task pane.

Word selects all the text in the document with the style of the selected text, which is Heading 2.

**10**  In the **Styles and Formatting** task pane, click **New Style**.

The **New Style** dialog box appears.

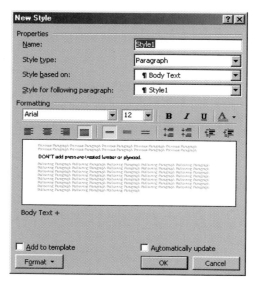

**11** In the **Name** box, type **Heading 2 Plus** to create a new name for the style.

**12** In the **Formatting** area, click the **Font Size** down arrow, click **16**, click the **Font Color** down arrow, click the **Blue** color box (sixth column, second row), and then click **OK**.

The Heading 2 Plus style appears in the **Styles and Formatting** task pane.

**13** In the **Styles and Formatting** task pane, click the **Heading 2 Plus** style.

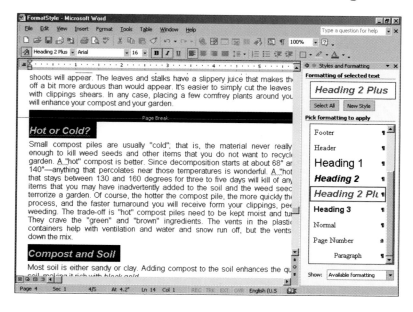

**14** In the **Styles and Formatting** task pane, point to the **Heading 2 Plus** style, click the **Heading 2 Plus** down arrow on the right, and then click **Modify**.

The **Modify Style** dialog box appears.

Italic

**15** In the **Formatting** area, click the **Italic** button to deselect the attribute, and then click **OK**.

The Heading 2 Plus style is updated along with all text with the style.

**16** In the **Styles and Formatting** task pane, click **Heading 2**.

The selected text is formatted with the selected style.

## Tip

You can use the **Find and Replace** dialog box to search for a specific style and replace it with a different style. On the **Edit** menu, click **Replace**, click **More**, click **Format**, and then click **Style**. In the **Find Style** dialog box, click the style that you want to find, and then click **OK**. Click in the **Replace With** box, click **Format**, click **Style**, click the style that you want to use, and then click **OK**. Click **Find Next** to search for the next occurrence of the style, and then click **Replace**.

**17** In the **Styles and Formatting** task pane, point to the **Heading 2 Plus** style, click the down arrow to the right, and then click **Delete**.

An alert dialog box appears, asking whether you want to delete the style.

**18** Click **Yes** to delete the Heading 2 Plus style.

**19** In the **Styles and Formatting** task pane, click the **Show** down arrow, and then click **Formatting in use**.

The styles used in the document appear in the task pane.

Close

**20** In the **Styles and Formatting** task pane, click the **Close** button to close the task pane.

## Tip

If a wavy blue line appears under a word or phrase as you type, Word detects inconsistent formatting. To remove the wavy blue line and not correct the inconsistency, right-click the word or phrase, and then click **Ignore Once** or **Ignore All**. To turn off the formatting options, on the **Tools** menu, click **Options**, click the **Edit** tab, clear **Keep track of formatting** check box, and clear the **Mark formatting inconsistencies** check box.

**21** On the Standard toolbar, click the **Save** button to save the document.

Close Window

**22** Click the **Close Window** button in the document window.

The FormatStyle document closes.

# Changing the Look of a Document with a Theme

You can change the entire look of a document by applying one of Word's 80 different themes. A **theme** is a unified look that incorporates the following: heading styles; text styles formatted with font effects, such as small caps and shading; lists with specially designed bullet characters; background colors; fill effects; and images. Each theme provides color schemes and graphical design elements that project a special image or tone. For example, the Axis theme uses a background that looks like parchment paper and text design elements that match. You can use a theme when designing Web pages, reports, and presentations.

FormatTheme

In this exercise, you apply a theme to an existing document and then display the theme styles in the **Styles and Formatting** task pane.

**1** On the Standard toolbar, click the **Open** button.

The **Open** dialog box appears.

Open

**2** Navigate to the **SBS** folder on your hard disk, double-click the **Word** folder, double-click the **FormattingDoc** folder, and then double-click the **Format-Theme** file.

The FormatTheme document opens.

**3** On the **Format** menu, click **Theme**.

The **Theme** dialog box appears.

**4** In the **Choose a Theme** list, scroll down until the **Nature** theme appears, and then click **Nature**.

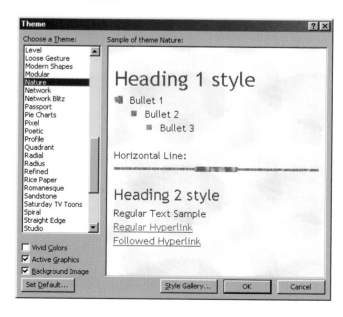

## Important

Some themes do not appear in the **Theme** dialog box until you install them from the Microsoft Office XP installation CD. To install a theme, click **Theme** on the **Format** menu, click a theme in the **Choose a Theme** list, and then click **Install**.

**5** Select the **Vivid Colors** check box to brighten the colors in the theme.

**6** Click **OK**.

The Nature theme is applied to the document.

**7** Select the line that starts with *Why Compost?*.

**8** On the **Format** menu, click **Styles and Formatting**.

The **Styles and Formatting** task pane appears, displaying the styles used in the Nature theme.

Close

**9** In the **Styles and Formatting** task pane, click the **Close** button to close the task pane.

**10** On the Standard toolbar, click the **Save** button to save the document.

Close Window

**11** Click the **Close Window** button in the document window.

The FormatTheme document closes.

## Chapter Wrap-Up

To finish this chapter:

Close

● On the **File** menu, click **Exit**, or click the **Close** button in the Word window.

Word closes.

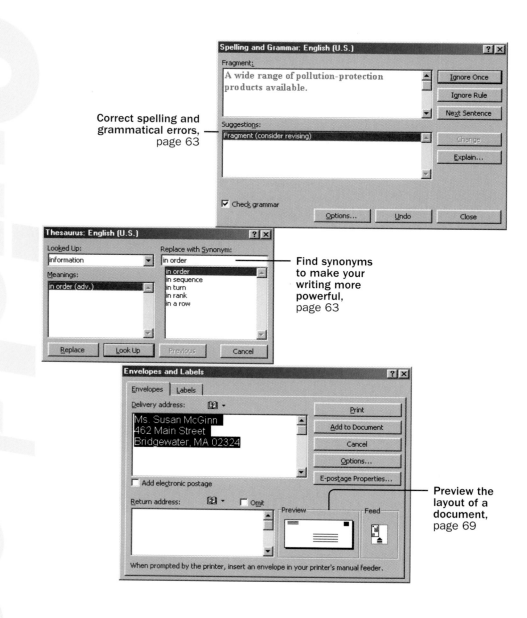

Correct spelling and grammatical errors, page 63

Find synonyms to make your writing more powerful, page 63

Preview the layout of a document, page 69

# Chapter 4
# Proofreading and Printing a Document

**After completing this chapter, you will be able to:**

✔ Check the spelling and grammar in a document.
✔ Preview and print a document.

Before you share your documents with others, you should take a few steps to ensure that the documents are ready for distribution. One of the most important steps to take is to check the document's grammar and spelling to ensure that the words are spelled correctly and that the text is grammatically correct. You can use Word's spelling and grammar checker and thesaurus to correct spelling and grammar errors, add new words to Word's online dictionary, and replace words with synonyms that improve readability and match the reading level of your audience. Because the online dictionary might not include specialized terms, proper names, or foreign words, you can use Word's AutoText feature to store and quickly insert these types of text. When you finish proofreading your document, you can preview the document to view and adjust the layout of your document before you print it. Then you're ready to print the document and any related materials, such as an envelope.

In this chapter, you'll proofread and print a letter for the assistant buyer at The Garden Company. You'll check the spelling and grammar in the Word document and then preview the document before you print it. You'll also create and insert an AutoText entry and print an envelope.

This chapter uses the practice files SpellCheck and PreviewPrint that you installed from this book's CD-ROM. For details about installing the practice files, see "Using the Book's CD-ROM" at the beginning of this book.

## Checking the Spelling and Grammar in a Document

W2002-1-1
W2002-1-3

Proofreading a document involves checking the spelling of words, correcting grammatical errors, and choosing language that best conveys your message to your audience. You should always proofread a document *before* you print and share it with others. Sending a document that is filled with spelling and grammatical errors creates a poor impression on your reader. You can use Word's **Spelling and Grammar** features to correct errors and maintain professional writing standards.

As you type the text of your document, by default Word underlines spelling and grammar errors with red or green wavy lines. A red wavy line indicates that Word does not recognize the spelling of the word; that is, the word is not included in Word's online dictionary. A green line indicates a possible grammar error. To fix individual spelling and grammar errors quickly, you can right-click a word underlined with a red or green wavy line to display a list of corrections from which you can choose.

In addition to correcting individual errors, you can check the entire document for spelling and grammar errors by clicking the **Spelling and Grammar** button on the Standard toolbar. When you start checking spelling and grammar, Word compares each word in the document with the words in its dictionary. Word stops at each red and green wavy line and displays the possible reason for the error. For example, if a word is misspelled, the **Spelling and Grammar** dialog box identifies the misspelled word and provides a list of possible replacements. If Word finds a potential grammar error, the **Spelling and Grammar** dialog box identifies the problem and provides suggestions for correcting the error.

The options that are displayed in the **Spelling and Grammar** dialog box depend on the type of error that Word encounters. The following table describes the options in the **Spelling and Grammar** dialog box:

| Button or Option | Function |
| --- | --- |
| **Ignore Once** | Leaves the highlighted error unchanged and finds the next spelling or grammar error. If you click in the document to edit it, this button changes to the **Resume** button. After you finish editing, click the **Resume** button to continue checking the spelling and grammar. |
| **Ignore All** or **Ignore Rule** | Leaves all occurrences of the highlighted spelling or grammar error unchanged throughout the document and continues to check the rest of the document. Word ignores the spelling or grammar of this word in this document and in all documents whose spelling is checked during the current Word session. |
| **Next Sentence** | Accepts manual changes in a document and continues to check the document. |
| **Add to Dictionary** | Adds the selected word in the **Not in dictionary** box to the custom dictionary. A custom dictionary contains your own words. |
| **Change** | Changes the highlighted error to the word that you select in the **Suggestions** box. |

| Button or Option | Function |
|---|---|
| **Change All** | Changes all occurrences of the highlighted error to the word that you select in the **Suggestions** box and then continues to check the rest of the document. |
| **Explain** | Provides more information about the grammar error. |
| **AutoCorrect** | Adds the spelling error and its correction to the **AutoCorrect** list so that Word corrects it automatically as you type. |
| **Undo** | Undoes the last spelling or grammar action that you performed. |
| **Options** | Opens the **Spelling and Grammar Options** dialog box. Use this dialog box to open a different custom dictionary or to change the rules that Word uses to check spelling and grammar. |

To make sure that you are using the exact words in your documents, you can use Word's **thesaurus**. For example, the language that you use in a letter to a friend is different from the language that you use in business correspondence. You can use the thesaurus to look up alternative words or synonyms for a selected word. To use the thesaurus, you select the word that you want to look up, point to **Language** on the **Tools** menu, and then click **Thesaurus**. The **Thesaurus** dialog box appears, displaying a list of synonyms with equivalent meanings.

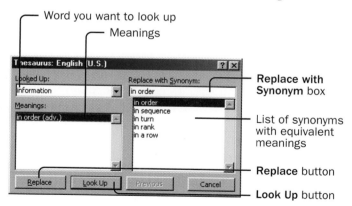

SpellCheck

In this exercise, you check the spelling in the document and add common terms that are not already in the online dictionary. You find, review, and correct a grammar error, and use the thesaurus to replace one word with another.

**1** Start Word, if necessary.

Open

**2** On the Standard toolbar, click the **Open** button.

The **Open** dialog box appears.

**3** Navigate to the **SBS** folder on your hard disk, double-click the **Word** folder, double-click the **ProofingPrint** folder, and then double-click the **SpellCheck** file.

The SpellCheck document opens, displaying red and green wavy lines.

Spelling and Grammar

**4** On the Standard toolbar, click the **Spelling and Grammar** button.

The **Spelling and Grammar** dialog box appears, highlighting the first word that Word does not recognize. The online dictionary contains many common first and last names, but it does not recognize unusual or foreign names.

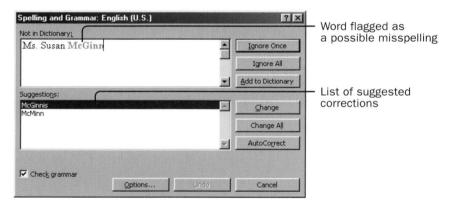

Word flagged as a possible misspelling

List of suggested corrections

## Troubleshooting

If the spelling and grammar checker doesn't find the errors in this document, you need to reset the spelling and grammar checker. On the **Tools** menu, click **Options**, click the **Spelling & Grammar** tab, click **Recheck Document**, and then click **Yes** to recheck words and grammar that were previously checked or that you chose to ignore.

**5** Click **Ignore Once** to skip the name.

Word stops at the next word that it does not recognize—*bot*.

**6** In the **Suggestions** box, click **both**, and then click **Change**.

Word corrects the misspelling. The next flagged word is *envrionmentally*.

**7** In the **Suggestions** box, click **environmentally**, and then click **AutoCorrect** to redefine the AutoCorrect entry.

Word adds the correction to the AutoCorrect list. The next time that you type *envrionmentally* by mistake, Word will correct the spelling for you as you type.

Word flags *harty* as a possible misspelling.

**8**  With the word *hearty* selected in the **Suggestions** box, click **Change All** to change this and subsequent occurrences of *harty* to *hearty*.

Word corrects both misspellings and then flags *crassula* as a word that it doesn't recognize.

**9**  Click **Ignore All**.

Because this is the correct spelling of crassula, a type of plant, you can skip any other instances of *crassula* in the letter.

Word stops at the next word that it does not recognize—this time a Latin word.

**10**  Click **Add to Dictionary** three times to add to the custom dictionary the next three Latin words that Word does not recognize.

The three Latin words in italics are spelled correctly. By adding them to the custom dictionary, you prevent Word from flagging them later.

Word flags a possible grammar error in green and indicates that this text could be a sentence fragment. The sentence is missing a verb.

Grammar error highlighted in green

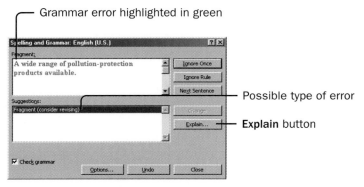

Possible type of error

**Explain** button

**11**  In the **Spelling and Grammar** dialog box, click before the word *available* in the highlighted text, type **are**, press    , and then click **Change**.

An alert message appears, indicating that Word has finished checking the spelling and grammar in the document.

**12**  Click **OK** to close the alert message.

**13**  Press `Ctrl`+`Home` to move the insertion point to the top of the document.

**14**  Double-click *important* near the end of the first paragraph to select the word.

**15** On the **Tools** menu, point to **Language**, and then click **Thesaurus**.

The **Thesaurus** dialog box appears, displaying a list of meanings associated with the word and suggested synonyms for *important*.

**16** With *significant* selected in the **Replace with Synonym** box, click the **Replace** button.

Word replaces *important* with *significant*.

**17** On the Standard toolbar, click the **Save** button to save the document.

Close Window

**18** Click the **Close Window** button in the document window.

The SpellCheck document closes.

# Translating Text in Another Language

Translate text
new for
**Office**XP

Word provides a basic multi-language dictionary and translation feature so that you can look up text in the dictionary of a different language, translate simple, short phrases, and insert the translated text into your document directly from the **Translate** task pane. You can often use these translations to determine the main ideas in a document written in a foreign language. If you need to translate longer sections of text, you can connect to translation services on the World Wide Web directly from the **Translate** task pane. For important or sensitive documents, you might want to have a trained person do the translation, since computer translation might not preserve the text's full meaning, detail, or tone. You can also look up words or phrases in the dictionary of a different language, provided that the language dictionary is installed on your computer and enabled through Microsoft Office XP Language Settings. To enable a language, click the **Start** button on the taskbar, point to **Programs**, point to **Microsoft Office Tools**, click **Microsoft Office XP Language Settings**, click the **Enabled Languages** tab, select a language, and then click **Add**.

To translate text in another language:

**1** Select the text in your document that you want to translate.

**2** On the **Tools** menu, point to **Language**, and then click **Translate**.

The **Translate** task pane appears.

**3** In the **Translate** task pane, click the **Current selection** option in the **Translate what?** section.

**4** In the **Dictionary** box, select the languages that you want to translate from and to, and then click **Go**.

The translated text appears in the **Results** box.

**5** In the **Results** box, select the translated text, and then click **Replace**.

The selected text in your document is replaced with the translated text.

# Previewing and Printing a Document

W2002-3-5

Before printing a document, you should verify that its pages look the way that you want. You save time, money, and paper by avoiding duplicate printing. Print Preview shows you exactly how your text will be placed on each page. This is especially helpful when you have a multi-page document. The Print Preview toolbar provides the tools that you need to check the presentation of each page. If you have headers and footers in your document, they also appear in Print Preview. You can change the layout of your document in Print Preview, and you can even change the text.

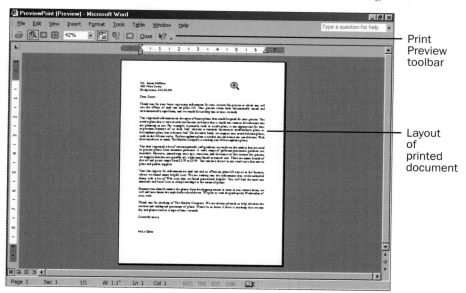

Print Preview toolbar

Layout of printed document

You can print your document by clicking the **Print** button on the Standard toolbar or the Print Preview toolbar. When you do, Word uses the current settings specified in the **Print** dialog box and prints to whichever printer that has been set as the default. To open the **Print** dialog box to view or change print settings, on the **File** menu, click **Print**. In the **Print** dialog box, you can choose to print the current page or select certain pages that you want to print. You can also choose to print more than one copy of a document or print other document components, such as the list of comments or styles associated with the document.

You can print envelopes and labels using addresses that you have entered in a document. To do this, you select the lines of the address (or the text that you want for the label), point to **Letters and Mailings** on the **Tools** menu, and then click **Envelopes and Labels** to open the **Envelopes and Labels** dialog box. You then choose the type of envelope or label that you need. You can also choose to print the envelope and label text in the font and font size that match those used in the document, and you can include a return address on the envelope.

## Tip

To provide a return address, Word uses the personalized information that you entered when you installed Word. You can change that information on the **User Information** tab in the **Options** dialog box, which you open by clicking **Options** on the **Tools** menu.

An assistant at The Garden Company wants to preview a letter before printing it and adjust the layout of the letter, if necessary. He wants to print the letter on a printer other than the one he normally uses and needs to print an envelope for the letter.

PreviewPrint

In this exercise, you preview a document, adjust the top margin in the print preview window, and select a new printer before sending the letter to be printed. After printing the document, you select the inside address and use it to print an envelope and label.

## Tip

To complete this exercise, you need a printer connected to your computer and the printer software installed.

Open

1   On the Standard toolbar, click the **Open** button.

The **Open** dialog box appears.

2   Navigate to the **SBS** folder on your hard disk, double-click the **Word** folder, double-click the **ProofingPrint** folder, and then double-click the **PreviewPrint** file.

The PreviewPrint document opens.

## Troubleshooting

If an information icon appears in the document window, you can ignore it for now. Words and phrases underlined with dotted lines have a Smart Tag. Smart Tags provide options for using text as data in other programs. For example, you might want to add Susan McGinn's name and address to your Contacts list in Microsoft Outlook. To do so, click the Smart Tag, and then select **Add to Contacts** from the list of Smart Tag options.

Print Preview

3   On the Standard toolbar, click the **Print Preview** button.

The letter appears in the print preview window, showing the entire page as it would appear on the printed page.

**4** Position the pointer (which changes to the two-headed arrow) over the **Top Margin** indicator on the vertical ruler, and then drag the pointer down about a half inch, making sure that the last line of text is not forced to another page, as shown in the following illustration:

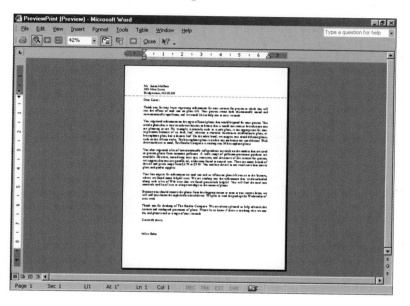

Magnifying Glass (+)

**5** Position the Magnifying Glass (+) pointer over the document, and then click near the top of the document.

The document view zoom percentage changes to 100%, the actual size of the page.

Magnifying Glass (-)

**6** Position the Magnifying Glass (-) pointer over the document, and then click near the top of the document.

The zoom percentage is reduced.

Close Preview

Close

**7** On the Print Preview toolbar, click the **Close Preview** button.

The print preview window closes, and the Word document window appears in Normal view.

## Tip

If you are satisfied with the current **Print** dialog box settings, you can click the **Print** button on the Standard toolbar to print directly without first viewing the settings.

**8** On the **File** menu, click **Print**.

The **Print** dialog box appears.

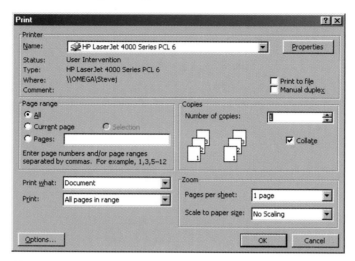

**9** Click the **Name** down arrow, select a printer, if necessary, and then click **OK** to send the document to the printer.

**10** Select the three lines of the inside address at the top of the document. (Do not select the blank line below the inside address.)

**11** On the **Tools** menu, point to **Letters and Mailings**, and then click **Envelopes and Labels**.

The **Envelopes and Labels** dialog box appears with the inside address selected in the **Delivery Address** box.

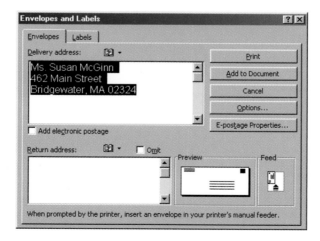

**12** Select the **Omit** check box, and then click **Options**.

This option excludes the return address when you print envelopes.

The **Envelope Options** dialog box appears, displaying envelope types and styles that your printer accepts. The default size is 10, which is acceptable.

**13** Click **OK**, insert an envelope in the printer according to your printer manufacturer's directions, and then click **Print**.

The envelope is printed.

**14** On the **Tools** menu, point to **Letters and Mailings**, click **Envelopes and Labels** to display the **Envelopes and Labels** dialog box, and then click the **Labels** tab.

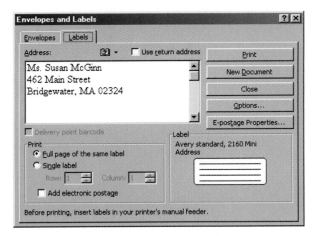

**15** Click the **Single label** option.

Row 1 and Column 1 appear under the **Single label** option.

**16** Click **Print**.

The label is printed.

**17** On the Standard toolbar, click the **Save** button to save the document.

Close Window

☒

**18** Click the **Close Window** button in the document window.

The PreviewPrint document closes.

# Chapter Wrap-Up

To finish this chapter:

Close

☒

● On the **File** menu, click **Exit**, or click the **Close** button in the Word window.

Word closes.

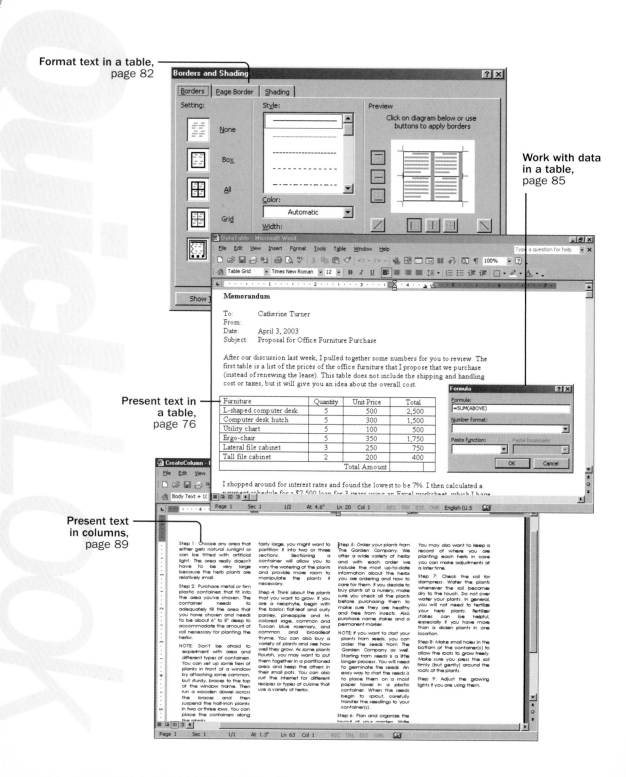

Format text in a table, page 82

**Borders and Shading**

Borders | Page Border | Shading

Setting:

None

Box

All

Grid

Style:

Color:

Automatic

Width:

Preview

Click on diagram below or use buttons to apply borders

Work with data in a table, page 85

Show

DataTable - Microsoft Word

File Edit View Insert Format Tools Table Window Help

Type a question for help

Table Grid | Times New Roman | 12 | B I U

**Memorandum**

To:        Catherine Turner
From:
Date:      April 3, 2003
Subject:   Proposal for Office Furniture Purchase

After our discussion last week, I pulled together some numbers for you to review. The first table is a list of the prices of the office furniture that I propose that we purchase (instead of renewing the lease). This table does not include the shipping and handling cost or taxes, but it will give you an idea about the overall cost.

Present text in a table, page 76

| Furniture | Quantity | Unit Price | Total |
|---|---|---|---|
| L-shaped computer desk | 5 | 500 | 2,500 |
| Computer desk hutch | 5 | 300 | 1,500 |
| Utility chart | 5 | 100 | 500 |
| Ergo-chair | 5 | 350 | 1,750 |
| Lateral file cabinet | 3 | 250 | 750 |
| Tall file cabinet | 2 | 200 | 400 |
| | | Total Amount | |

**Formula**

Formula:
=SUM(ABOVE)

Number format:

Paste function:          Paste bookmark:

OK        Cancel

I shopped around for interest rates and found the lowest to be 7%. I then calculated a payment schedule for a $7,500 loan for 3 years using an Excel worksheet, which I have

CreateColumn -

File Edit View

Body Text + 1

Present text in columns, page 89

Page 1    Sec 1    1/2    At 4.6"   Ln 20  Col 1    REC TRK EXT OVR  English (U.S

Step 1: Choose any area that either gets natural sunlight or can be fitted with artificial light. The area really doesn't have to be very large because the herb plants are relatively small.

Step 2: Purchase metal or firm plastic containers that fit into the area you've chosen. The container needs to adequately fill the area that you have chosen and needs to be about 6" to 8" deep to accommodate the amount of soil necessary for planting the herbs.

NOTE: Don't be afraid to experiment with area and different types of containers. You can set up some tiers of planks in front of a window by attaching some common, but sturdy, braces to the top of the window frame. Then run a wooden dowel across the braces and then suspend the half-inch planks in two or three rows. You can place the containers along the planks.

fairly large, you might want to partition it into two or three sections. Sectioning a container will allow you to vary the watering of the plants and provide more room to manipulate the plants if necessary.

Step 4: Think about the plants that you want to grow. If you are a neophyte, begin with the basics: flat-leaf and curly parsley, pineapple and tri-colored sage, common and Tuscan blue rosemary, and common and broadleaf thyme. You can also buy a variety of plants and see how well they grow. As some plants flourish, you may want to put them together in a partitioned area and keep the others in their small pots. You can also surf the internet for different recipes or types of cuisine that use a variety of herbs.

Step 5: Order your plants from The Garden Company. We offer a wide variety of herbs and with each order we include the most up-to-date information about the herbs you are ordering and how to care for them. If you decide to buy plants at a nursery, make sure you check all the plants before purchasing them to make sure they are healthy and free from insects. Also purchase name stakes and a permanent marker.

NOTE: If you want to start your plants from seeds, you can order the seeds from The Garden Company as well. Starting from seeds is a little longer process. You will need to germinate the seeds. An easy way to start the seeds is to place them on a moist paper towel in a plastic container. When the seeds begin to sprout, carefully transfer the seedlings to your container(s).

Step 6: Plan and organize the layout of your garden. Write

You may also want to keep a record of where you are planting each herb in case you can make adjustments the area so you can make adjustments later time.

Step 7: Check the soil for dampness. Water the plants whenever the soil becomes dry to the touch. Do not over water your plants. In general, you will not need to fertilize your herb plants. Fertilizer stakes can be helpful, especially if you have more than a dozen plants in one location.

Step 8: Make small holes in the bottom of the container(s) to allow the roots to grow freely. Make sure you press the soil firmly (but gently) around the roots of the plants.

Step 9: Adjust the growing lights if you are using them.

Page 1    Sec 1    1/1    At 1.3"   Ln 63  Col 1    REC TRK EXT OVR

# Chapter 5
# Presenting Information in Tables and Columns

**After completing this chapter, you will be able to:**

✔ Present and format text in a table.

✔ Work with data in a table.

✔ Present text in columns.

You can use a table to group and organize the information in your document in a concise, consistent, and easy-to-read format. A table organizes information neatly into rows and columns. The intersection of a row and column is called a cell. You can create a uniform table with standard-sized cells or draw a custom table with various-sized cells, or you can create a table from existing text. Once you create your table, you can enter text, numbers, and graphics into cells. To help readers interpret the information in your table, you can arrange, or **sort**, the information in a logical order.

Once you have created a table, you can change the size of the table or of individual columns and rows. You can also insert and delete columns and rows as needed. To make the table visually appealing, you can format table text and add borders and shading to part or all of the table.

Tables often present numerical data. To perform standard mathematical calculations on numbers in a table, you can use the **Formula** command on the **Table** menu to add the numbers in a column or row, for example, or to find the average of the numbers. For more complex calculations, you can insert a Microsoft Excel worksheet into your document. Excel is a Microsoft Office program that you can use to perform complex calculations or statistical analysis.

Columns of text are another way that you can group and organize information in a document. Dividing text into columns is useful when you are creating a newsletter or brochure. In Word, you can define the number of columns that you want on a page. You can then choose to allow the text to flow from the bottom of one column to the top of the next column, as you see in newspapers. Or you can choose to end the column of text in a specific location, moving the subsequent text to the next column.

This chapter uses the practice files CreateTable, FormatTable, DataTable, InsertTable, and CreateColumn that you installed from this book's CD-ROM. For details about installing the practice files, see "Using the Book's CD-ROM" at the beginning of this book.

# Presenting Text in a Table

W2002-3-4
W2002e-1-2
W2002e-3-2

To add a simple table to a document, you can use the **Insert Table** button on the Standard toolbar and then select the number of rows and columns you want from the menu that appears. If you want to set the size of the table along with other options, such as table formatting, you use the **Insert** command on the **Table** menu to open the **Insert Table** dialog box. You can also add a table by converting existing plain text to a table.

Once you create a table, you enter text or numbers into cells just as you would in a paragraph, except pressing the Tab key in a table moves the insertion point from cell to cell instead of indenting a paragraph. In addition to Tab, you can also use the arrow keys or the mouse pointer to move from cell to cell. The leftmost cell in a row is considered the first cell in the row. The first row in the table is good for column headings, whereas the leftmost column is good for row labels.

After you have created a table, you can modify its structure by inserting or deleting columns and rows. If the insertion point is positioned in the rightmost cell in the last row of the table, you can press Tab to quickly add another row to the bottom of the table. You can also use the **Table** menu to insert, delete, and select rows and columns. To insert a row or column, you click to place the insertion point in the row or column where you want to insert one, point to **Insert** on the **Table** menu, and then click **Rows Above**, **Rows Below**, **Columns to the Right**, or **Columns to the Left**. If you select more than one row or column and use one of the **Insert** commands, Word adds that number of rows or columns to the table.

Selection
handle
new for
**Office**XP

You can resize an entire table or each column or row individually to accommodate the text that you are presenting. To resize a table quickly, you can click and then drag the selection handle that appears in the lower-right corner of the table.

You can also merge cells to create cells of varying sizes. For example, if you want the title to be in the first row of your table, you can merge the cells in that row to create one cell that spans the table's width. If you need to divide a cell into smaller cells, you can split a cell into additional columns or rows. You can use the **Merge Cells** and **Split Cells** commands on the **Table** menu to combine or separate cells.

To change a table, you might need to select the entire table or specific rows or columns. The following table explains how to select part or all of a table.

| To select | Action |
| --- | --- |
| A table | Click the **Select Table** button in the upper-left of the first cell in the table. Or on the **Table** menu, point to **Select**, and then click **Table**. |
| A column or a row | Point to the first row in a column or the first column in a row, and when the pointer changes to an arrow, click to select the column or row. |

| To select | Action |
|---|---|
| A cell | Double-click the cell. |
| Multiple cells | Click the first cell, hold down the ⎵shift⎵ key, and then press the ⬇ or ➡ key to select cells in a column or row, respectively. |

## Tip

The document must be in Print Layout view before you can use the **Select Table** button and the selection handle.

To move a table in a document, you can click the **Select Table** button and drag the table to another location in the document. You can also use the **Cut** and **Paste** buttons on the Standard toolbar to move a table.

You will often create a table to accommodate multiple columns or lists of information. After you enter the text, you can sort the information in ascending or descending order, and you can sort the information by column or row by using the **Sort** command on the **Table** menu. For example, if you have a table with column headings for name, address, and phone number, you can sort the table in alphabetical order by name to make it easier to find a person in the table.

The Garden Company needs to design an insert for its catalog, *The Garden Company Herbs*. The owner of the Garden Company wants the insert to include three tables: an order form, a table of shipping and handling fees, and a table of delivery services.

CreateTable

In this exercise, you create three tables. In the first table, you merge cells, enter text, and add rows. To create the second table, you convert existing plain text to a table. Finally, you sort information in a third table.

**1**   Start Word, if necessary.

Open

**2**   On the Standard toolbar, click the **Open** button.

The **Open** dialog box appears.

**3**   Navigate to the **SBS** folder on your hard disk, double-click the **Word** folder, double-click the **AddingTables** folder, and then double-click the **CreateTable** file.

The CreateTable document opens.

**4**   Press ⬇ to position the insertion point in the blank line below the *Please complete this form* sentence.

**5**   On the **Table** menu, point to **Insert**, and then click **Table**.

The **Insert Table** dialog box appears.

6   Make sure that the **Number of columns** box displays 5, click the **Number of rows** up arrow to display 5, and then click **OK**.

A blank table with five columns and five rows appears. The insertion point appears in the first cell.

7   Position the pointer in the selection area to the left of the first row, and then click to select the row.

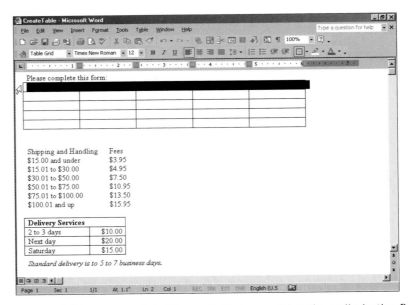

8   On the **Table** menu, click **Merge Cells** to combine the cells in the first row into one cell.

9   Type **The Garden Company Herb Plant Order Form**.

The text appears in the first row.

**10** Click in the first cell in the second row, and then type **Page No.**

**11** Press <kbd>Tab</kbd> and type **Description**, press <kbd>Tab</kbd> and type **Quantity**, press <kbd>Tab</kbd> and type **Unit Price**, press <kbd>Tab</kbd> and type **Total**, and then press <kbd>Tab</kbd> to move the insertion point to the first cell in the next row.

**12** Type **25**, press <kbd>Tab</kbd> and type **Lemon Basil**, press <kbd>Tab</kbd> and type **3**, press <kbd>Tab</kbd> and type **2.29**, and then press <kbd>Tab</kbd> and type **6.87**.

The text appears in the second row.

**13** Position the pointer in the selection area to the left of the fourth row, and then drag to select the last two rows.

**14** On the **Table** menu, point to **Insert**, and then click **Rows Below** to add two more rows to the table.

Two rows appear below the two selected rows.

**15** In the last row, click in the first cell, hold down <kbd>Shift</kbd>, and then press <kbd>→</kbd> four times to select the first four cells in the row.

**16** On the **Table** menu, click **Merge Cells** to combine the cells in the first row into one cell.

**17** Type **Total Order Amount**, and then press <kbd>Tab</kbd> twice.

A new row is added to the bottom of the table. Note that the new row uses the structure of the preceding row.

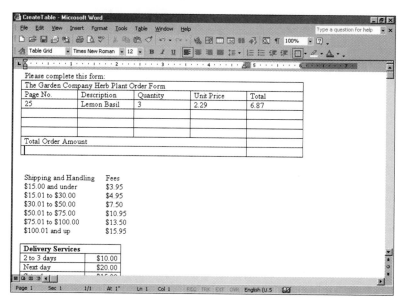

**18** Type **Add Shipping and Handling Fee**, press <kbd>Tab</kbd> twice to add a new row, and then type **Add Delivery Service Fee, if necessary**.

**19** Press [Tab] twice to add a new row, and then type **Total Amount Due**.

**20** In the paragraphs below the table, select the block of text that begins *Shipping and Handling* and ends with *$15.95*.

**21** On the **Table** menu, point to **Convert**, and then click **Text to Table**.

The **Convert Text to Table** dialog box appears.

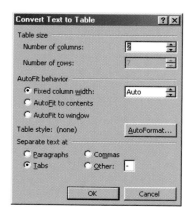

**22** Make sure that the **Number of columns** box displays *2*, and then click **OK**.

The selected text appears in a table with two columns and seven rows.

Resize pointer

**23** Click in the table to deselect the cells, point to the right edge of the table until the pointer changes to a resize pointer, and then double-click to resize the table to the width of the text in the cell.

**24** Scroll down, and then click anywhere in the Delivery Services table to place the insertion point.

**25** On the **Table** menu, click **Sort**.

The **Sort** dialog box appears.

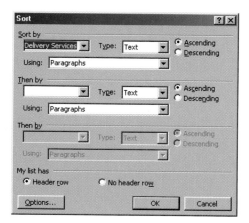

**26** Click the **Sort by** down arrow, and then click **(Column2)**, if necessary, click the **Descending** option, make sure the **Header row** option in the **My list has** area is selected, and then click **OK** to sort the table in descending order by Column2

Print Layout
View

**27** Click the **Print Layout View** button, and then scroll down the document window to bring the Delivery Services table, the Shipping and Handling Fees table, and the bottom of the Order Form table into view.

Select Table

**28** Hold down the **Select Table** button in the upper-left corner of the Delivery Services table to select the table.

**29** Drag the outline of the table up and to the right of the Shipping and Handling Fees table, aligning the top of the Delivery Services table with the top of the Shipping and Handling table and the right side of the Delivery Services table with the right side of the Order Form table.

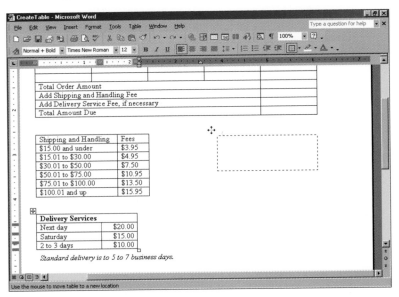

**30** When the Delivery Services table is positioned correctly, release the mouse button.

**31** Point to the Delivery Services table, and then drag the selection handle in the lower-right corner down, releasing the mouse button when the lower-edge of the Delivery Services table is aligned with the lower-edge of the Shipping and Handling Fees table to align the tables.

**32** On the Standard toolbar, click the **Save** button to save the document.

Close Window

**33** Click the **Close Window** button in the document window.

The CreateTable document closes.

# Formatting Text in a Table

W2002-3-4

To enhance the appearance of the text in a table, you can format it using the buttons on the Formatting toolbar, just as you would when formatting any text in a Word document. You can also format the structure of the table by adding borders and shading.

You can use the buttons on the Formatting toolbar to change the appearance and the alignment of the text in a cell. To modify the table or cell borders, you use the **Borders and Shading** command on the **Format** menu, which opens the **Borders and Shading** dialog box. You can also add shading to the table or cells using the options on the **Shading** tab in the **Borders and Shading** dialog box.

Table styles
new for
**Office**XP

To format a table and its text quickly, you can apply a **Table AutoFormat** using the **Table AutoFormat** command on the **Table** menu. The **Table AutoFormat** dialog box provides 18 predesigned table formats that include a variety of borders, colors, and attributes, such as italics, that will give your table a professional look. This is useful for quickly formatting a table. You can also create your own table style to quickly make one table look like another. Select a table, open the **Table AutoFormat** dialog box, click **New** or select a table style and click **Modify**, and then use the formatting options to define the table style.

To make sure that the tables in The Garden Company's catalog are easily distinguishable from one another, but also complementary, the owner will format the tables.

FormatTable

In this exercise, you format the text in a table and add shading to a cell. You also apply an AutoFormat and add a border to a table.

**1** On the Standard toolbar, click the **Open** button.

Open

The **Open** dialog box appears.

**2** Navigate to the **SBS** folder on your hard disk, double-click the **Word** folder, double-click the **AddingTables** folder, and then double-click the **FormatTable** file.

The FormatTable document opens.

# Troubleshooting

The document should open in Print Layout view. If the document is in Normal view, click the **Print Layout View** button.

**3** Position the pointer in the selection area to the left of the first row in the Order Form table, and then click to select the first row.

**4** On the Formatting toolbar, click the **Font** down arrow, and then click **Arial**. Click the **Font Size** down arrow, and then click **16**.

The font style changes to Arial, and the size changes to 16 points.

**Center**

**5** On the Formatting toolbar, click the **Bold** button, and then click the **Center** button.

The text appears in the center of the cell with the bold formatting style.

**6** On the **Format** menu, click **Borders and Shading**.

The **Borders and Shading** dialog box appears.

**7** Click the **Shading** tab.

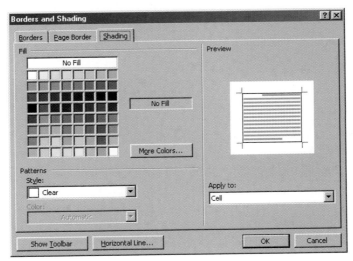

**8** Click the **Light Yellow** color box in the color palette (last row, third column), and then click **OK**.

Word adds light yellow shading to the background of the first row.

**9** Select the third row in the table.

**Italic**

**10** On the Formatting toolbar, click the **Italic** button to change the selected text to italic.

**Font Color**

**11** On the Formatting toolbar, click the **Font Color** down arrow, and then click the **Red** color box in the color palette (third row, first column) to change the selected text to red.

**12** Select the last four rows in the Order Form table.

**Align Right**

**13** On the Formatting toolbar, click the **Align Right** button.

Word aligns the text in the last four rows of the table along the right margin.

**14** Click anywhere in the Shipping and Handling table to place the insertion point.

**15** On the **Table** menu, click **Table AutoFormat**.

The **Table AutoFormat** dialog box appears.

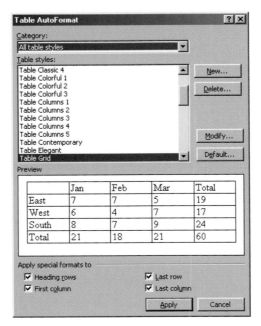

**16** Scroll down the **Table styles** list, click **Table List 8**, and then click **Apply**.

The Shipping and Handling Fees table is formatted in contrasting colors with a dark border.

**17** Click anywhere in the Delivery Services table to place the insertion point.

**18** On the **Format** menu, click **Borders and Shading** to open the **Borders and Shading** dialog box, and then click the **Borders** tab.

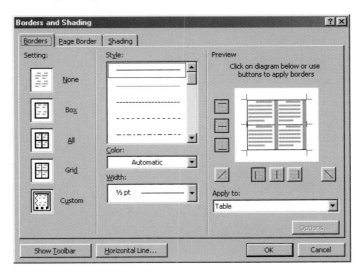

**19** In the **Setting** area, click the **All** icon, if necessary, to select it.

**20** In the **Style** list, click the down scroll arrow twice, and then click the double line border style.

**21** Click the **Color** down arrow, click the **Red** color box in the color palette (third row, first column), and then click **OK**.

Word adds a red double border to the entire table.

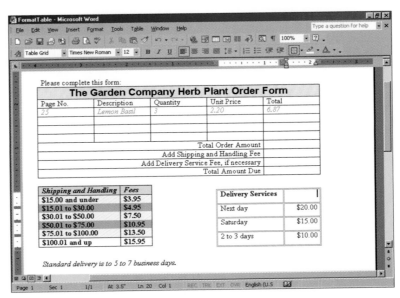

**22** On the Standard toolbar, click the **Save** button to save the document.

Close Window

**23** Click the **Close Window** button in the document window.

The FormatTable document closes.

# Working with Data in a Table

W2002e-3-1
W2002e-3-2

You can perform certain calculations on the numbers in a Word table using one of Word's built-in formulas. A **formula** is a mathematical expression that performs calculations, such as adding or averaging values. To insert a formula, you use the **Formula** command on the **Table** menu to display the **Formula** dialog box. A formula starts with an equal sign. After the equal sign, you insert a function, such as (SUM), which performs a calculation.

Word anticipates what you want to calculate. In the illustration on the next page, the formula in the **Formula** dialog box will add (SUM) the values in the cell that appear above the current cell (the cell that contains the insertion point).

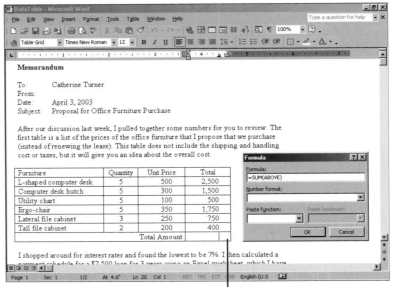

The total will be inserted in the cell
that contains the insertion point.

To insert other functions into the **Formula** box in the **Formula** dialog box, click the **Paste function** down arrow, and then click a function. You can use other built-in functions to count (COUNT) the number of values or find the maximum (MAX) or minimum (MIN) value in a series of cells. Many Word formulas refer to the cells in the table; you can also specify cell references or values that are used as constants. To reference a cell in a formula, you type the cell location in parentheses in the formula. For example, the formula =SUM(b2, b3) uses cell references to cell b2 and b3. The formula adds the numbers in the two cells.

Although you can perform many standard calculations in a Word table, the available formulas might not address all your needs. For complex calculations or analyses, such as determining a payment schedule for a loan, you can include a Microsoft Excel worksheet in a Word document. Excel is an electronic spreadsheet program that provides extensive mathematical and financial capabilities.

**Important**

In a Word table, you must recalculate formulas manually if you change a value in the Word table. In an Excel worksheet, the formulas are automatically recalculated when you change a value in the worksheet.

To include an Excel worksheet in a Word document, you need to understand how Microsoft Office programs integrate data. You can insert data from an Excel worksheet into a Word document in a few ways. Copy and paste the data if you do not need to maintain a connection between the source file and the destination file. You can use the **Object** command on the **Insert** menu to link or embed objects, such as graphics, slide presentations files, charts, graphs, and spreadsheets. You can also use the **Paste Special** command on the **Edit** menu to embed or link the object. Paste Special allows you to copy information from one location and paste it in another location using a different format, such as a Microsoft Excel Object, Picture, or Web format.

To update a linked or embedded object, you double-click the object. If the object is linked, the source file opens in the source program. When you save any changes that you've made, the linked object is updated. If the object is embedded, the source program opens, but the source file does not. You can use the source program commands to update the embedded object, saving the changes in the destination file.

# Object Linking and Embedding

To insert information from one Office program into another, you can use Microsoft's **object linking and embedding (OLE)** technology. OLE allows you to insert a file created in one program into a document that was created in another program. For example, you can insert an Excel file into a Word document. The object that you are inserting is called the **source file**, which is created in the **source program**. The file into which you are inserting the information is called the **destination file**.

The difference between linking and embedding is the type of connection that is maintained between the source and the destination. A **linked object** is an object that maintains a direct connection (or link) to the source file. The linked data is stored in the source file, not in the destination file; the destination file displays only a representation of the linked data. An **embedded object** is an object that becomes part of the destination file and is no longer a part of the source file.

When you link an object, the linked object is updated only when you update the source file. The update occurs when you open the destination file that includes the linked object. When you embed an object, you can make changes to the embedded object using the source program, but the source file is not updated. Determining whether to link or embed an object depends on whether the information in the destination file must be synchronized with the information in the source file. If more than one person needs to update a file, you can place the file in a central location and then link to the file so that both people will always get the latest information in the file.

If you do not need to maintain a connection between the source file and the destination file, you can copy and paste information between programs using the **Copy** and **Paste** buttons on the Standard toolbar. If you use this method, the source files and the destination files are not connected. The pasted information becomes part of the destination file, and you can use the tools in the destination file to edit the pasted information.

The office manager at The Garden Company has written a memo outlining a proposal to purchase office furniture. The memo includes a table listing furniture and prices. The office manager has also created an Excel worksheet that provides the payment schedule for a loan needed to purchase the furniture. She wants to embed the worksheet because this is a preliminary proposal. She also wants to see how the payment schedule changes if the loan amount changes.

In this exercise, you calculate data in a table. You embed an Excel worksheet in a Word document and then change the worksheet data.

DataTable
InsertTable

Open

1   On the Standard toolbar, click the **Open** button.

The **Open** dialog box appears.

2   Navigate to the **SBS** folder on your hard disk, double-click the **Word** folder, double-click the **AddingTables** folder, and then double-click the **DataTable** file.

The DataTable document opens.

3   Click in the lower-right cell of the Furniture table (after *Total Amount*).

4   On the **Table** menu, click **Formula** to open the **Formula** dialog box.

The **Formula** dialog box shows the formula *=SUM(ABOVE)*, meaning that the formula will add the numbers in the cells above the current cell.

5   Click **OK** to display the total amount for the furniture in the cell.

## Tip

To add a column or row of numbers quickly and easily, you can click the last cell in a column of numbers and then click the **AutoSum** button on the **Tables and Borders** toolbar.

6   Move to the end of the document by pressing ⌃Ctrl+End or otherwise moving the insertion point to the correct position.

7   On the **Insert** menu, click **Object** to open the **Object** dialog box, and then click the **Create from File** tab.

8   Click **Browse**, navigate to the **SBS** folder on your hard disk, double-click the **Word** folder, double-click the **AddingTables** folder, and then double-click the **InsertTable** file.

The InsertTable file appears in the **File name** box.

9   Click **OK**.

The Excel worksheet appears in the document.

10  Press the ↑ key to see the beginning of the inserted Excel worksheet.

**11** Double-click anywhere in the Excel worksheet table, click cell **B4**, type **10000**, and then press the Enter key.

Excel recalculates the data in the table to show how the payment schedule would change if the loan were for $10,000.

**12** Scroll up, and then click just above the Excel worksheet table.

The worksheet table is updated with the costs for a loan of $10,000.

**13** On the Standard toolbar, click the **Save** button to save the document.

Close Window

**×**

**14** Click the **Close Window** button in the document window.

The DataTable document closes.

# Presenting Text in Columns

W2002-3-2

When you want to create a document, such as a newsletter, columns are a useful way to present information. In Word, a column is a block of text that has its own margins. You can divide a document into two, three, or more columns of text. (If you decide that you don't want to divide your document into multiple columns, you can format the document as one column—which is the default setting for any Word document.) When you divide a document into columns, the text flows, or snakes, from the top of one column to the top of the next. If you want the columns to be equal in length, you can insert a column break to force the text to move to the top of the next column.

After you break text into columns, you can change the width of a column. You can also format column text as you would any other text. For example, you can change the indentation or the alignment of text in a column using the horizontal ruler or the alignment buttons on the Formatting toolbar.

The owner of The Garden Company has written a nine-step procedure for cultivating an herb garden. The document must be set up in four columns to match other marketing materials.

CreateColumn

In this exercise, you format text into four columns and reduce the amount of space between the columns and indent column text. You also break the columns at specific locations rather than allowing the text to flow naturally from one column to the next.

**1** On the Standard toolbar, click the **Open** button.

Open

The **Open** dialog box appears.

**2** Navigate to the **SBS** folder on your hard disk, double-click the **Word** folder, double-click the **AddingTables** folder, and then double-click the **CreateColumn** file.

The CreateColumn document opens.

**3** On the **Format** menu, click **Columns**.

The **Columns** dialog box appears.

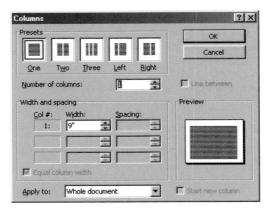

4   Click the **Number of columns** up arrow until **4** appears, and then click **OK**.

The document view changes to Print Layout view, and the document is divided into four columns.

5   On the **Edit** menu, click **Select All** to select all the text in the document.

Justify

6   On the Formatting toolbar, click the **Justify** button to align the text in the columns, and then click in the document to deselect the text.

Zoom

75%

7   On the Standard toolbar, click the **Zoom** down arrow, and then click **75%** so that more of the document is displayed in the document window.

**Hanging Indent** marker ———————————  ——— **Right Margin** indicator

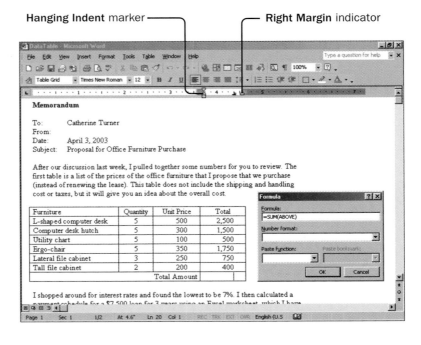

**8** Point to the **Right Margin** indicator for the second column on the horizontal ruler. The pointer changes shape.

**9** Click and drag the pointer 1/6 inch (one tick mark) to the right, and then release the mouse button to resize the columns.

By dragging the pointer to the right, you decrease the spacing between the columns, which decreases the amount of white space on the page, visually enhancing the overall appearance of the layout of the document.

**10** Click in the *NOTE* paragraph that appears after the *Step 2* paragraph.

**11** Drag the **Hanging Indent** marker on the ruler 1/6 inch (one tick mark) to the right.

All lines except the first line of text in the *NOTE* paragraph are indented, which offsets this text from the step text.

**12** Click in the *NOTE* paragraph that appears after the *Step 5* paragraph, and then press the ⌨F4 key to apply the same formatting to this paragraph.

**13** Click to the left of the text *Step 5* to place the insertion point.

**14** On the **Insert** menu, click **Break** to open the **Break** dialog box, click the **Column break** option, and then click **OK**.

The text that appears after the column break moves to the top of the next column.

**15** Click to the left of the text *Step 6*, and then press ⌨F4.

The Step 6 paragraph moves to the top of the fourth column. The columns are now more evenly divided across the page.

Print Preview

**16** On the Standard toolbar, click the **Print Preview** button to view the document formatted in columns.

Close Preview

**17** On the Print Preview toolbar, click the **Close Preview** button to close the print preview window.

**18** On the Standard toolbar, click the **Save** button to save the document.

Close Window

**19** Click the **Close Window** button in the document window.

The CreateColumn document closes.

# Chapter Wrap-Up

To finish this chapter:

Close

● On the **File** menu, click **Exit**, or click the **Close** button in the Word window.

Word closes.

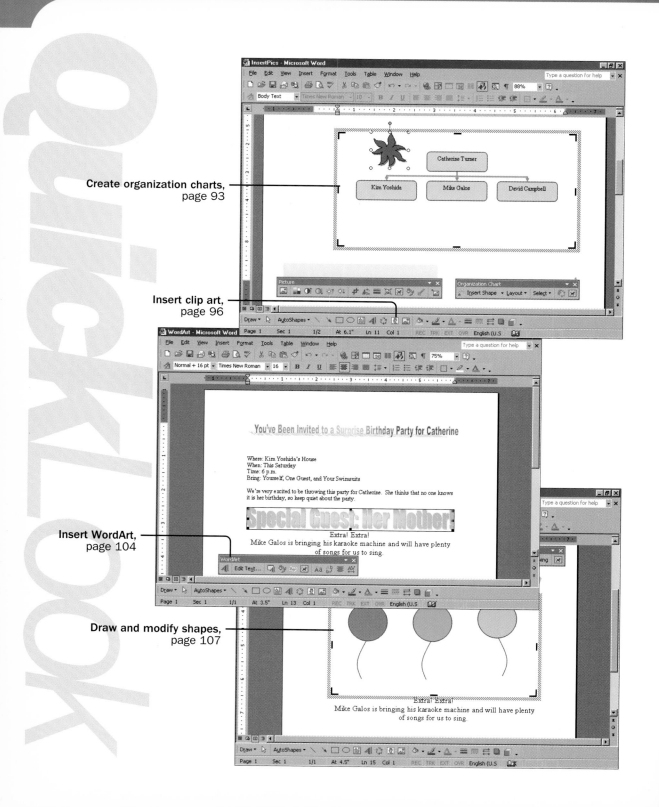

**Create organization charts,**
page 93

**Insert clip art,**
page 96

**Insert WordArt,**
page 104

**Draw and modify shapes,**
page 107

# Chapter 6
# Working with Graphics

**After completing this chapter, you will be able to:**

✔ Create a diagram.

✔ Insert and modify pictures.

✔ Align text and pictures.

✔ Create WordArt.

✔ Draw and modify shapes.

You can insert and modify graphics in Word to make your documents more visually appealing and to convey information that is difficult to provide in textual form. A **graphic** is a picture or a drawing object. You can use the options on the Drawing toolbar to insert pictures and draw numerous objects without leaving Word. A **picture** is a photograph, a scanned picture, a bitmap, or clip art that was created outside of Word. Drawing objects are created within Word and include AutoShapes, diagrams, curves, lines, and WordArt drawing objects. After you add a graphic to a document, you can enhance it with a variety of colors and special effects. You can also change the position of graphics in a document by using various layout options and changing how the text and graphics work together on the page.

In this chapter, you'll create a diagram to communicate information visually and relationally, insert pictures, change a picture to appear faintly in the background, change how text and graphics are laid out, insert WordArt, and draw and modify shapes.

This chapter uses the practice files OrgChart, InsertPics, Gardenco, AlignPics, WordArt, and DrawShape that you installed from this book's CD-ROM. For details about installing the practice files, see "Using the Book's CD-ROM" at the beginning of this book.

## Creating a Diagram

W2002-5-2

To help you organize personnel data or other types of information, you can insert and modify diagrams in your documents. A **diagram** is a visual and relational representation of information. A common diagram is an organization chart. You can also create cycle diagrams, radial diagrams, pyramid diagrams, Venn diagrams, and target diagrams.

Diagram
new for
**Office**XP

OrgChart

When you insert an organization chart into a document, the chart has placeholder text that you click and replace with your own. The boxes and the lines of the organization chart are objects that you can move and change.

In this exercise, you insert and modify an organization chart.

**1** Start Word, if necessary.

**2** On the Standard toolbar, click the **Open** button.

Open

The **Open** dialog box appears.

**3** Navigate to the **SBS** folder on your hard disk, double-click the **Word** folder, double-click the **Drawing** folder, and then double-click the **OrgChart** file.

The OrgChart document opens.

**4** Press Ctrl+End to place the insertion point at the end of the document.

Insert Diagram
or Organiza-
tion Chart

**5** On the Drawing toolbar, click the **Insert Diagram or Organization Chart** button.

## Tip

If the Drawing toolbar is not open on your screen, on the **View** menu, point to **Toolbars**, and then click **Drawing**.

The **Diagram Gallery** dialog box appears, with the Organization Chart selected by default.

**6** Click **OK**.

An organization chart is inserted into the document, and the Organization Chart toolbar appears.

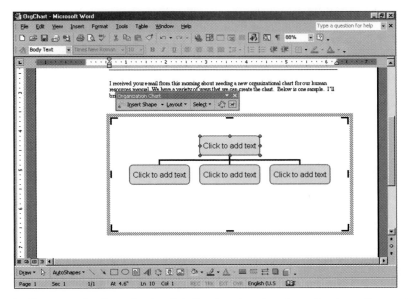

**7**    In the organization chart, click the top box to place the insertion point, and then type **Catherine Turner**.

**8**    Click the first box in the second row, type **Kim Yoshida**, click the second box in the second row, type **Mike Galos**, click the third box in the second row, and then type **David Campbell**.

All boxes contain names. The last box is still selected.

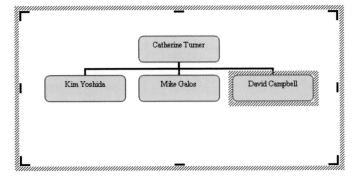

**9**    On the Organization Chart toolbar, click the **Select** down arrow, and then click **All Connecting Lines**.

All connecting lines in the organization chart are selected.

10   On the **Format** menu, click **AutoShape**.

The **Format AutoShape** dialog box appears.

11   In the **Line** area, click the **Color** down arrow, and then click the **Red** color box (row 3, column 1).

The line color selection is now red.

12   In the **Arrows** area, click the **Begin style** down arrow, click the second option in the first row, and then click **OK**.

The lines in the organization chart are now red with arrows attached.

## Tip

Autoformat

You can quickly format an organization chart using a predefined style by clicking the **Autoformat** button on the Organization Chart toolbar.

13   Click a blank area of the document to deselect the organization chart.

14   On the Standard toolbar, click the **Save** button to save the document.

Close Window

15   Click the **Close Window** button in the document window.

The OrgChart document closes.

# Inserting and Modifying Pictures

W2002-5-1

You can insert nearly any picture, scanned photograph, photo, or artwork from a CD-ROM or other program into a document in Word. When you use the **Picture** submenu on the **Insert** menu, you specify the source of the picture—a file, Word's clip art collection, or a scanner.

To insert a picture from a file on your hard disk, removable disk, or network, you use the **From File** command on the **Picture** submenu. To insert a picture from the clip art collection that comes with Word, you click the **Clip Art** command on the **Picture** submenu or click the **Insert Clip Art** button on the Drawing toolbar, which opens the **Insert Clip Art** task pane. Microsoft Office XP provides hundreds of professionally designed pieces of clip art that you can use in your documents. For example, you can insert clip art pictures of scenic backgrounds, maps, buildings, or people. If you have a scanner connected to the computer that you are using, you can scan and insert a picture using the **From Scanner** command. Once you insert clip art or any picture into your document, you can modify it by using the Picture toolbar.

The following table describes the buttons on the Picture toolbar:

| Button Name | Button | Description |
| --- | --- | --- |
| **Insert Picture** |  | Allows you to insert a picture |
| **Color** |  | Allows you to change the coloring of the picture |
| **More Contrast** |  | Applies more contrast |
| **Less Contrast** |  | Reduces contrast |
| **More Brightness** |  | Applies more brightness |
| **Less Brightness** | 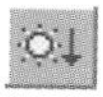 | Reduces brightness |
| **Crop** |  | Crops the picture |
| **Rotate Left** |  | Rotates the picture to the left |
| **Line Style** | 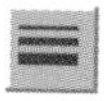 | Allows you to change the line style |
| **Compress Pictures** |  | Enables you to reduce the size of pictures |
| **Text Wrapping** |  | Allows you to wrap text around a picture |
| **Format Picture** |  | Allows you to change features such as colors, size, and lines |
| **Set Transparent Color** |  | Allows you to make selected colors in the picture see-through |
| **Reset Picture** |  | Resets the picture to its original state |

Watermarks
new for
**Office**XP

**Watermarks** are dimmed pictures or text that appear faintly in the background of your printed document. You can use a picture such as a company logo as a watermark, or you can use words such as *ASAP, CONFIDENTIAL,* or *DRAFT.*

The head buyer at The Garden Company wants to send a memo that contains a sample organization chart. She will insert clip art to enhance the chart and a watermark to indicate that the memo is confidential.

InsertPics
Gardenco

Open

In this exercise, you insert and modify clip art and then insert a watermark.

**1** On the Standard toolbar, click the **Open** button.

The **Open** dialog box appears.

**2** Navigate to the **SBS** folder on your hard disk, double-click the **Word** folder, double-click the **Drawing** folder, and then double-click the **InsertPics** file.

The InsertPics document opens, showing the insertion point to the left of the text *Memorandum*.

**3** Press the ⌈Enter⌋ key, and then press the ⌈↑⌋ key to place the insertion point in a blank line at the beginning of the document.

**4** On the **Insert** menu, point to **Picture**, and then click **From File**.

The **Insert Picture** dialog box appears.

## Tip

Insert Picture

You can also click the **Insert Picture** button on the Drawing toolbar to open the **Insert Picture** dialog box.

**5** Navigate to the **SBS** folder on your hard disk, double-click the **Word** folder, double-click the **Drawing** folder, and then double-click the **Gardenco** file.

The picture is inserted into the document.

**6** Click The Garden Company logo to select it.

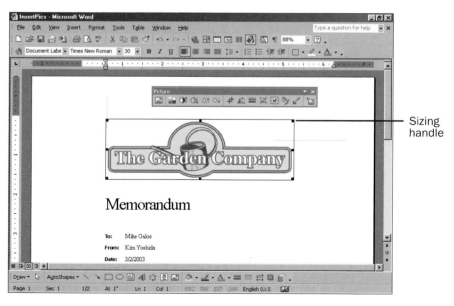

Sizing handle

## Tip

If the Picture toolbar is not open on your screen, on the **View** menu, point to **Toolbars**, and then click **Picture**.

**7**   Drag the lower-right-corner sizing handle (which changes to a diagonal double-arrow) up and to the left until you reach the 4-inch mark on the ruler to resize the picture.

Color

**8**   On the Picture toolbar, click the **Color** button, and then click **Washout**.

The picture is now washed out.

Less Brightness

**9**   On the Picture toolbar, click the **Less Brightness** button four times to reduce the brightness of the picture.

More Contrast

**10**   On the Picture toolbar, click the **More Contrast** button two times to sharpen the picture.

**11**   Scroll down the document to display the organization chart.

Insert Clip Art

**12**   On the Drawing toolbar, click the **Insert Clip Art** button.

The **Insert Clip Art** task pane opens.

**13**   In the **Insert Clip Art** task pane, type **plant** in the **Search text** box, and then click **Search**.

The task pane displays graphics associated with the keyword *plant*.

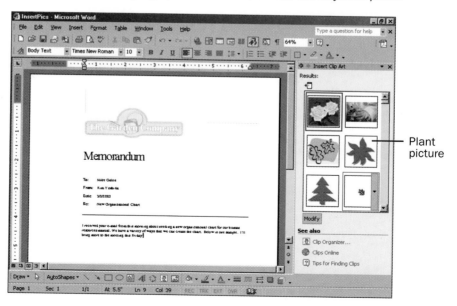

Plant picture

**14** In the **Results** area, click the plant picture, and then click **Close** to close the **Insert Clip Art** task pane.

The picture is inserted into the document.

**15** Click the plant picture to select it, point to the lower-right circular handle until the pointer changes to a double arrow, and then drag up and to the left until the picture is about 1 inch by 1 inch in size.

The picture appears smaller.

**16** Point to the plant picture until the pointer changes to the four-headed arrow, and then drag the picture to the left of the Catherine Turner box in the organization chart.

The picture appears in the organization chart and the Organization Chart toolbar appears

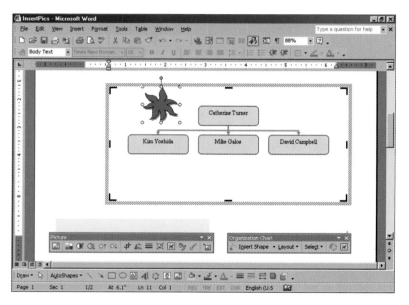

## Troubleshooting

If the Drawing and Organization Chart toolbars are blocking your view of the document, drag their title bars to move them out of the way.

**17** Hold down [Ctrl], click the plant picture, and then drag it to the right of the Catherine Turner box to copy it there.

**18** Click outside of the drawing canvas to deselect it.

**19** On the **Format** menu, point to **Background**, and then click **Printed Watermark.**

The **Printed Watermark** dialog box appears.

**20** Click the **Text watermark** option, click the **Text** down arrow, and then click **CONFIDENTIAL** to select a watermark style.

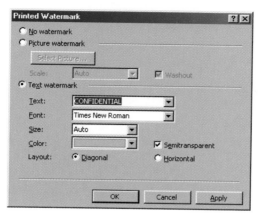

**21** Click **OK**.

A *CONFIDENTIAL* watermark now appears faintly in the background at an angle.

**22** On the Standard toolbar, click the **Save** button to save the document.

Close Window

**23** Click the **Close Window** button in the document window.

The InsertPics document closes.

# Aligning Text and Pictures

W2002e-4-1
W2002e-4-3

After you insert a picture or graphic into a document, you can change its position in the document and in relation to the text that surrounds it. When you insert a picture into a document, it appears as a separate object, and text doesn't wrap around it. You can use the **Layout** tab on the **Format Picture** dialog box to help you align and wrap text around pictures. The **Format Picture** dialog box provides options for placing a picture or wrapping text around a picture. For instance, you can choose from seven different text wrapping styles: **Square**, **Tight**, **Through**, **Top** and **Bottom**, **Behind text**, **In front of text**, and **In line with text**. You can wrap text on both sides of the picture, on one side of the picture, or on the largest side of the picture. In addition, you can set the distance between the edge of your picture and the text itself.

You can also specify that a picture be positioned absolutely or relatively. When a picture is positioned **absolutely**, its position is determined by measurements that you set. When a picture is positioned **relatively**, its position is determined by its relation to other specified parts of the document, such as the margin, the page, a column, or a particular character.

As you add text to a document with a picture wrapped around the text, you can choose how the picture moves with the text. You can specify that your picture move with text, stay locked to its anchor, or overlap the text.

The owner of The Garden Company has awarded an employee the Employee of the Month award. She is preparing an announcement that publicizes the award and includes The Garden Company logo.

AlignPics

In this exercise, you modify the placement and text wrapping attributes of a picture already inserted into a document.

**1** On the Standard toolbar, click the **Open** button.

Open

The **Open** dialog box appears.

**2** Navigate to the **SBS** folder on your hard disk, double-click the **Word** folder, double-click the **Drawing** folder, and then double-click the **AlignPics** file.

The AlignPics document opens.

**3** Click the logo to select it.

The Picture toolbar appears.

**4** On the **Format** menu, click **Picture**.

The **Format Picture** dialog box appears.

**5** Click the **Layout** tab, and then click **Advanced**.

The **Advanced Layout** dialog box appears.

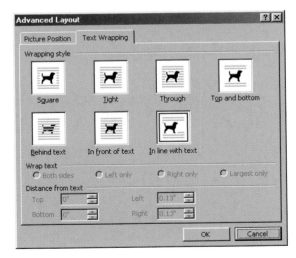

**6**    Click the **Tight** option, click the **Both sides** option, and then click the **Picture Position** tab.

**7**    In the **Horizontal** area, click the **Alignment** option, click the **Alignment** down arrow, click **Right**, click the **relative to** down arrow, click **Margin**, and then click **OK**.

The **Advanced Layout** dialog box closes.

**8**    Click **OK** to close the **Format Picture** dialog box.

The picture is repositioned so that it is flush with the right margin, with the paragraph text wrapped tightly around its left and bottom edges.

## Tip

You might have to move the Picture toolbar out of the way to see the picture.

**9**    Click to the left of the word *The* at the beginning of the first paragraph, and then press ⌷Enter⌷ three times.

The graphic moves with the text.

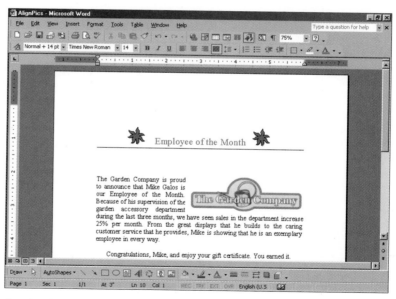

**10**   On the Standard toolbar, click the **Save** button to save the document.

Close Window

✕

**11**   Click the **Close Window** button in the document window.

The AlignPics document closes.

# Creating WordArt

W2002-5-1

**WordArt** allows you to change the shape and appearance of text in your document. Use WordArt to create special effects for your text. You can make WordArt text appear curved, outlined, shadowed, or three-dimensional.

To create WordArt out of existing text in your document, select the text that you want to enhance, click the **Insert WordArt** button on the Drawing toolbar, click a selection in the **WordArt Gallery** dialog box, and then click **OK**. The **Edit WordArt Text** dialog box appears with your text selection highlighted.

When you work with WordArt, you can use the WordArt toolbar, which opens when you insert or select a WordArt object. The following table lists the WordArt toolbar buttons and a brief description of each.

| Button Name | Button | Description |
|---|---|---|
| **Insert WordArt** | | Inserts WordArt |
| **Edit Text** | Edit Text... | Edits text within WordArt |
| **WordArt Gallery** | | Provides graphical options for your WordArt |
| **Format WordArt** | | Allows you to change the color, size, and layout of the WordArt |
| **WordArt Shape** | Abc | Changes the shape of the WordArt |
| **Text Wrapping** | | Changes the text wrapping around your WordArt |
| **WordArt Same Letter Heights** | Aa | Makes the letters in the WordArt the same height |
| **WordArt Vertical Text** | Ab b | Changes the alignment of the text from horizontal to vertical |
| **WordArt Alignment** | | Changes the alignment of the WordArt |
| **WordArt Character Spacing** | AV | Changes the spacing between characters in the WordArt |

The head buyer of the Garden Company is throwing a surprise birthday party for the owner. She is preparing a flyer about the party, which she will distribute to all The Garden Company employees.

WordArt

In this exercise, you insert and modify WordArt.

**1** On the Standard toolbar, click the **Open** button.

The **Open** dialog box appears.

Open

**2** Navigate to the **SBS** folder on your hard disk, double-click the **Word** folder, double-click the **Drawing** folder, and then double-click the **WordArt** file.

The WordArt document opens.

**3** Press the ↓ key twice to move the insertion point to the third line of the document.

Insert WordArt

**4** On the Drawing toolbar, click the **Insert WordArt** button.

The **WordArt Gallery** dialog box appears.

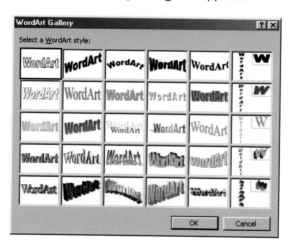

## Tip

If the Drawing toolbar is not open on your screen, on the **View** menu, point to **Toolbars**, and then click **Drawing**.

**5** Click the WordArt style in row 3, column 1, and then click **OK**.

The **Edit WordArt Text** dialog box appears, displaying *Your Text Here* as a placeholder.

**6**    Type **Special Guest: Her Mother!**. Click the **Size** down arrow, click **44**, click the **Bold** button, and then click **OK**.

The text is inserted as an object.

**7**    Click the WordArt object to select it.

The WordArt toolbar appears, and sizing handles surround the object.

**8**    Drag the **WordArt object** down so that it appears above the text *Extra! Extra!*, as shown in the following illustration:

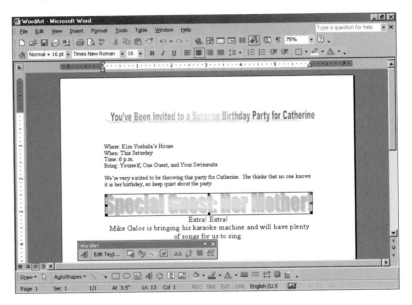

WordArt Character Spacing

**9**    On the WordArt toolbar, click the **WordArt Character Spacing** button, and then click **Very Loose**.

The spacing between the letters in the WordArt increases.

WordArt Shape

**10**    On the WordArt toolbar, click the **WordArt Shape** button, and then click **Arch Up (Curve)** on the submenu (row 2, column 1).

The WordArt shape changes to an arch.

**11**    Click in a blank area of the document to deselect the WordArt.

**12**    On the Standard toolbar, click the **Save** button to save the document.

Close Window

**13**    Click the **Close Window** button in the document window.

The WordArt document closes.

# Drawing and Modifying Shapes

You can use Word's drawing tools to add shapes, or objects, to your documents. Drawing shapes in your documents can add interest and provide impact to your message. Popular drawing objects include ovals, rectangles, lines, curves, and AutoShapes, which are more complex shapes, such as stars and banners. To draw a shape, you select a drawing tool from the Drawing toolbar or from the **AutoShapes** menu on the Drawing toolbar, and then you drag the pointer to create the shape.

Once you draw a shape, you can change or enhance it. A shape has attributes, such as fill, color, border, and shadow, that affect how it appears. Shapes that you draw usually have a default fill—the color inside the shape—and a border or frame, which you can set by using the **Set AutoShape Defaults** command on the **Draw** menu on the Drawing toolbar. Before you can modify these attributes, you must first select the shapes that you want to change. When you draw a shape, it is automatically selected. Often you will draw a shape or import a picture that isn't the right size. You can change the size of an object by dragging its sizing handles.

Drawing canvas
new for
**Office**XP

Word uses a drawing canvas to simplify inserting, changing, and manipulating drawing shapes and pictures. A **drawing canvas** is an area that contains drawing shapes and pictures. You can create a drawing canvas by selecting a drawing tool from the Drawing toolbar or **AutoShapes** menu on the Drawing toolbar. When you draw within the drawing canvas, you can resize and move the drawing canvas and the objects that it contains as a unit. This allows you to make design decisions once and then apply them to all related objects.

## Tip

Word inserts a drawing canvas by default when you select a drawing tool. If you find that the feature has been turned off in Word, click **Options** on the **Tools** menu, and then click the **General** tab. Select the **Automatically create drawing canvas when inserting AutoShapes** check box, and then click **OK**.

When you first insert a drawing canvas into your document, you see no border or shading around the canvas. However, because the drawing canvas is an object, you can apply borders and shading to it just as you would to any other object in Word.

When you work with a drawing canvas, you can use the tools on the Drawing toolbar. These tools let you fit a drawing canvas to its contents, expand a drawing canvas on the document, scale the drawing canvas, or apply text-wrapping features. You can also fit the drawing canvas to the document environment so that you use only as much space in your document as you need.

You can move drawing objects or pictures on the drawing canvas by dragging them. You can also move them by selecting them within the drawing canvas, clicking the **Draw** button on the Drawing toolbar, and then selecting an option from the menu.

Options include nudging the objects up or down by small increments, rotating or flipping them, or applying text-wrapping features to them.

The head buyer at The Garden Company is throwing a surprise birthday party for the owner. She wants to add balloons to the flyer about the party.

DrawShape

In this exercise, you open a drawing canvas, insert additional drawing objects, and then modify those objects.

**1** On the Standard toolbar, click the **Open** button.

Open

The Open dialog box appears.

**2** Navigate to the **SBS** folder on your hard disk, double-click the **Word** folder, double-click the **Drawing** folder, and then double-click the **DrawShape** file.

The DrawShape document opens.

**3** Press Ctrl+End to place the insertion point at the end of the document.

Oval

○

**4** On the Drawing toolbar, click the **Oval** button.

A drawing canvas and the Drawing Canvas toolbar appear.

## Tip

If the Drawing toolbar is not open on your screen, on the **View** menu, point to **Toolbars**, and then click **Drawing**.

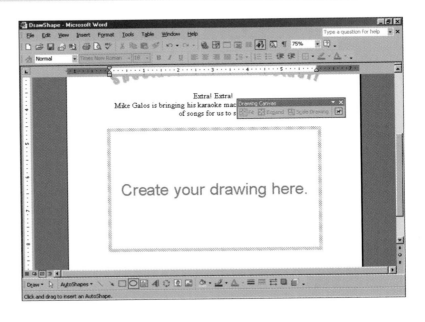

**5**     Draw a circle about 1.5 inches high in the left half of the drawing canvas.

A circle appears on the drawing canvas with sizing handles around it.

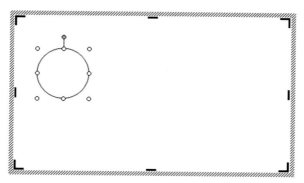

# Tip

To draw objects with equal heights and widths, such as a square or circle, click the **Rectangle** or **Oval** button on the Drawing toolbar, and then hold down the ⟨Shift⟩ key while you draw.

**6**     Hold down ⟨Ctrl⟩, and then drag from the circle to create a copy of the circle in the middle of the drawing canvas.

**7**     Hold down ⟨Ctrl⟩, and then drag from the second circle to create a copy of the circle in the right half of the drawing canvas.

The drawing canvas has three circles on it. The last circle is selected, so its sizing handles are visible.

Fill Color

**8**     Click the first circle on the left, click the **Fill Color** down arrow on the Drawing toolbar, and then click the **Pink** color box (fourth row, first column).

The circle is now filled with color.

**9**     Click the middle circle, click the **Fill Color** down arrow on the Drawing toolbar, and then click the **Lime** color box (third row, third column).

**10**     Click the right circle, click the **Fill Color** down arrow on the Drawing toolbar, and then click the **Turquoise** color box (fourth row, fifth column).

All circles are now filled with color.

Curve

**11**     On the Drawing toolbar, click **AutoShapes**, point to **Lines**, and then click the **Curve** button.

**12** Position the pointer over the bottom of the left balloon, click the canvas, drag down and left about an inch, click the canvas, drag down and right about an inch, and then double-click the canvas.

A curved line appears below the left balloon.

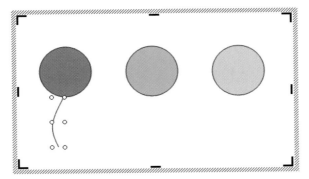

**13** Hold down Ctrl and then drag to copy the line to the other two circles.

All the balloons now have strings—diagonal lines. The last line is still selected.

**14** Hold down Ctrl and then click the turquoise circle.

Both the circle and the curved line are selected.

**15** On the Drawing toolbar, click **Draw**, and then click **Group**.

The circle and curved line are grouped. One set of resize handles appears around the grouped object.

**16** On the Drawing toolbar, click **Draw**, point to **Rotate or Flip**, and then click **Flip Horizontal**.

The grouped object flips horizontally.

**17** Press the ↑ key, and then click in a blank area of the drawing canvas to deselect the object.

The circle and line are now positioned slightly higher in the drawing canvas.

**18** Point to the edge of the drawing canvas.

The mouse pointer changes to the four-headed arrow, indicating that you can move the canvas.

**19** Drag the drawing canvas to the left of the *Extra! Extra!* text in the document.

The drawing canvas moves, along with the objects that it contains.

Drawing sizing
handle
⊦

**20** In the drawing canvas area, drag the top-middle drawing sizing handle down to match the following illustration.

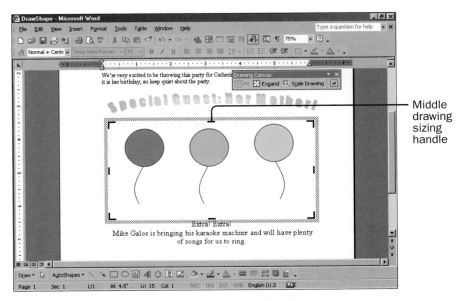

Middle
drawing
sizing
handle

**21** Click outside of the drawing canvas to deselect it.

**22** On the Standard toolbar, click the **Save** button to save the document.

Close Window
×

**23** Click the **Close Window** button in the document window.

The WordArt document closes.

## Chapter Wrap-Up

To finish the chapter:

Close
×

● On the **File** menu, click **Exit**, or click the **Close** button in the Word window.

Word closes.

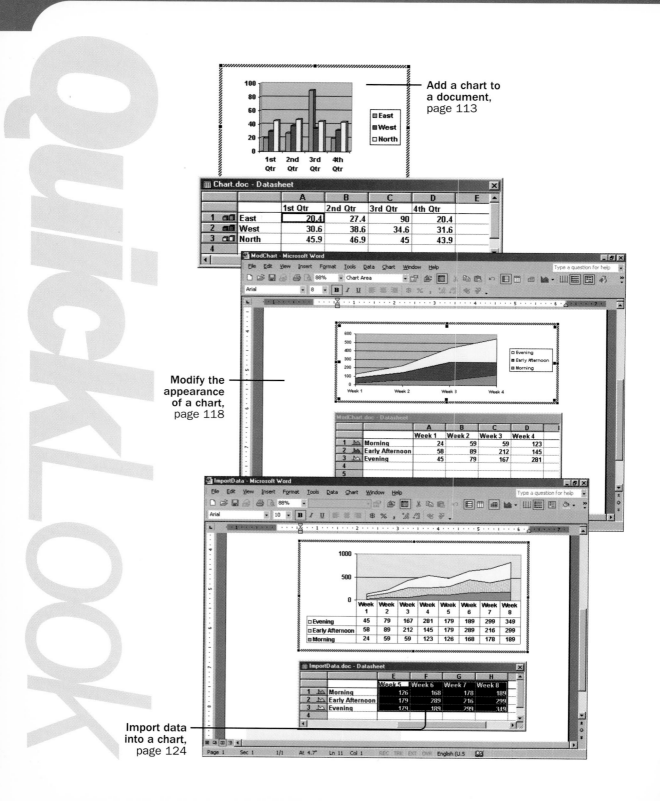

Add a chart to a document, page 113

Modify the appearance of a chart, page 118

Import data into a chart, page 124

# Chapter 7
# Working with Charts

**After completing this chapter, you will be able to:**

✔ **Add a chart to a document.**

✔ **Modify the appearance of a chart.**

✔ **Import data into a chart.**

When you want to compare numeric information, such as last year's quarterly sales or the time that you spent on projects last week, you can create a **chart**. Charts are graphics that use lines, bars, columns, pie slices, or other markers to represent numbers and other values. Adding a chart to a document creates visual interest and shows trends, illustrates relationships, or demonstrates how information changes over time. Microsoft Word and other Microsoft Office XP programs include Microsoft Graph Chart, a program that lets you insert and modify a chart directly in a document.

In this chapter, you'll add a chart to a memo from The Garden Company regarding its customer traffic. You'll start by creating a chart in a Word document, typing data into that chart, modifying the appearance of the chart, and then importing additional data from an Excel workbook to add to the chart.

This chapter uses the practice files AddChart, ModChart, ImportData, and FileImport that you installed from this book's CD-ROM. For details about installing the practice files, see "Using the Book's CD-ROM" at the beginning of this book.

## Adding a Chart to a Document

W2002-5-2

To add a chart to a Word document, you use Microsoft Graph Chart, a program integrated with Word and other Office XP programs that lets you add, modify, and format various types of charts. When you insert a chart, Microsoft Graph Chart adds a sample chart and a datasheet to the document. A **datasheet** looks similar to a table; it initially displays sample data in rows and columns. You can type to replace the sample data with your own labels and values. Because the datasheet is linked to the chart, when you change the values in the datasheet, the chart changes as well.

Your first step after inserting a datasheet and chart is to replace the sample data with your own. To do so, you work in the datasheet, entering values and labels in cells. A **cell** is where a row and column intersect.

A datasheet also contains gray buttons across the top for **column headings** and gray buttons along the left for **row headings**. When you click a heading, you select the entire column or row. To select the entire datasheet, you can click the **Select All** button, a gray box in the upper-left corner of the datasheet.

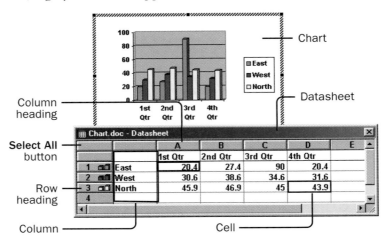

Column heading

Chart

Datasheet

Select All button

Row heading

Column

Cell

## Tip

If you can see your chart but not the accompanying datasheet, double-click the chart to open the datasheet.

When you insert a chart into a document, the Microsoft Graph Chart commands become available on the menu bar and toolbars so that you can work with the chart directly in your Word document.

## Tip

You always change data in the datasheet, but not in the chart itself. You can change the appearance of the chart, but not the values that it contains.

The owner of the Garden Company wants to add a chart to a memo that demonstrates customer traffic patterns during the first eight weeks of the year.

AddChart

In this exercise, you open a document and then add a chart to the document.

**1**  Start Word, if necessary.

**2**  On the Standard toolbar, click the **Open** button.

Open

The **Open** dialog box appears.

**3** Navigate to the **SBS** folder on your hard disk, double-click the **Word** folder, double-click the **Charting** folder, and then double-click the file **AddChart**.

The AddChart document opens.

**4** Press ⌷Ctrl⌷+⌷End⌷.

The insertion point moves to the end of the document.

**5** On the **Insert** menu, point to **Picture**, and then click **Chart**.

A sample chart and datasheet appear.

**6** Drag the title bar of the datasheet window so that it is positioned below the sample chart.

**7** Click the **Select All** button on the datasheet (the upper-left button), and then press the ⌷Del⌷ key.

The sample data and sample chart are deleted.

**8** Click in the first cell in row 1 to the left of column A, type **Morning**, and then press the ⌷Enter⌷ key.

The heading is entered, and the insertion point moves to the cell below *Morning*.

**9** Type **Early Afternoon**, and then press ⌷Enter⌷.

The insertion point moves to the cell below *Early Afternoon*.

**10** Type **Evening**, and then press ⌷Enter⌷.

The insertion point moves to the cell below *Evening*.

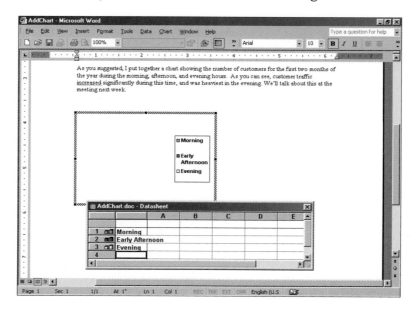

**11** In the column heading area of the datasheet, place the mouse pointer on the line to the left of the column A heading until it changes to a double-headed resize pointer, and then drag the line to the right, stretching the column until the text fits in the cells.

| ▦ AddChart.doc - Datasheet | | ✛ A | B | C | D | ▲ |
|---|---|---|---|---|---|---|
| 1 ▣ | Morning | | | | | |
| 2 ▣ | Early Afternoon | | | | | |
| 3 ▣ | Evening | | | | | |
| 4 | | | | | | ▼ |

## Tip

You can also double-click the vertical line between column headings to resize the column to fit the longest item in the column cells.

**12** Click in the cell in column A in the row above row 1. Type **Week 1**, and then press the ⌨Tab key.

*Week 1* is added to the chart, and the insertion point moves one cell to the right.

**13** Type **Week 2**, and then press ⌨Tab.

*Week 2* is added to the chart, and the insertion point moves one cell to the right.

**14** Type **Week 3**, and then press ⌨Tab.

*Week 3* is added to the chart, and the insertion point moves one cell to the right.

**15** Type **Week 4**, and then press ⌨Enter.

*Week 4* is added to the chart. The data labels for the chart appear in columns A through D.

| ▦ AddChart.doc - Datasheet | | A | B | C | D | ▲ |
|---|---|---|---|---|---|---|
| | | Week 1 | Week 2 | Week 3 | Week 4 | |
| 1 ▣ | Morning | | | | | |
| 2 ▣ | Early Afternoon | | | | | |
| 3 ▣ | Evening | | | | | |
| 4 | | | | | | ▼ |

**16** Click the first empty cell in the second row under column A, and then type the following data into the chart's datasheet:

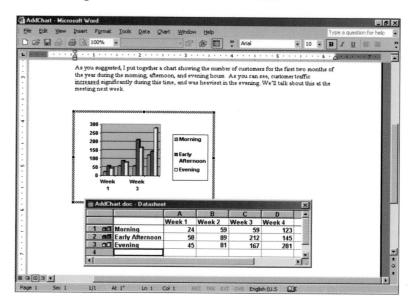

## Tip

You can use the keyboard to help you move around the datasheet. You can press [Enter] to move the insertion point down one row, or [Shift]+[Enter] to move up one row. Press [Tab] to move the insertion point to the right one column, or [Shift]+[Tab] to move to the left one column. To move up, down, left, and right within the datasheet, use the arrow keys.

**17** Click in the cell in column B, in row 3 (which contains *81*), type **79** to change the data, and then press [Enter].

## Tip

To edit individual characters in a cell, double-click the cell to place the insertion point, and then edit the text as you would in Word.

**18** Click a blank area of the document to deselect the chart.

The datasheet closes, and the chart is deselected.

**19** On the Standard toolbar, click the **Save** button to save the document.

Close Window

**×**

**20** Click the **Close Window** button in the document window.

The AddChart document closes.

# Modifying the Appearance of a Chart

W2002-5-2

If the appearance of your chart doesn't fit your needs, you can change the chart's type, colors, borders, fonts, font sizes, and chart elements. When you change the chart type, you choose one of 18 different ways to present your data. Choose the chart type that best suits the purpose of your data. For example, to show how data changes over time, you can choose a column chart. To show how parts relate to the whole, choose a pie chart. You can use the **Chart Type** list on the Standard toolbar or the **Chart Type** dialog box to choose one of the chart types. To create a customized chart, use the **Chart Type** dialog box.

In addition to changing a chart's type, you can change the appearance of the chart and its elements, such as the title, gridlines, legend, and colors. You start by selecting the chart and then selecting the element that you want to modify. You can then move, resize, or format the selected element. To move a selected chart or chart item, you point to the chart or element and then drag it to another location. To resize a selected chart or chart item, you drag a sizing handle.

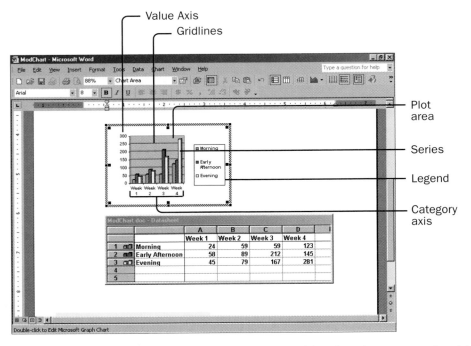

When you select part or all of a chart, you can use the chart buttons on Graph's Standard toolbar to format the chart, including those elements. For example, use the **Fill Color** button to change the color of chart elements, such as a **data marker**—the bar or area that represents a value in the datasheet—and the **plot area**—the area that includes the data markers and the category (x) and value (y) axes. Besides changing the color of an element, you can change its pattern, called a **fill effect**. For example, you can apply a striped pattern to a **data series**, which is a group of related data markers.

Some chart elements in Microsoft Graph Chart help you interpret the chart data. For example, if your chart contains a lot of data, you can add **gridlines** to make it easier to view and evaluate the data. If the gridlines make the chart cluttered, you can remove them. A **legend** identifies the patterns or colors assigned to the data. By default, the legend appears to the right of the chart, but you can change this position. You can also clarify the data in a chart by adding labels to identify what each data series represents. If you have a small set of data, you might find it helpful to see the numeric values along with the graphic representations of the data. For line, area, column, and bar charts, you can display a **data table**, a grid attached to a chart that shows the data used to create the chart.

Now that the owner of The Garden Company has added a chart to her memo, she wants to enhance its appearance and make it easier to interpret.

ModChart

In this exercise, you modify the appearance of a chart by changing its chart type and resizing it. Then you change the color of the plot area and apply a pattern to a data series. You hide and show gridlines, move the legend, and add labels to identify the data series. In addition, you add a data table to show the numeric values along with the graphic representations of the data, and then you format the data table.

Open

**1**  On the Standard toolbar, click the **Open** button.

The **Open** dialog box appears.

**2**  Navigate to the **SBS** folder on your hard disk, double-click the **Word** folder, double-click the **Charting** folder, and then double-click the **ModChart** file.

The ModChart document opens.

**3**  Scroll down the document, and then double-click the chart to activate it.

The chart and datasheet appear along with Graph's toolbars and menus.

Toolbar Options

**4**  Click **Toolbar Options** on one of the toolbars, and then click **Show Buttons on Two Rows**.

The Standard and Formatting toolbars appear on two rows.

Chart Type

**5**  On the Standard toolbar, click the **Chart Type** down arrow.

The list of chart types appears, as shown in the following illustration.

Area Chart

**6** Click the **Area Chart** button (the first button in the first row).

The chart type changes to an area chart, which compares data with areas of color instead of columns.

**7** On the right border of the chart, drag the middle sizing handle to the right until the chart is roughly as wide as your memo.

Now the labels for the weeks have more space between them, making the chart easier to read.

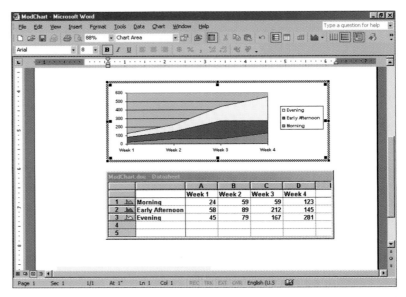

**8** Point to the gray area of the chart to display the *Plot Area* ScreenTip.

**9** Click the gray plot area to select the area.

Fill Color

**10** On the Standard toolbar, click the **Fill Color** down arrow to display a color menu.

**11** Click the **Light Green** color box (fifth row, fourth column).

The background of the chart changes to light green.

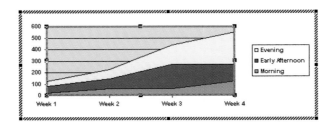

**12** Point to the middle series (maroon color) area of the chart to display the *Series "Early Afternoon"* ScreenTip, and then click the Early Afternoon series in the chart to select it.

Small black squares appear around the selected area.

Format Data
Series

**13** On the Standard toolbar, click the **Format Data Series** button.

The **Format Data Series** dialog box appears, showing the **Patterns** tab.

## Tip

You can double-click a chart element to display the **Format Data Series** dialog box.

**14** Click **Fill Effects** to open the **Fill Effects** dialog box.

**15** Click the **Pattern** tab to display pattern fill effects, and then click the 25% pattern (first column, fourth row).

Click this
pattern

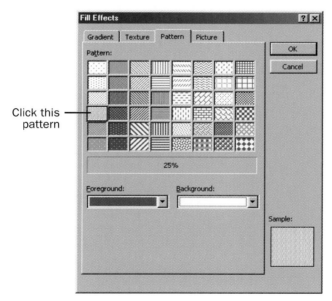

**16** Click **OK** to close the **Fill Effects** dialog box, and then click **OK** to close the **Format Data Series** dialog box.

The Early Afternoon series changes to a light dotted pattern.

Value Axis
Gridlines

**17** On the Standard toolbar, click the **Value Axis Gridlines** button to remove the horizontal gridlines from the chart.

**18** On the **Chart** menu, click **Chart Options**.

The **Chart Options** dialog box appears, showing the **Gridlines** tab.

**19** In the **Value (Y) axis** area, select the **Major gridlines** check box to show horizontal gridlines.

**20** Click the **Legend** tab, and then click the **Top** option.

The legend is moved to the top of the chart.

**21** Click the **Data Labels** tab, select the **Series name** check box, and then click **OK**.

The **Chart Options** dialog box closes, and a label appears next to each data series.

**22** Drag the lower-middle resize handle down to increase the size of the chart.

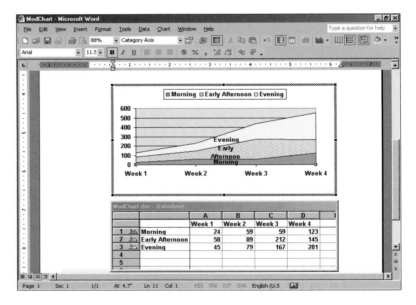

Legend

**23** On the Standard toolbar, click the **Legend** button to hide the legend.

**24** On the Standard toolbar, click the **Data Table** button.

Data Table

A data table is inserted below the chart.

**25** Double-click the data table.

The **Format Data Table** dialog box appears, showing the **Patterns** tab.

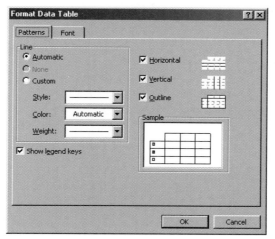

**26** Click the **Color** down arrow, and then click the **Blue** color box (second row, sixth column).

**27** Click the **Font** tab, click **10** in the **Size** box, and then click **OK**.

The data table text is smaller, allowing it all to fit in the table.

View Datasheet

**28** On the Standard toolbar, click the **View Datasheet** button to hide the datasheet, and then click outside the chart to deselect it.

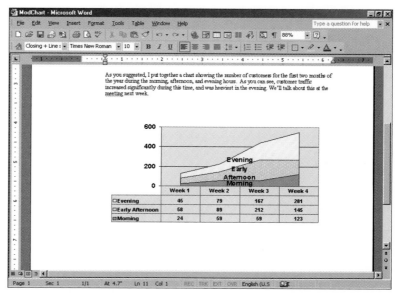

**29** On the Standard toolbar, click the **Save** button to save the document.

Close Window
**30** Click the **Close Window** button in the document window.

The ModChart document closes.

# Importing Data into a Chart

W2002e-4-2

Instead of typing data directly into a datasheet to create a chart, you can also enter data for a chart by importing it from another source, such as a Word table, a Microsoft Excel workbook, or a Microsoft Access database. To import data, select the cells in the datasheet where you want the data to be placed, click the **Import File** button on the Standard toolbar to place the data, and then select a data file. The **Import Data Options** dialog box opens and asks you to choose the data that you want to import. If you do not want the incoming data to overwrite existing chart data, it is important that you clear the **Overwrite existing cells** check box in the **Import Data Options** dialog box.

Instead of importing a chart from another source, you might find it easier to copy and paste information from the data source into your chart's datasheet. If that data source is a Word table, for example, you can select the data in the table, right-click the selection, and then click **Copy**. In your chart's datasheet, you can click the cell in which you want the copied data to begin, and then click the **Paste** button on the Standard toolbar. Copying and pasting from an Excel worksheet to a chart's datasheet is just like copying and pasting from a Word table to a chart's datasheet.

The owner of The Garden Company has been maintaining additional data about customer traffic in an Excel worksheet and wants to import the Excel information to the chart in a memo.

ImportData
FileImport

In this exercise, you import data from an Excel worksheet into a chart in a Word document so that you have a broader view of the trend.

**1** On the Standard toolbar, click the **Open** button.

Open

The **Open** dialog box appears.

**2** Navigate to the **SBS** folder on your hard disk, double-click the **Word** folder, double-click the **Charting** folder, and then double-click the **ImportData** file.

The ImportData document opens.

**3** Scroll down the document, and then double-click the chart to activate it.

The datasheet appears along with Microsoft Graph toolbars and menus.

## Tip

View
Datasheet

If the datasheet doesn't appear when you activate the chart, on Graph's Standard toolbar, click the **View Datasheet** button.

**4**   If necessary, drag the datasheet to position it below the chart.

**5**   Click in the datasheet, and then press the ➡ key until you see the **E**, **F**, **G**, and **H** columns.

**6**   Click the first empty cell under column E, and then drag to the right and down to select the first four rows in columns E through H, as shown below.

**Import File**

**7**   On the Standard toolbar, click the **Import File** button.

The **Import File** dialog box appears.

**8**   Navigate to the **SBS** folder, double-click the **Word** folder, double-click the **Charting** folder, and then double-click the **FileImport** file.

The **Import Data Options** dialog box appears, which lets you choose the data that you want to import. This workbook contains three worksheets. You want to import the worksheet named *weeks 5-8*, which is already selected.

**9**   Clear the **Overwrite existing cells** check box to prevent the incoming data from overwriting your existing chart data.

**10**  Click **OK** to accept the default worksheet, *weeks 5-8*.

The data from the Excel worksheet, including the new column headings for *Week 5* through *Week 8*, appears in the datasheet. The chart also now shows the imported data.

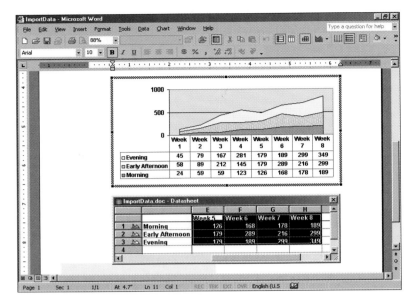

**11** On the Standard toolbar, click the **View Datasheet** button to hide the datasheet.

**12** Drag the bottom-middle resize handle down to increase the size of the chart, and then click outside the chart to deselect it.

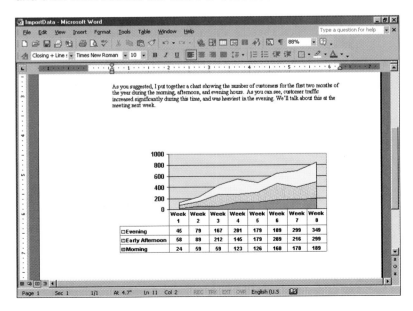

**13** On the Standard toolbar, click the **Save** button to save the document.

Close Window

**14** Click the **Close Window** button in the document window.

The ImportData document closes.

# Chapter Wrap-Up

To finish the chapter:

Close

● On the **File** menu, click **Exit**, or click the **Close** button in the Word window.

Word closes.

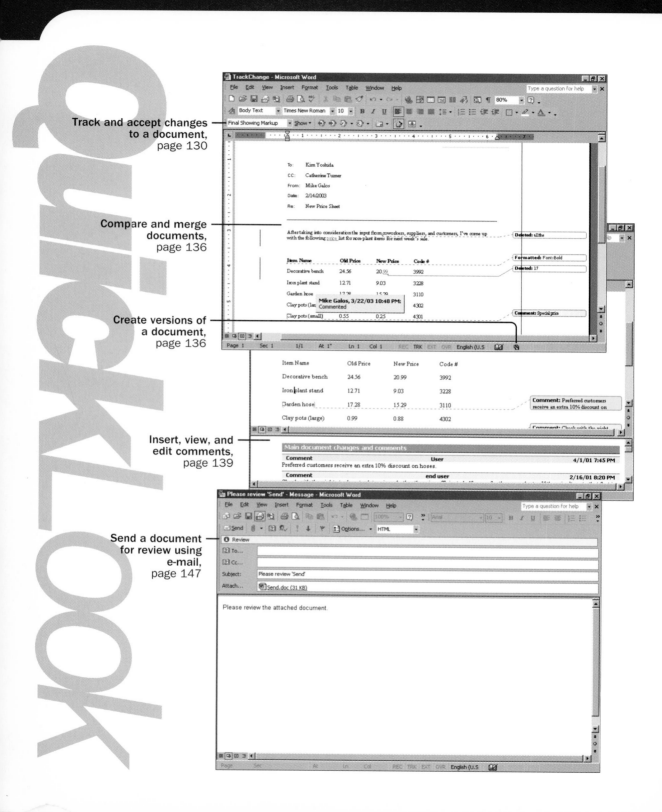

Track and accept changes to a document, page 130

Compare and merge documents, page 136

Create versions of a document, page 136

Insert, view, and edit comments, page 139

Send a document for review using e-mail, page 147

# Chapter 8
# Collaborating with Others

**After completing this chapter, you will be able to:**

✔  **Track and manage changes in a document.**
✔  **Compare and merge documents.**
✔  **Review comments in a document.**
✔  **Protect a document.**
✔  **Send a document for review using e-mail.**

After you create a draft of a document, you might distribute it to your coworkers and ask for their comments and revisions. Collaborating with others in this way helps you produce accurate and thorough documents.

Word lets you distribute a document to reviewers electronically so that they can read, revise, and comment on the document without printing it. Reviewers edit the document using the Track Changes feature so that you can see what they've changed. Reviewers can also insert **comments**, which are notes about text or other parts of the document. If you don't want reviewers to edit your work, you can protect a document so that others can only read it. For greater protection, you can assign a password so that only those who know the password can open the document. When reviewers return their comments and changes to you, you can merge all the revisions and comments into the original document and then review the changes, accepting or rejecting the changes and comments as appropriate.

You can review changes in Word by using the **Reviewing toolbar**, which contains buttons that let you accept and reject changes and comments, and by using the **Reviewing Pane,** which shows information related to the changes and comments in your document.

In this chapter, an assistant at The Garden Company collaborates with the head buyer to revise a memo and related documents. The assistant tracks his changes, reviews comments, and merges, accepts, and rejects other changes. He also protects other documents, and then he sends all the documents to the head buyer via e-mail.

 This chapter uses the practice files TrackChange, CompareMerge, Merge1, Merge2, RevComment, ProtectDoc, Attach1, Attach2, and Send that you installed from this book's CD-ROM. For details about installing the practice files, see "Using the Book's CD-ROM" at the beginning of this book.

# Tracking and Managing Changes in a Document

W2002e-6-1
W2002e-6-5

Revision
balloons
new for
**Office**XP

When you share your documents with others, you can track changes to see exactly what additions and deletions they made. Then you can accept or reject their revisions one at a time or all at once. If reviewers return their changes in separate documents, you can merge all their revisions into a single document and then review them. If you want a record of changes made to a document, you can save different versions of a document within the same document.

Tracking changes in a document allows you to make revisions to a document without losing the original text. When you track changes, Word shows changed text in a different color from the original text and uses **revision marks**, such as underlines, to distinguish the revised text from the original text. To preserve the layout of your document, Word also identifies the change and its type, such as a deletion, in a balloon that appears in the margin of the document.

By default, Word underlines and changes the color of inserted text. It also includes a vertical changed line in the margin to the left of any changed text to help you locate changes in the document.

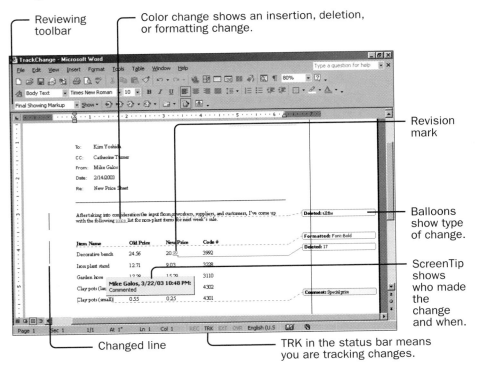

Reviewing toolbar

Color change shows an insertion, deletion, or formatting change.

Revision mark

Balloons show type of change.

ScreenTip shows who made the change and when.

Changed line

TRK in the status bar means you are tracking changes.

Track Changes

To turn on change tracking, you right-click any toolbar, click **Reviewing** on the menu to open the Reviewing toolbar, and then click the **Track Changes** button. Any changes that you make are then indicated by revision marks.

Display for
Review and
Show lists
new for
**Office**XP

If the revision marks are distracting, you can track changes without highlighting them on the screen. To hide the revision marks, click the **Track Changes** button on the Reviewing toolbar, if necessary, to start tracking changes. Click the **Display for Review** down arrow, and then click **Final**. When you're finished working on a document, click the **Display for Review** down arrow, and then click **Final Showing Markup** to see the changes identified in the document. While the **Display for Review** list changes whether you see the revisions identified, you also use the **Show** list to choose the types of revisions that you see in the document window.

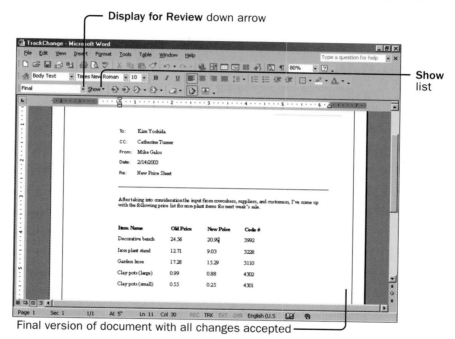

Final version of document with all changes accepted

As you review the tracked changes, you can accept or reject them one at a time, or you can accept or reject all the changes at once. When you accept a change, Word removes the typographical revision marks. If you have deleted text, it also removes the text from the document. If you have inserted text, it leaves the new text in the document. When you reject a change, Word restores the original text.

To review changes, you use the Reviewing toolbar. You can review changes one at a time by using the **Next Change** and **Previous Change** buttons. Then use the **Accept Change** or **Reject Change** buttons to respond to the revisions. To accept all the changes at once, click the **Accept Change** down arrow, and then click **Accept All**

**Changes in Document**. To reject all the changes at once, click the **Reject Change** down arrow, and then click **Reject All Changes in Document**.

If you want a record of changes made to a document, you can save different **versions** of a document within the same document. When you save different versions within Word, you also save disk space because Word saves only the differences between versions, not an entire copy of each document. After you've saved several versions of the document, you can go back and review, open, print, and delete earlier versions. You can also have Word save a version of your document each time the document is closed, which is useful when you need a record of who made changes and when, as in the case of a legal document. To save a version every time that you close a document, use the **Versions** command on the **File** menu to open the **Versions in TrackChange** dialog box, and then select the **Automatically save a version on close** check box.

An assistant at The Garden Company is ready to revise a memo for the head buyer. The memo lists price changes for non-plant products within the store.

TrackChange

In this exercise, you open a document, turn on change tracking, make changes to the document, accept and reject changes, and create a second version of the document.

**1** Start Word, if necessary.

Open

**2** On the Standard toolbar, click the **Open** button.

The **Open** dialog box appears.

**3** Navigate to the **SBS** folder on your hard disk, double-click the **Word** folder, double-click the **Collaborating** folder, and then double-click the **TrackChange** file.

The TrackChange document opens.

**4** On the **View** menu, point to **Toolbars**, and then click **Reviewing.**

The Reviewing toolbar appears.

Track Changes

**5** On the Reviewing toolbar, click the **Track Changes** button.

Any changes that you make will now be tracked.

## Tip

When track changes is turned on, the **Track Changes** button has a blue border, and the letters *TRK* are highlighted on the status bar; when track changes is turned off, the **Track Changes** button has no border, and *TRK* is gray on the status bar.

**6** Scroll down the document to see the product information, click to the right of the new price *20.17* for the decorative bench, and then press the [Backspace] key twice.

Word inserts a callout—*Deleted: 17*—that describes the type and content of your change.

**7** Type **99**.

The price changes from $20.17 to $20.99, and *99* appears in a different color.

**8** Click to the right of the new price *$15.29* for the garden hose.

**9** Press [Backspace] twice to delete *29*.

The document shows two callouts, each identifying text that has been deleted.

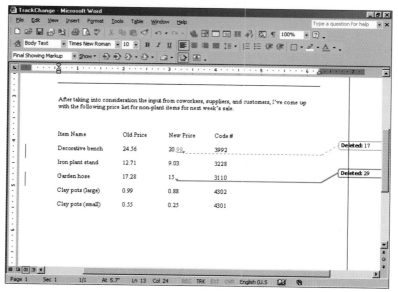

**10** Type **99**.

The document shows the two corrected prices, *$20.99* and *$15.99*, with the revisions in a different color.

**11** In the text, point to the first change that you made for the decorative bench price, the price that you changed to $20.99.

A ScreenTip tells you the name of the person who made the change, when the change was made, and the type of change that was made. In this case, the ScreenTip displays *Inserted*.

**12** Press [Ctrl]+[Home] to move the insertion point to the beginning of the document.

Next

**13** On the Reviewing toolbar, click the **Next** button.

The first change in the document is selected—the number 99 in the decorative bench price.

Accept Change

**14** On the Reviewing toolbar, click the **Accept Change** button, and then click the price again to deselect it.

Word accepts the change, and the price of the decorative bench now appears as $20.99 without revision marks. A balloon still shows that you deleted 17 from this text.

## Tip

To accept a change, you can also right-click the change and then click **Accept Insertion** or **Accept Deletion** on the shortcut menu that appears.

**15** Click in the middle of 99 in the new garden hose price to place the insertion point.

Reject
Change/
Delete
Comment

**16** On the Reviewing toolbar, click the **Reject Change/Delete Comment** button, and then click the **Reject Change/Delete Comment** button again.

The first click rejects the new price that you entered; the second click rejects the deletion that you made.

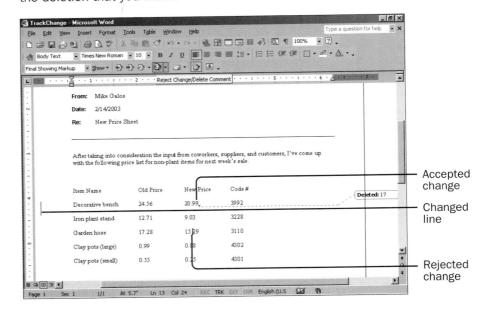

## Tip

When you point to a change on the screen, the name that appears in the ScreenTip is the user name that was entered when the operating system was installed. If no name was entered, the ScreenTip shows *User* as the name. You can change the user name in the **Options** dialog box. On the **Tools** menu, click **Options**, click the **User Information** tab, type a user name in the **Name** box, and then click **OK**.

**17** On the **File** menu, click **Versions**.

The **Versions in TrackChange** dialog box appears, showing that Mike Galos saved the original version of the document.

**18** Click **Save Now** to open the **Save Version** dialog box, type **New price for decorative bench** in the **Comments on version** box, and then click **OK**.

The **Versions in TrackChange** dialog box closes, and the version is saved.

**19** On the **File** menu, click **Versions** to open the **Versions in TrackChange** dialog box again.

The new version appears in the **Existing versions** area.

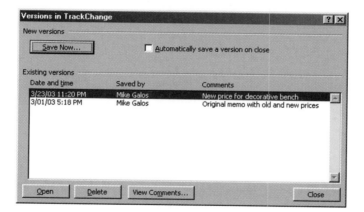

## Tip

Versions icon

You can also double-click the **Versions** icon on the status bar to open the **Versions in TrackChange** dialog box.

**20** Click the **Close** button to close the **Versions in TrackChange** dialog box.

**21** On the Standard toolbar, click the **Save** button to save the document.

Close Window

**22** Click the **Close Window** button in the document window.

The TrackChanges document closes.

# Comparing and Merging Documents

W2002-6-1
W2002e-6-2

If you want to compare an earlier version of a document with the current version of a document, you can compare the documents and then merge the changes into one document. For example, if you ask an associate to edit a document, but he doesn't track changes while editing, you can compare his edited document to your original to see what changes he made.

When you compare and merge documents, Word shows the differences between them as tracked changes. If multiple reviewers return their changes and comments in separate documents, you can merge all their changes into a single document and review their changes from that single document. You then can review changes from a specific reviewer.

CompareMerge
Merge1
Merge2

An assistant at The Garden Company is ready to revise the memo for the head buyer. The memo lists price changes for non-plant products within The Garden Company.

In this exercise, you merge the document with two other versions of the document.

**1**   On the Standard toolbar, click the **Open** button.

The **Open** dialog box appears.

**2**   Navigate to the **SBS** folder on your hard disk, double-click the **Word** folder, double-click the **Collaborating** folder, and then double-click the **Compare-Merge** file.

The CompareMerge document opens.

Compare
and merge
documents
**new for**
**Office**XP

**3**   On the **Tools** menu, click **Compare and Merge Documents**.

The **Compare and Merge Documents** dialog box appears.

**4**   Navigate to the **Collaborating** folder.

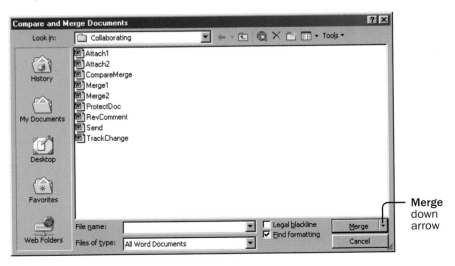

Merge
down
arrow

**5** Click **Merge1**, click the **Merge** down arrow, and then click **Merge into current document**.

The deletions and changes from the document appear on the screen in the current document. The color of each revision indicates a different reviewer.

## Tip

When you compare versions of a document, you see reviewers' changes even if the reviewers did not track their changes as they edited.

**6** On the **Tools** menu, click **Compare and Merge Documents**, navigate to the **Collaborating** folder, click **Merge2**, click the **Merge** down arrow, and then click **Merge into current document**.

The deletions and changes from the documents appear on the screen in the current document with the other changes.

**7** Scroll down the document to see the product information.

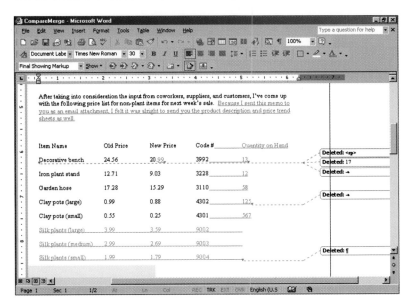

## Important

The colors of the tracked changes above might not be the same as the ones that you see on your screen.

**8**     On the Reviewing toolbar, click the **Show** down arrow, point to **Reviewers**, and then click **Jill B**.

The revisions made by the *Jill B.* reviewer are hidden.

**9**     On the Reviewing toolbar, click the **Show** down arrow, point to **Reviewers**, and then click **All Reviewers**.

The revisions made by all reviewers appear.

**10**     Type **132**, **139**, and **167** as the *Quantity On Hand* for the large, medium, and small silk plants.

**11**     Scroll up to the top of the document, if necessary.

The title of the document has been changed by one of the reviewers.

**12**     On the Reviewing toolbar, click the **Show** down arrow, and then click **Formatting**.

Only insertions and deletions, not formatting changes, appear in the document.

**13**     Triple-click the *Memorandum* paragraph to select the entire paragraph, and then press the ⌈Del⌋ key.

The second title from the document is deleted, leaving the one merged from the Merge1 document.

Next

**14**     On the Reviewing toolbar, click the **Next** button.

The added text *for Next Sales Period* is selected.

Accept Change

**15**     On the Reviewing toolbar, click the **Accept Change** button to accept the change, and then click the **Next** button to find the next revision.

The added sentence in the first paragraph is selected.

Reject Change/Delete Comment

**16**     On the Reviewing toolbar, click the **Reject Change/Delete Comment** button to reject the change.

The added sentence change is removed.

**17**     On the Reviewing toolbar, click the **Display for Review** down arrow, click **Final**, and then scroll through the document.

The document appears with all the current changes and without the revision marks.

**18**     On the Reviewing toolbar, click the **Display for Review** down arrow, and then click **Final Showing Markup**.

The document appears with all the revision marks.

**19**     On the Reviewing toolbar, click the **Accept Change** down arrow, and then click **Accept All Changes in Document**.

The changes are accepted in the document.

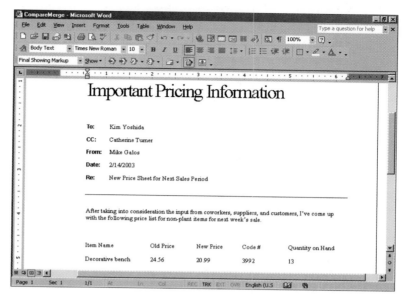

**20** On the Standard toolbar, click the **Save** button to save the document.

Close Window

**21** Click the **Close Window** button in the document window.

The CompareMerge document closes.

# Reviewing Comments in a Document

W2002-6-2

Reviewing
toolbar
new for
**Office**XP

In addition to tracking changes, you can insert **comments**, which are notes or annotations that you or a reviewer adds to a document without changing the document text. To insert a comment, you select the text that you want to comment on and then click the **New Comment** button on the Reviewing toolbar. Type your comment in the comment balloon or the Reviewing Pane. Word inserts colored brackets around commented text and displays comments in a balloon in the margin of the document or in the Reviewing Pane.

To view comments, read the text in the comment balloons. You can also point to commented text to see a ScreenTip showing both the name of the person who made the comment and the date and time of the comment. To edit or delete a comment, right-click the commented text and then click **Edit Comment** or **Delete Comment**. To review comments, you click the **Next Comment** and **Previous Comment** buttons to move from one comment to another. To respond to a comment, you click in the comment balloon or the comment text in the document and then click the **New Comment** button. Type your response in the new comment balloon that appears.

If Word cannot display the complete text of a comment in a balloon, you can open the Reviewing Pane to see the entire comment. If you find the comment balloons distracting, you can turn them off and work with comments only in the Reviewing Pane. To show or hide balloons, on the **Tools** menu, click **Options** to open the **Options** dialog box, click the **Track Changes** tab, and then select or clear the **Use balloons** check box. To show or hide the Reviewing Pane, you click the **Reviewing Pane** button on the Reviewing toolbar. In addition to providing information about comments in the document, the Reviewing Pane tracks changes to the main part of the document, to headers and footers and their text boxes, to text boxes themselves, and to footnotes and endnotes.

In this exercise, you show and review comments in a document, add a comment, delete one that is no longer needed, and then hide the remaining comment.

RevComment

**1** On the Standard toolbar, click the **Open** button.

Open

The **Open** dialog box appears.

**2** Navigate to the **SBS** folder on your hard disk, double-click the **Word** folder, double-click the **Collaborating** folder, and then double-click the **RevComment** file.

The RevComment document opens.

Web Layout View

**3** Click the **Web Layout View** button to switch to Web Layout view.

**4** On the **View** menu, click **Markup** to show comments and changes and to display the Reviewing toolbar.

Next

**5** On the Reviewing toolbar, click the **Next** button to display the first comment in the document, and then scroll down to display the entire comment.

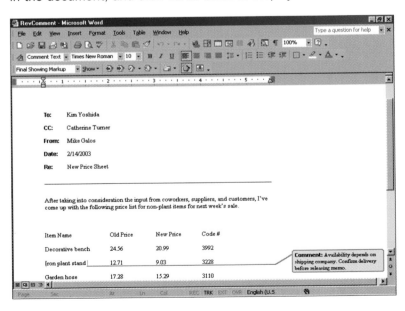

The insertion point appears in the first balloon comment, and brackets appear around the text *Iron plant stand*. The brackets show where comments have been inserted.

**6** On the Reviewing toolbar, click the **Next** button to display the next comment in the document.

The insertion point appears in the next balloon comment, and brackets appear around the text *Clay pots (small)*.

**7** Point to the text *Iron plant stand*, and then read the ScreenTip.

The ScreenTip displays information about who inserted the comment and when.

**8** Drag the horizontal scroll bar to the right, if necessary, to read the comments along the right side of the document.

**9** Drag to select the *Garden hose* text.

New Comment

**10** On the Reviewing toolbar, click the **New Comment** button.

Word adds brackets around the *Garden hose* text and inserts a comment balloon in the right margin.

**11** In the comment balloon, type **Preferred customers receive an extra 10% discount on hoses**.

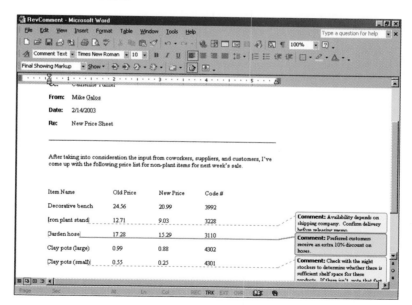

**12** Click a blank area of the document to deselect the comment.

**13** Right-click anywhere on the *Iron plant stand* text, and then click **Delete Comment** to delete the comment from the screen.

Reviewing Pane

**14** On the Reviewing toolbar, click the **Reviewing Pane** button.

The Reviewing Pane opens at the bottom of the Word window, showing the remaining comments about the garden hoses and clay pots.

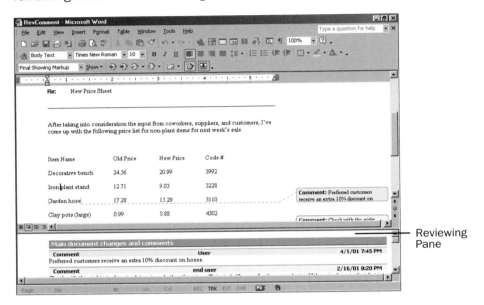

Reviewing Pane

## Tip

Resize pointer

To change the size of the Reviewing Pane, point to the top edge of the Reviewing Pane until the pointer changes to a resize pointer, and then drag the edge.

**15** Click to the right of the last word (*intact*) in the second comment, press `Space`, type your initials, type a colon (:), press `Space`, and then type **I'm not sure if there is enough shelf space.**

The text appears in the Reviewing Pane for the selected comment.

**16** On the Reviewing toolbar, click the **Reviewing Pane** button to close the Reviewing Pane.

**17** Right-click the *Clay pots (small)* text, and then click **Edit Comment**.

The insertion point appears at the end of the comment attached to the *Clay pots (small)* text.

New Comment

**18** On the Reviewing toolbar, click the **New Comment** button to create a new balloon comment in response to the other comment.

Dotted lines connect both comments.

**19** Type **I checked with the shipping company. They are ready to go**.

The text appears in the balloon comment.

**20** Double-click *3992* in the decorative bench code to select the number.

**21** On the Reviewing toolbar, click the **New Comment** button to create a new balloon comment.

**22** Type **Kim, Is this product code correct?**.

The text appears in the balloon comment.

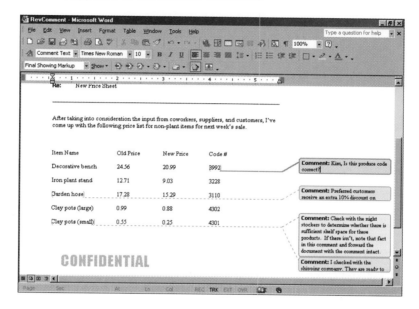

## Tip

If you have a sound card and a microphone installed on your computer, you can record voice comments, which are attached as sound objects to the text in the document. To insert a voice comment, on the Reviewing toolbar, click the **New Comment** down arrow, click **Voice Comment**, and then record the voice comment. If an alert appears, asking whether you want to update the sound object, click **Yes**.

**23** On the Reviewing toolbar, click the **Show** down arrow, and then click **Comments** to hide them.

**24** On the Standard toolbar, click the **Save** button to save the document.

Close Window

**25** Click the **Close Window** button in the document window.

The RevComment document closes.

# Protecting a Document

W2002e-6-6

You can use the security options in Word to protect the integrity of your document as others review it. At times, you will want the information in a document to be used, but not changed; at other times, you might want only specific people in your office to be able to view the document. To protect a document, you use the options on the **Security** tab in the **Options** dialog box.

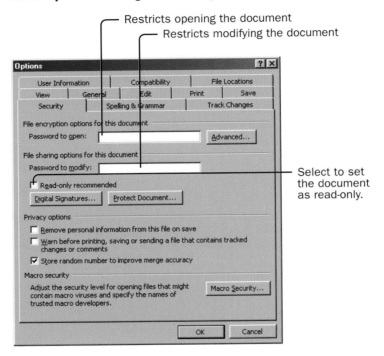

Restricts opening the document

Restricts modifying the document

Select to set the document as read-only.

Password protection

new for **Office**XP

In this dialog box, you can set a password that must be entered before someone can open or modify your document. Selecting the **Read-only recommended** check box allows you to display a message that suggests that the user open the document as **read-only**, a setting that lets someone read or copy the file, but not change or save it. Setting a document as read-only is useful when you want a document, such as a company-wide bulletin, to be distributed and read, but not changed. You can also use the **Protect Document** button on the **Security** tab to set passwords so that you can restrict who can track changes or enter comments.

When you set a password, take a moment to write it down. Word doesn't keep a list of passwords. If you lose or forget the password for a protected document, you will not be able to open it. To open a protected document, you need to enter the password in the exact same way that it was set, including spaces, symbols, and uppercase and lowercase characters.

An assistant at The Garden Company wants to protect the pricing memo so that no one can change it while he distributes it for review. Then he plans to remove the protection so that the head buyer can update it as necessary.

ProtectDoc

In this exercise, you set a password for a document. You save and close the document, and then you test the security of the document by entering an incorrect password. You open the document as read-only and then reopen it with the correct password. Finally, you remove the protection from the document.

Open

**1** On the Standard toolbar, click the **Open** button.

The **Open** dialog box appears.

**2** Navigate to the **SBS** folder on your hard disk, double-click the **Word** folder, double-click the **Collaborating** folder, and then double-click the **ProtectDoc** file.

The ProtectDoc document opens.

**3** On the **Tools** menu, click **Options**.

The **Options** dialog box appears.

**4** Click the **Security** tab to display security options.

**5** In the **Password to modify** box, type **tgc3**.

As you type the password, asterisks appear instead of the characters you type to keep your password confidential.

## Tip

Passwords should never be common words or phrases, and the same password should never be used for multiple documents.

**6** Click **OK** to close the **Options** dialog box.

The **Confirm Password** dialog box appears.

**7** In the **Reenter password to modify** box, type **tgc3**.

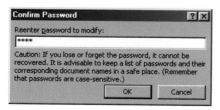

**8** Click **OK** to set the password.

**9** On the Standard toolbar, click the **Save** button to save the document.

Close Window

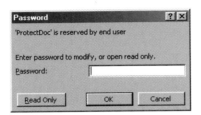

**10**  Click the **Close Window** button in the document window.

The ProtectDoc document closes. Next, you will open the protected document with read-only and then full privileges.

**11**  On the Standard toolbar, click the **Open** button.

The **Open** dialog box appears.

**12**  Navigate to the **Collaborating** folder, and then double-click the **ProtectDoc** file.

The **Password** dialog box appears. This document is now protected by the password that you just set.

**13**  In the **Password** box, type **tgc1**, and then click **OK**.

A message appears, indicating that you typed an incorrect password.

**14**  In the message box, click **OK**.

**15**  In the **Password** dialog box, click **Read Only**.

The ProtectDoc document opens as a read-only document. *(Read-Only)* appears in the title bar.

Close Window

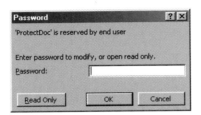

**16**  Click the **Close Window** button in the document window.

The read-only document closes.

**17**  On the Standard toolbar, click the **Open** button.

The **Open** dialog box appears.

**18**  Navigate to the **Collaborating** folder, and then double-click the **ProtectDoc** file.

The **Password** dialog box appears.

**19**  Type **tgc3**, and then click **OK**.

After you type the correct password, the document opens.

**20**  On the **Tools** menu, click **Options**.

The **Options** dialog box appears.

**21**  Click the **Security** tab, if necessary, select the contents in the **Password to modify** box, press ⌫, and then click **OK**.

The password protection is removed.

**22** On the Standard toolbar, click the **Save** button to save the document.

Close Window

**23** Click the **Close Window** button in the document window.

The ProtectDoc document closes.

# Sending a Document for Review Using E-Mail

W2002e-6-2

After you finish making changes to a document, you can quickly send it to another person for review using e-mail. Word allows you to distribute documents for review using e-mail from within Word so that you do not have to start your e-mail program. To share your documents with others, on the **File** menu, point to **Send To**. The **Send To** submenu includes the **Mail Recipient (for Review)** and **Mail Recipient (as Attachment)** commands. Click one of these commands to open a message window with the current document as an attachment. If you use the **Mail Recipient (for Review)** command, the message also includes the text *Please review the attached document.* To send the document, enter the destination e-mail address for anyone who should receive a copy of the message and its attachments. The subject line of the e-mail will already contain the name of the document that you are sending.

## Important

To complete this exercise, you need to have an e-mail program installed on your computer and an e-mail account set up. Microsoft Outlook 2002 or later is recommended. You can use another e-mail program, but the functionality and settings might be different.

Send
Attach1
Attach2

An assistant at The Garden Company is ready to distribute the pricing memo to other staff. From within Word, he'll send the memo as an attachment to an e-mail message.

In this exercise, you send three documents for review attached to an e-mail message.

**1** On the Standard toolbar, click the **Open** button.

The **Open** dialog box appears.

**2** Navigate to the **SBS** folder on your hard disk, double-click the **Word** folder, double-click the **Collaborating** folder, and then double-click the **Send** file.

The Send document opens.

Send for review
new for
**Office**XP

**3** On the **File** menu, point to **Send To**, and then click **Mail Recipient (for Review)**.

The **Choose Profile** dialog box might appear, showing information about your Internet or network profile.

**4** Click **OK**, if necessary, to accept the profile and display the message window.

Box for the e-mail address of your recipient

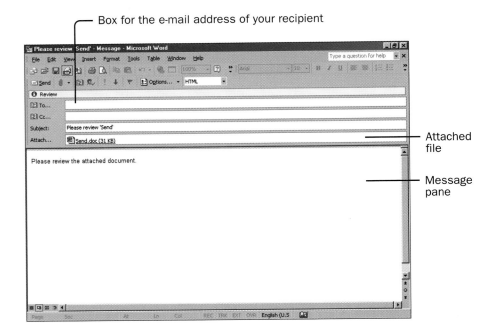

Attached file

Message pane

## Tip

To send a copy of the current document as the message body in an e-mail message, click the **E-Mail** button on the Standard toolbar. A toolbar appears in the Word document with e-mail commands from which you can send the current document.

**5** Click in the **To** box, if necessary, and then type someone@microsoft.com.

Insert File

**6** Click the **Insert File** button, and then navigate to the **Collaborate** folder, if necessary.

**7** Click **Attach1**, hold down [Ctrl], click **Attach2**, and then click **Insert**.

The Attach box shows three files.

**8** On the Message toolbar, click the **Importance: High** button.

The message is set for delivery with the Importance: High flag.

**9** Click anywhere in the message pane.

Highlight

**10** On the Formatting toolbar, click the **Highlight** button.

The pointer changes to a highlight pen in text areas.

**11** Drag the pointer over the text in the message pane.

The text is highlighted with yellow, making it stand out.

Send

**12** On the Message toolbar, click the **Send** button.

When you try this with a real e-mail address, the e-mail message with the attached documents is sent out for review. In this case, the e-mail message is sent to an e-mail account at Microsoft, which automatically sends a response to the sender. You'll receive an e-mail response in your Inbox. The Send document appears in the document window.

**13** On the Standard toolbar, click the **Save** button to save the document.

Close Window

**14** Click the **Close Window** button in the document window.

The Send document closes.

## Chapter Wrap-Up

To finish the chapter:

Close

● On the **File** menu, click **Exit**, or click the **Close** button in the Word window.

Word closes.

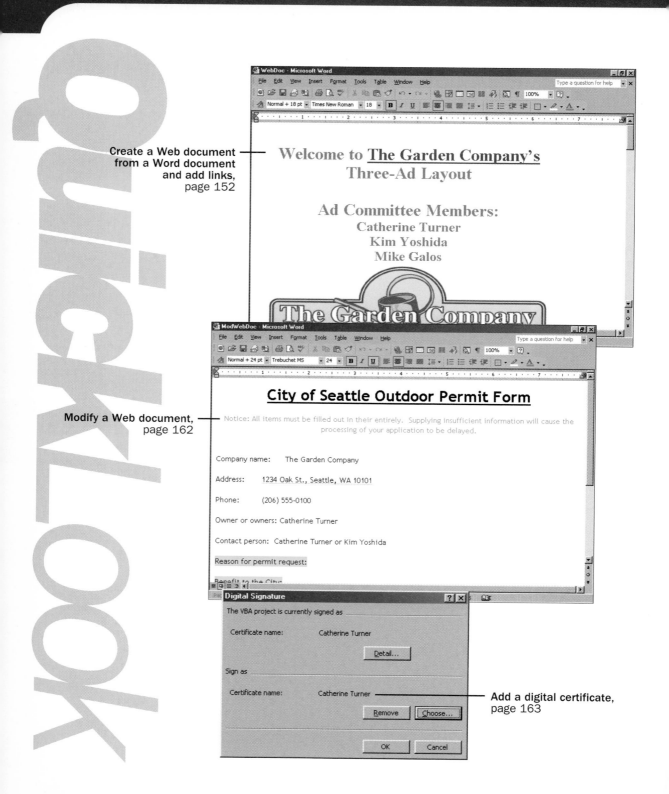

Create a Web document from a Word document and add links, page 152

Welcome to **The Garden Company's** Three-Ad Layout

**Ad Committee Members:**
Catherine Turner
Kim Yoshida
Mike Galos

Modify a Web document, page 162

**City of Seattle Outdoor Permit Form**

Notice: All items must be filled out in their entirely. Supplying insufficient information will cause the processing of your application to be delayed.

Company name:    The Garden Company

Address:    1234 Oak St., Seattle, WA 10101

Phone:    (206) 555-0100

Owner or owners: Catherine Turner

Contact person:  Catherine Turner or Kim Yoshida

Reason for permit request:

Add a digital certificate, page 163

# Chapter 9
# Working with Documents on the Web

**After completing this chapter, you will be able to:**

✔ **Create a Web document containing links.**

✔ **Modify a Web document.**

✔ **Add a digital signature.**

If you have ever explored the Web to find sports scores or to research a topic, you know that the Web is an appealing, informative, and immediate medium. Your documents can find a broader audience if you transform them into Web pages and let others read them on the Web. For example, if you develop materials such as newsletters, brochures, and flyers, you can publish them on the Web, and your readers can view them in a browser such as Microsoft Internet Explorer.

Although professional Web page designers use special programs, such as Microsoft FrontPage, to design sophisticated Web pages, Word is a good choice for creating simple Web pages or for converting existing documents to Web pages. Word lets you save a document as a Web page, preview it in your Web browser, and then modify it as necessary. You can also add **hyperlinks** to the document, which you and others can click to link to other documents, Web pages, or e-mail addresses. To help others explore your Web pages, you can create a **link bar**, which includes **Back** and **Next** buttons to guide users through a series of pages. You can also apply a **digital signature** to confirm that your Web document has not been changed since you created it.

In this chapter, you'll create a Web document from a Word document and then add links to it. You'll also open an existing Web document and modify it. Then you'll add a digital signature to a document.

This chapter uses the practice files CreateWeb, OtherLogos, ModWebDoc, WebSignature, and AddSignature that you installed from this book's CD-ROM. For details about installing the practice files, see "Using the Book's CD-ROM" at the beginning of this book.

# Creating a Web Document Containing Links

W2002-6-3
W2002e-6-3
W2002e-6-4

You can save any Word document as a **Web page**, which is a special document designed to be viewed in a program called a Web browser. Most of the formatting in your Word document will be preserved when you view the document as a Web page in your browser. However, some formatting is not converted, such as text wrapping around pictures and objects, and other features are not supported by all Web browsers, for example table formatting, character formatting, page layout features, and security and document protection.

If you know which Web browser your viewers will be using, it's a good idea to optimize your Web page for that browser. Word lets you specify the browser that viewers of your Web documents are using, and then it disables any features that won't appear in that Web browser. To see how your document will appear in a Web browser, you can preview it as a Web page and then edit as necessary. When you're satisfied with the results, you save the document as a Web page. You can also click the **Web Layout View** button above the status bar to see how a document appears as a Web page.

You can convert existing Word documents to Web pages using the **Save as Web Page** command on the **File** menu. To create a new Web page, you can use the **Web Page Wizard** or a Web page template. For a multipage **Web site** (a collection of related Web pages), complete with navigation tools and a professionally designed theme, you can use the **Web Page Wizard**, which guides you through the steps of creating Web pages. To create a particular kind of Web page, such as one for frequently asked questions or personal information, you can use a Web template. To use the **Web Page Wizard** or a Web page template, on the **File** menu, you click **New**, click **General Templates** in the **New Document** task pane, click the **Web Pages** tab, double-click **Web Page Wizard**, and then follow the instructions in the wizard, or you double-click a Web template.

Filtered Web page and Web archive
new for **Office**XP

You can save a Word document as a Web page, a filtered Web page, or a Web archive. A Web page is a document in HTML (Hypertext Markup Language, the markup language of tags, which determine how text and graphics are displayed in a browser), while a **filtered Web page** is a document in HTML optimized without Microsoft Office-specific HTML tags. A **Web archive** saves all the elements of a Web site, including text and graphics, into a single document with the .mht extension. When you save a Word document as a Web page, Word changes any unsupported formatting, such as table borders, background, and animated text, so that Web browsers can display the information. To make your Web page viewable by others over the Internet, you need to save it on a **Web server**, a process known as **publishing**. To publish a Web document to a Web server, your computer needs to have access to a Web server using an Internet or network connection. Once you have a connection, you can use the **Web Folders** icon in the **Save As** dialog box to navigate to a Web server and then save the Web document in the same way that you save a document to your hard disk.

Web pages use hyperlinks—text, graphics, or other objects—that you can click to perform an action, such as opening another Web page or document. You can insert hyperlinks (also called **links**) into a Web document or any other type of Word document to link to another Web page, file, e-mail address, or **bookmark**, which is a location in a document that you identify and name for future reference. To insert a hyperlink, you click the **Insert Hyperlink** button on the Standard toolbar to display the **Insert Hyperlink** dialog box. Use the buttons in the **Link to bar** to set up a link to another file or Web page, to another place in the document, such as a heading or bookmark, to a new document, or to an e-mail address. To link to another Web page, you specify a **Uniform Resource Locator** (URL), which is a unique address for the Web page, such as *www.microsoft.com*. A URL consists of three parts: the prefix *http://*, which indicates a Web address; a network identification, such as *www* for World Wide Web; and a Web site name, or domain name, such as *microsoft.com*.

Hyperlinks appear in Word documents as blue underlined text, which is similar to the way that they appear in browsers. To edit a hyperlink, you right-click it and then choose a command from the shortcut menu to change the destination of the hyperlink, to change the display text, or to convert the hyperlink to regular text.

When you insert a hyperlink into a document, you can use the **Set Target Frame** dialog box to control how the linked page is displayed in the document. You can display the linked page in the same window as the original page, in a new window, or in a **frame**, which is a window region on a Web page. You can follow a hyperlink in any Word document by holding down the [Ctrl] key and then clicking the link. When you view the Web document in your browser, you can simply click the link to follow it.

The head buyer for the Garden Company created a document containing sales ads and wants to convert the document into a Web document. To make it easy to access logos that are mentioned in the sales ads document, the buyer will insert hyperlinks to a document that contains company logos.

CreateWeb
OtherLogos

In this exercise, you set options for displaying a document in Microsoft Internet Explorer 5.0 or later, preview and save the document as a Web page, and insert, test, and modify a hyperlink.

**Important**

To complete this exercise, you need a Web browser; Internet Explorer 5.0 or later is recommended. You can use another browser, but the functionality and settings might be different.

**1**   Start Word, if necessary.

Open

**2**   On the Standard toolbar, click the **Open** button.
The **Open** dialog box appears.

**3** Navigate to the **SBS** folder on your hard disk, double-click the **Word** folder, double-click the **WorkingWeb** folder, and then double-click the **CreateWeb** file.

The CreateWeb document opens in Print Layout view.

**4** On the **Tools** menu, click **Options**.

The **Options** dialog box appears.

**5** Click the **General** tab, if necessary, and then click **Web Options**.

The **Web Options** dialog box appears.

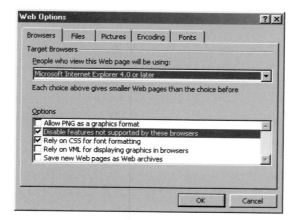

**6** Click the **Browsers** tab, if necessary, click the **People who view this Web page will be using** down arrow, and then click **Microsoft Internet Explorer 5.0 or later**.

**7** In the **Options** list, verify that the **Disable features not supported by these browsers** check box is selected, and then click **OK** to close the **Web Options** dialog box.

**8** Click **OK** to close the **Options** dialog box.

**9** On the **File** menu, click **Web Page Preview**.

The CreateWeb document opens in your Web browser.

Maximize

**10** Click the **Maximize** button to maximize the Internet Explorer window.

**11** On the **File** menu, click **Close** to close the Internet Explorer window.

The Word window appears.

**12** On the **File** menu, click **Save as Web Page**.

The **Save As** dialog box appears.

## Tip

When you save a document as a Web page, you can specify a page title for the document. This title appears in the title bar of the Web browser, and it can be different from the file name. To specify a Web page title, click **Change Title** in the **Save As** dialog box, and then type the title in the **Page title** box.

**13** Navigate to the **WorkingWeb** folder, and then type **WebDoc** in the **File name** box.

**14** Click the **Save as type** down arrow, and then click **Web page**.

**15** Click **Save**.

A message box appears, indicating that some features in this document are not supported by Internet Explorer 5.0.

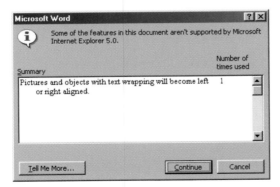

**16** Click **Continue**.

The document appears in Word, this time in Web Layout view. The Word document is now a Web document.

**17** Scroll down to see The Garden Company logo, if necessary, right-click the logo, and then click **Hyperlink**.

The **Insert Hyperlink** dialog box appears, displaying the **WorkingWeb** folder.

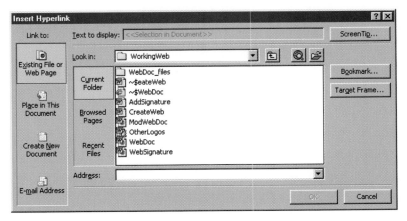

**18** In the list of folders and file names, click the **OtherLogos** file, and then click **Target Frame**.

The **Set Target Frame** dialog box appears with **Page Default (none)** as the current frame setting.

When you view your Web document in a browser and click the company logo, the OtherLogos document will open in the same window.

**19** Click **OK** to accept the default selection, click **OK** to close the **Insert Hyperlink** dialog box, and then point to the logo again.

Word displays a ScreenTip that shows the path of this hyperlink to the OtherLogos file.

**20** Hold down Ctrl, and then click the logo.

The OtherLogos file is displayed in your browser window.

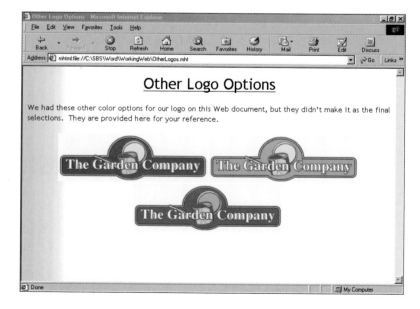

**21** On the **File** menu, click **Close** to close the Internet Explorer window.

The Word window appears. In the first line of the document, the phrase *The Garden Company's* is underlined to indicate that it is a hyperlink.

**22** Click to the left of The Garden Company's hyperlink to select the text box containing it, point to the hyperlink, and then read the ScreenTip.

The ScreenTip shows the target Web address as *http://www.msn.com.*

**23** Right-click the hyperlink, and then click **Edit Hyperlink**.

The **Edit Hyperlink** dialog box appears with the current Web address for this link in the **Address** box.

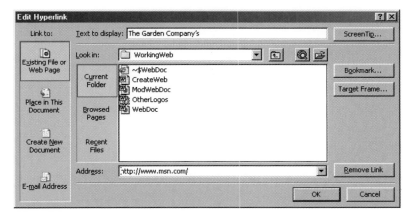

**24** In the **Address** box, click before the letters *msn*, and then type **gardenco.**

You changed the link to connect to The Garden Company's Web address—*www.gardenco.msn.com*.

## Tip

When you type a URL as a hyperlink, you do not have to type the *http://* protocol. If you omit the protocol, your browser will add *http://* for you automatically. You only need to add the protocol—the letters before the colon—if it is something other than *http*, such as *ftp*.

**25** Click **OK** to close the **Edit Hyperlink** dialog box, and then point to the hyperlink again.

The ScreenTip shows that the Web address is *http://www.gardenco.msn.com*.

**26** On the Standard toolbar, click the **Save** button to save the document.

Close Window
**27** Click the **Close Window** button in the document window.

The WebDoc document closes.

## Adding a Link Bar

Link bar

new for
**Office**XP

Once you convert a Word document to a Web or Web archive document and save it to a Web server that is running Microsoft FrontPage 2002 Server Extensions or Microsoft SharePoint, you can insert a link bar into the document. A link bar is a collection of graphic or text buttons representing hyperlinks to pages in your Web site and external Web sites. A link bar gives you and others who use your document a way to easily navigate around the content and features of your Web document. For example, link bars include Next and Back links, which you can click to move from one page to another in sequence. You also can add custom links in a link bar, such as one to your home page, and arrange them in any order you like.

You can format and style the link bar to match the design of your Web site. For example, you can change the font of the text, add images, and apply themes. You can also choose a bar type, such as rounded or rectangular, a bar style, such as 2-D or 3-D, and an orientation to specify whether the link bar resides across the top or along the left side of your Web page.

You can create a link bar from scratch or create one based on an existing link bar.

*You need access to a server running Microsoft FrontPage Version 2002 Server Extensions or Microsoft SharePoint to create link bars.*

To add a link bar to a Web page:

1   On the **File** menu, click **Save as Web Page**.

    The **Save As** dialog box appears.

2   In the **Places Bar**, click **Web Folders**, and then navigate to a Web server that is running Microsoft FrontPage 2002 Server Extensions or Microsoft Share-Point.

    See your network administrator or the Microsoft SharePoint documentation for instructions to access a Web server.

3   In the **File name** box, type a name, and then click **Save**.

    Word saves the document to a Web server.

4   On the **Insert** menu, click **Web Component**.

    The **Insert Web Component Wizard** appears.

5   In the **Component type** list, click **Link Bars**.

6   In the **Choose a bar type** list, click a link bar type, and then click **Next** to display the next page.

**7** In the **Choose a bar style** list, click a bar style.

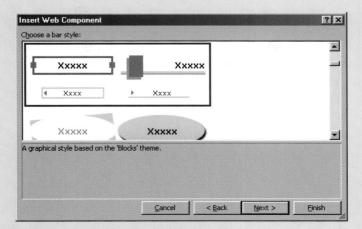

**8** Click **Next** to display the next page.

**9** In the **Choose an orientation** list, click an orientation (the location of the link bar on the Web page), and then click **Finish**.

The **Link Bar Properties** dialog box appears.

**10** In the **Choose existing** list, click **Create New**, type a name for your link bar in the **Name** box, and then click **OK** to create a new link bar or click the name of a link bar to reuse an existing link bar.

**11** Click **Add link**.

**12** Select the link that you want, and then type the text for the link in the **Text to display** box.

**13** Click **OK**, and then click **Add link** to add any more links that you want.

**14** Click **Move up** or **Move down** to change the order of your links.

**15** Click **OK** to add the link bar to your document.

# Modifying a Web Document

W2002e-6-4

Once you create and save a Word document as a Web document, you can open it in Word and change it, just as you would change a normal Word document. You can also use Word to open Web pages created in other programs that save Web pages with an .htm or .html file extension. Changes can be as simple as changing text and alignment or as complicated as moving and inserting graphics. When you finish changing the document, you can save the document as a Web page or a Word document.

The Garden Company needs to fill out a form on a Web page to request a permit for an outdoor sale.

ModWebDoc

In this exercise, you open a Web document, add some text, remove some highlighting, and then save it.

**1** On the Standard toolbar, click the **Open** button.

Open

The **Open** dialog box appears.

**2** Navigate to the **SBS** folder on your hard disk, double-click the **Word** folder, double-click the **WorkingWeb** folder, and then double-click the **ModWebDoc** file.

The ModWebDoc Web document opens.

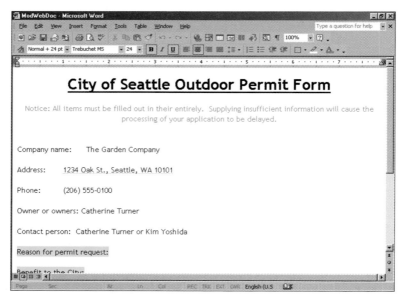

**3** Click to the right of the first line of yellow-highlighted text, press [Space], and then type **Semi-Annual Sale for The Garden Company**.

Highlight

**4** Select the text *Reason for permit request:* and then on the Formatting toolbar, click the **Highlight** button to remove the highlighting.

**5** Click to the right of the remaining line of yellow highlighted text (scroll down, ifnecessary),press ⌞Space⌟ andthentype We'llhaveeventsotherthanthesale. It will be a relaxing outing for neighborhood residents.

**6** Select the text *Benefit to the City:* and then on the Formatting toolbar, click the **Highlight** button to remove the highlighting.

**7** On the Standard toolbar, click the **Save** button to save the Web document.

Close Window

**8** Click the **Close Window** button in the document window.

The ModWebDoc document closes.

# Attaching a Digital Signature

W2002e-6-8

For any Web document that you create, you might want to consider adding a digital signature, which is an secure electronic stamp of authentication on a document. When you apply your digital signature to a document, you verify the contents of the file and confirm that the file has not changed since you attached the signature. If someone else then modifies the file, the digital signature is removed. It's a good idea to apply a digital signature to important documents that you plan to send over the Internet; the digital signature lets the recipient know that no one tampered with it.

Digital signature
new for
**Office**XP

When you add a digital signature, you sign either a file or a macro project. When you work with a regular Word document, you sign a file. When you work with a Web document, you sign a macro project. To sign a file, you click **Options** on the **Tools** menu, click the **Security** tab in the **Options** dialog box, click **Digital Signatures**, click **Add**, click a certificate, and then click **OK** twice. To sign a macro project, you open the Visual Basic Editor using the **Macro** submenu on the **Tools** menu.

The Visual Basic Editor lets you view and edit Microsoft Visual Basic for Applications (VBA) code. VBA is a macro-language version of Microsoft Visual Basic that is used to program many applications for Microsoft Windows 95 and later, and it is included with several Microsoft applications. The Visual Basic Editor window shows the programming needed to create a Web document. If you were a developer, you would need to know the parts more closely. However, to apply a digital signature, you need only to confirm that you see the name of your file in the Project pane of the window.

The Garden Company needs to complete a Web form requesting a permit for an outdoor sale. Because this is an important document that cannot be altered, the owner will apply a digital signature to it before she submits it over the Web.

AddSignature
WebSignature

In this exercise, you assign a digital signature to a Web document.

**Important**

Before you can start this exercise, you must install and run the Selfcert.exe file. This file enables you to create a digital signature that you will apply to your Web document in this exercise. The file is not installed during the normal Office installation. To install the file after you have already installed Office, insert the Office CD into your CD-ROM drive, run the Setup program, click the **Add or Remove Features** option, if necessary, click **Next**, click the plus sign (+) next to Office Shared Features to expand that option, click the **Digital Signatures for VBA Projects** down arrow, and then click **Update**. To run the Selfcert.exe file, start Windows Explorer using the **Start** button on the taskbar, and then locate and double-click the **Selfcert.exe** file. The program is typically located in the Programs Files\Microsoft Office\Office folder. In the **Create Digital Certification** dialog box, type your name as instructed, and then click **OK**.

Open

**1** On the Standard toolbar, click the **Open** button.

The **Open** dialog box appears.

**2** Navigate to the **SBS** folder on your hard disk, double-click the **Word** folder, double-click the **WorkingWeb** folder, and then double-click the **WebSignature** file.

The WebSignature Web document opens.

**3** On the **Tools** menu, point to **Macro**, and then click **Visual Basic Editor**.

The Visual Basic Editor window opens.

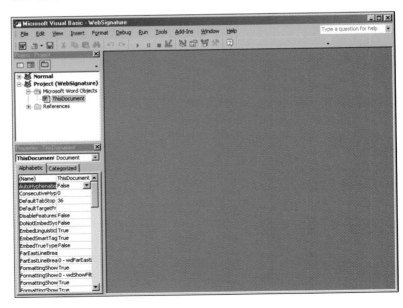

**4** In the Project window, under **Project (WebSignature)**, click **ThisDocument**, if necessary, to select the current document in Word.

Close

**5** If a window is open in the right pane of the Visual Basic Editor window, click its **Close** button to close it.

**6** On the **Tools** menu in the Visual Basic Editor window, click **Digital Signature**.

The **Digital Signature** dialog box appears, indicating that no certificate is assigned to the document.

**7** Click **Choose**, select a certificate in the list, and then click **View Certificate**.

The **Certificate** dialog box appears.

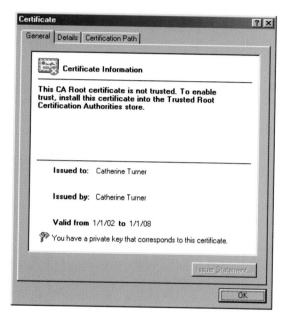

**8** Click **OK** to close the **Certificate** dialog box, and then click **OK** to close the **Select Certificate** dialog box.

The document now contains a secure and authentic digital signature.

**9** Click **OK** to close the **Digital Signature** dialog box.

**10** Click the **Close** button in the Visual Basic Editor window.

The document appears in Word.

**11** On the Standard toolbar, click the **Save** button to save the document.

Close Window

**12** Click the **Close Window** button in the document window.

The WebSignature Web document closes.

**13** On the Standard toolbar, click the **Open** button.

The **Open** dialog box appears.

**14** Navigate to the **SBS** folder on your hard disk, double-click the **Word** folder, double-click the **WorkingWeb** folder, and then double-click the **AddSignature** file.

The AddSignature document opens.

**15** On the **Tools** menu, click **Options**, and then click the **Security** tab.

The **Options** dialog box appears, showing the **Security** tab.

**16** Click **Digital Signatures**.

The **Digital Signature** dialog box appears.

**17** Click **Add**.

The **Select Certificate** dialog box appears.

**18** Select a certificate in the list, and then click **OK** to close the **Select Certificate** dialog box.

The **Digital Signature** dialog box appears with a digital signature.

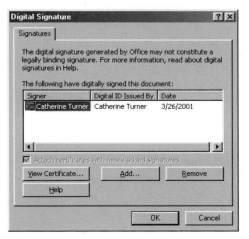

**19** Click **OK** to close the **Digital Signature** dialog box, and then click **OK** to close the **Options** dialog box.

The document appears in Word and the text *(Signed)* appears in the title bar.

**20** On the Standard toolbar, click the **Save** button to save the document.

Close Window

**21** Click the **Close Window** button in the document window.

The AddSignature document closes.

## Chapter Wrap-Up

To finish the chapter:

Close

● On the **File** menu, click **Exit**, or click the **Close** button in the Word window.

Word closes.

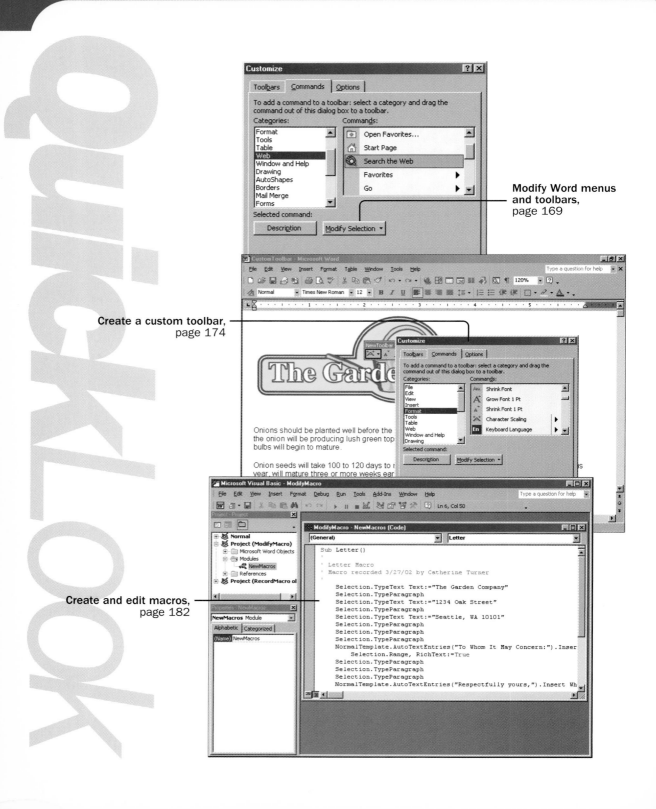

QuickLook

**Modify Word menus and toolbars,** page 169

**Create a custom toolbar,** page 174

**Create and edit macros,** page 182

# Chapter 10
# Customizing Word for the Way You Work

After completing this chapter, you will be able to:

✔ **Customize menus.**

✔ **Customize toolbars.**

✔ **Automate tasks using macros.**

✔ **Customize macro tasks.**

As you work with Microsoft Word, you'll develop your own preferences and styles for working in documents. To match the way that you like to work, you can customize Word by adjusting the way your screen looks, changing what you see on menus and toolbars, and using macros to automate repetitive tasks.

This chapter explains how to customize Word. Specifically, you will modify the existing Word toolbars and menus to show the buttons and commands that you access most frequently, and you'll create custom toolbars and menus showing only those commands that you select. Additionally, you will move toolbars to different locations on the screen. Finally, you will create, run, edit, and delete macros.

 This chapter uses the practice files CustomMenu, CustomToolbar, RecordMacro, and ModifyMacro that you installed from this book's CD-ROM. For details about installing the practice files, see "Using the Book's CD-ROM" at the beginning of this book.

## Customizing Menus

W2002e-5-2

The first time that you start Word, the menus list only the most basic commands. For example, the **File** menu lists the **New**, **Edit**, **Save**, **Save As**, and **Print** commands, but not the **Send To** and **Properties** commands. To see the full menu, click the double arrow at the bottom of the menu, or wait a few seconds until Word expands the menu for you. As you work, the menus adjust so that only the commands that you use most often appear on the short menus; that is, Word **personalizes** your menus. You can always see the complete list of commands by waiting or clicking the double arrow at the bottom of the menu.

In addition to personalizing menus to show the commands that you use most often, Word also lets you customize the menu contents with the **Customize** dialog box. If the standard Word menus do not contain the commands that you want, you can change them. For example, you can remove infrequently used commands to free space on your menus, add other commands that you access more often, and create new menus for specialized tasks.

After you add commands to a menu or add a new menu to the menu bar, you can remove the commands or menus if you like. You might want to create a menu for a particular project and then delete it when you are finished.

Custom Menu

In this exercise, you add and delete menu commands, create a custom menu, delete it, and then restore Word to its original menu settings.

**1** Start Word, if necessary.

Open

**2** On the Standard toolbar, click the **Open** button.

The **Open** dialog box appears.

**3** Navigate to the **SBS** folder on your hard disk, double-click the **Word** folder, double-click the **Customizing** folder, and then double-click **CustomToolbar**.

The CustomToolbar document opens.

**4** On the **Tools** menu, click **Customize** to open the **Customize** dialog box, and then click the **Options** tab, if necessary.

## Tip

To show only long menus, not personalized menus, on the **Tools** menu, click **Customize**, click the **Options** tab, select the **Always show full menus** check box, and then close the **Customize** dialog box.

## Tip

You can customize the way menus appear in Word by adding a menu animation, such as a slide or unfold effect. You can animate the display of menus in Word by clicking the **Menu animations** down arrow in the **Options** tab of the **Customize** dialog box and then clicking an animation.

**5** Click **Reset my usage data**, and then click **Yes** to reset Word menus and toolbars to their default settings.

**6** Click the **Commands** tab, and then click **Drawing** in the **Categories** list.

The Drawing commands appear in the **Commands** list.

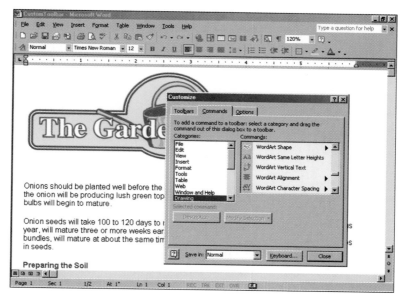

Move command pointer

**7** Scroll down in the **Commands** list, click **WordArt Shape**, and then drag it to the **Format** menu without releasing the mouse button.

As you drag the command to the menu, the pointer changes to the move command pointer and an insertion bar appears.

Insertion bar

I

**8** When the **Format** menu opens, drag to position the insertion bar after the **Object** command at the end of the menu, and then release the mouse button to lock this position.

**9** Click the **Format** menu again to close it.

**10** In the **Customize** dialog box, click **Close**.

The menu command is now placed and available for all currently open documents and those that you create in the future.

## Tip

Some menu commands include icons that match icons on a corresponding toolbar button. To pick a new icon for any menu command, open the **Customize** dialog box, click the **Commands** tab, click the appropriate category, click the command, click the **Modify Selection** down arrow, click **Change Button Image**, and then click an image.

**11** Right-click the menu bar or any toolbar to display a submenu with a list of available toolbars.

**12** On the **Tools** menu, click **Customize** to open the **Customize** dialog box.

**13** Click the **Commands** tab, scroll down to the end of the **Categories** list, and then click **New Menu**.

The **New Menu** appears in the **Commands** list.

**14** Drag **New Menu** from the **Commands** list to the right end of the **Word** menu bar next to the **Help** menu.

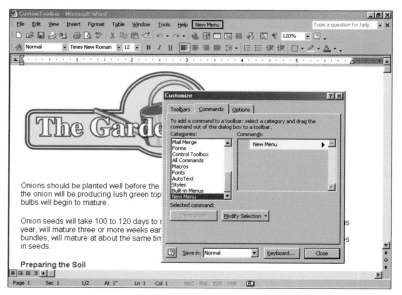

**15** On the menu bar, right-click **New Menu**.

**16** In the **Name** box on the shortcut menu, select the text *New Menu*, and then type **CustomMenu**.

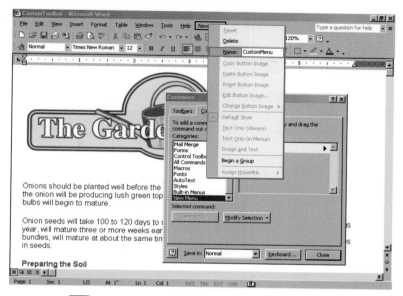

**17** Press the Enter key to change the menu name to *CustomMenu* and close the menu.

**18** On the menu bar, click **CustomMenu.**

A blank menu appears under the **CustomMenu** menu.

**19** In the **Categories** list of the **Customize** dialog box, scroll up, and then click **Format**.

The Format commands appear in the **Commands** list.

**20** In the **Commands** list, scroll down, and then drag **Double Underline** onto the empty **CustomMenu** menu.

The **Double Underline** command appears on the **CustomMenu** menu.

**21** In the **Commands** list, drag **Word Underline** onto the **CustomMenu** menu, and then position it below the **Double Underline** command by using the horizontal black insertion bar.

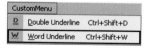

**22** Click **Close** to close the **Customize** dialog box.

**23** In the document window, select the text heading *Preparing the Soil*, and then on the **CustomMenu** menu, click **Double Underline**.

**24** Right-click any toolbar, and then click **Customize** to open the **Customize** dialog box.

**25** Right-click the **CustomMenu** menu, and then click **Delete** to delete the **CustomMenu** menu.

### Important

You cannot delete the standard Word menus—**File**, **Edit**, **View**, **Insert**, **Format**, **Tools**, **Table**, **Window**, and **Help**—only the custom menus that you create.

**26** Click the **Format** menu to open it.

**27** Drag the **Word Art Shape** command to a blank area in the open document.

The **Word Art Shape** command is removed from the **Format** menu.

**28** Click the **Format** menu again to close it.

**29** Click **Close** to close the **Customize** dialog box.

### Tip

You can also move or remove a menu without using the **Customize** dialog box by holding down the Alt key while you drag the menu to a new location or into an open document window to remove it.

**30** On the Standard toolbar, click the **Save** button to save the document.

Close Window

**31** Click the **Close Window** button in the document window.

The CustomMenu document closes.

## Customizing Toolbars

W2002e-5-2

There are two types of toolbars in Word: docked and floating. A **docked toolbar** is attached to the top, bottom, left, or right edge of the Word window. When you first start Word, the Standard and Formatting toolbars are docked to the top of the window. A **floating toolbar** is not attached to an edge of the Word window. The Picture toolbar is a floating toolbar by default.

Toolbar Options

You can click any edge of the toolbar and drag to resize it. The buttons within the toolbar shift accordingly. Although you cannot resize docked toolbars, you can move them on the edge of the Word window where they are attached. Point to the vertical move handle at the left end of the toolbar until the four-headed move pointer appears, and then drag to reposition the toolbar. As with personalized menus, Word also modifies the toolbars as you work, showing only the buttons that you use most often. To see all buttons on a toolbar, click the **Toolbar Options** button with double arrows at the right end of a toolbar. You also can hide or change the order of visible buttons by dragging them to different positions within the toolbar.

You can add buttons to a toolbar using the **Toolbar Options** button. This button appears at the end of a docked toolbar or in the top-right corner of a floating toolbar. You click the arrow to display a list of buttons that are not visible on the toolbar. The **Toolbar Options** menu also includes the **Add or Remove Buttons** command. In the button list, those buttons that now appear on any toolbar are checked.

You also can use an option on the **Toolbar Options** menu to display toolbars on separate rows. This is useful when you want to access any button quickly. When you first install Word, it shows the Standard and Formatting toolbars on one row. To separate them, on the Standard or Formatting toolbar, click the **Toolbar Options** button and then click **Show Buttons on Two Rows**.

Alternately, you can use the **Customize** command to add or remove buttons on any toolbar. Right-click any toolbar, click **Customize**, click the **Commands** tab, click a category, and then click the button that you want to use. Drag the button to a toolbar, use the insertion bar to place it, and then release the mouse button. To remove a button, open the **Customize** dialog box, drag the button from a toolbar to a blank area of the window, and then release the mouse button.

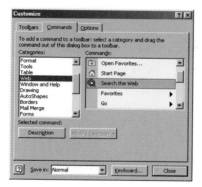

You can create a custom toolbar to house your most frequently used commands or to combine buttons from several toolbars onto a single custom toolbar and close the unused portions of the other toolbars to free up space in the Word window. By using custom toolbars, you can avoid jumping between multiple menus or toolbars to complete your work.

The owner of The Garden Company wants to customize her Word window. She'll experiment by customizing toolbars and then restoring them to their default settings. After she's comfortable customizing toolbars, she will create a custom toolbar so that she can use it to format a document for The Garden Company. When she's completed the document, she'll delete the custom toolbar.

CustomToolbar

In this exercise, you hide and show a toolbar, change the display of the Standard toolbar from one row to two, remove a number of buttons from the Standard toolbar and add some others, and then restore the Standard toolbar to its default settings. You also create a custom toolbar, use the toolbar to format a document, and then delete the custom toolbar.

Open

**1** On the Standard toolbar, click the **Open** button.

The **Open** dialog box appears.

**2** Navigate to the **SBS** folder on your hard disk, double-click the **Word** folder, double-click the **Customizing** folder, and then double-click **CustomToolbar**.

The CustomToolbar document opens.

**3** On the **View** menu, point to **Toolbars**, and then click **Drawing**.

The Drawing toolbar appears at the bottom of the screen.

**4** Right-click any toolbar, and then click **Drawing** to close the Drawing toolbar.

**5** Point to the left edge of the Standard toolbar. (The Standard toolbar is the one below the menu bar. It contains the **Open** and **Save** buttons, among others.)

Four-headed arrow pointer

The four-headed arrow pointer appears.

**6** Drag the Standard toolbar into a blank area of the document, and then release the mouse.

The Standard toolbar appears as a floating toolbar.

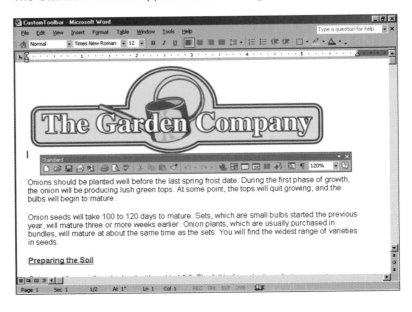

**7** Point to the title bar of the **Standard** toolbar, drag it to the right edge of the Word window until it is docked as a vertical toolbar, and then drag it to the left of the Formatting toolbar below the menu bar until it is docked as a toolbar on the same row as the Formatting toolbar.

**8** Point to the left edge of the **Formatting** toolbar, and then drag the toolbar to the left, as shown in the following illustration.

Toolbar Options

**9** On the right edge of the Standard toolbar, click the **Toolbar Options** button.

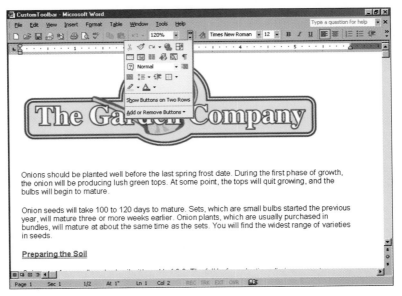

**10** Click **Show Buttons on Two Rows**.

The Standard and Formatting toolbars appear on two rows.

**11** On the Standard toolbar, click the **Toolbar Options** button.

**12** Point to **Add or Remove Buttons**, and then point to **Standard** to see all the possible buttons that you can assign to the Standard toolbar.

**13** Clear the **Format Painter**, **Drawing**, and **Document Map** check boxes, scroll down the list, if necessary, select the **Print** and **Envelopes and Labels** check boxes, and then click in the open document window to save your changes.

The Standard toolbar is updated to reflect your changes.

**14** On the Standard toolbar, click the **Toolbar Options** arrow, point to **Add or Remove Buttons**, point to **Standard**, scroll down the list, if necessary, and then click **Reset Toolbar**.

The Standard toolbar is restored to its default settings.

**15** Right-click any toolbar, and then click **Customize** to open the **Customize** dialog box.

**16** Click the **Toolbars** tab, and then click **New** to open the **New Toolbar** dialog box.

**17** In the **Toolbar name** box, type NewToolbar.

**18** Click the **Make toolbar available to** down arrow, click **CustomToolbar** to make the new toolbar available only to this document, and then click **OK**.

An empty floating toolbar appears next to the **Customize** dialog box with the name *NewToolbar*. Only part of the *NewToolbar* title may be showing.

**19** In the **Customize** dialog box, click the **Commands** tab.

The **Categories** and **Commands** lists appear in the dialog box.

**20** In the **Categories** list, click **Format**, scroll down the **Commands** list, and then drag the **Grow Font** button to the blank NewToolbar toolbar.

The **Grow Font** button appears on the NewToolbar toolbar.

**21** Drag the **Shrink Font, Grow Font 1 Pt**, **Shrink Font 1 Pt**, and **Character Scaling** buttons from the **Commands** list to the NewToolbar toolbar. (Scroll within the **Commands** list as necessary to select all the buttons.)

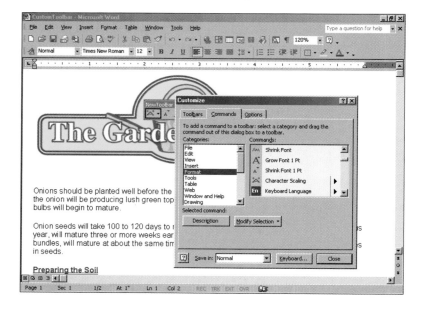

**22** Click **Close** to close the **Customize** dialog box.

## Tip

If the **Customize** dialog box is not open, you can still remove buttons from the toolbar or alter the sequence of buttons on a toolbar by holding down ⁅Alt⁆ and then dragging a button.

Grow Font 1 Pt

**23** In the document window, select the text heading *Preparing the Soil*, and then click the **Grow Font 1 Pt** button on the NewToolbar toolbar twice.

The text increases in size by two points.

**24** Right-click the menu bar to open the list of toolbars, and then click **NewToolbar** to hide the toolbar.

## Tip

To delete a custom toolbar, on the **Tools** menu, click **Customize**, and then click the **Toolbars** tab. In the **Toolbars** box, click the name of the custom toolbar that you want to delete, and then click **Delete**. You can delete only custom toolbars, not built-in toolbars.

**25** Right-click any toolbar, and then click **Customize** to open the **Customize** dialog box, and then click the **Toolbars** tab.

**26** In the **Toolbars** list, scroll down, click the **NewToolbar**, click **Delete**, click **OK** to confirm the deletion, and then click **Close** to close the **Customize** dialog box.

The NewToolbar toolbar is deleted.

**27** On the Standard toolbar, click the **Save** button to save the document.

Close Window

**28** Click the **Close Window** button in the document window.

The CustomToolbar document closes.

# Automating Tasks Using Macros

W2002e-5-1

Instead of performing a long set of Word commands to perform a task, you can create a macro to automate and simplify the process, which will reduce the number of steps involved in a task and save you time. A **macro** is a recorded series of Word commands (keystrokes and instructions) that are treated as a single command. You can use macros to automate many tasks in Word, such as creating form letters, inserting AutoText, formatting text, creating tables, and turning command options on and off. For example, suppose your company uses a special format and design for any tables that you insert in your documents. Instead of inserting a table, adding shading and borders, applying different fonts to column and row headings, and then adjusting the line spacing, you could create a macro to perform all these steps, which would save you time and reduce the number of steps involved in the task.

To record a macro, on the **Tools** menu, point to **Macro**, and then click **Record New Macro**. In the **Record Macro** dialog box, type a macro name, click **Toolbars** or **Keyboard** to assign a quick way to access the macro, specify a location to store the macro, click **OK**, perform a series of commands in Word, and then click the **Stop Recording** button. While you record a macro, you use the mouse to select menu commands, click toolbar buttons, and scroll through the document window, and you use the keyboard instead of the mouse to select text or move the insertion point.

Macros are not separate files, and they work only in conjunction with the document or template for which they were created. Only the template or document that is currently active will be modified by any macros that you create. When you create a new document, Word uses the Normal template by default. Because you will use the Normal template most frequently, record your macros so that the Normal.dot template file is updated accordingly. When you store macros in the Normal template, the macros are always available when you use the template.

Before you run a macro, position the insertion point where you want the result of the macro to be displayed. For example, if you are creating a macro to insert a table, click where you want the table to appear. To run a macro from the list of macros, on the **Tools** menu, point to **Macro** and then click **Macros**. In the **Macros** dialog box, click the appropriate macro in the **Macro name** box and then click **Run** (or double-click the macro name). You can also assign a macro to one of your active toolbars or to a shortcut key so that the macro is readily available and easily executed.

The owner of The Garden Company wants to create a macro that automatically inputs the normal elements of a business correspondence so that all she needs to do is focus on the bodies of the letters themselves. She will create a macro that inputs the company address, salutation, closing, and her name and title information.

RecordMacro

In this exercise, you create a macro that automatically formats the basic elements of a letter.

Open

**1**  On the Standard toolbar, click the **Open** button.

The **Open** dialog box appears.

**2**  Navigate to the **SBS** folder on your hard disk, double-click the **Word** folder, double-click the **Customizing** folder, and then double-click **RecordMacro**.

The RecordMacro document opens.

**3**  Press Ctrl+End to move the insertion point to the blank line below the logo for The Garden Company.

**4** On the **Tools** menu, point to **Macro**, and then click **Record New Macro** to open the **Record Macro** dialog box.

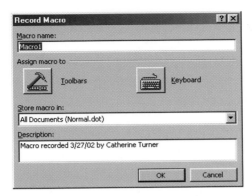

**5** In the **Macro name** box, type Letter.

**6** Click the **Store macro in** down arrow, and then click **RecordMacro (document)**.

**7** Click the **Keyboard** button to open the **Customize Keyboard** dialog box, press Alt+L to place the key combination in the **Press new shortcut key** box, click **Assign**, and then click **Close**.

The **Customize Keyboard** dialog box closes, and the **Stop Recording** toolbar appears with buttons to stop and pause the recording.

**8** In the document, type The Garden Company, and then press Enter.

# Tip

You can assign a macro to a toolbar or menu before or after you record the macro. If you aren't sure that you want to assign your macro, you can create it first and assign it to a toolbar or menu later.

**9** Type 1234 Oak Street, and then press Enter.

**10** Type Seattle, WA 10101, and then press Enter three times.

**11** On the **Insert** menu, point to **Autotext**, point to **Salutation**, and then click **To Whom it May Concern**.

The text *To Whom it May Concern* is inserted into the document.

**12** Press Enter three times.

**13** On the **Insert** menu, point to **Autotext,** point to **Closing,** and then click **Respectfully yours,**.

The text *Respectfully yours,* is inserted into the document.

**14** Press Enter three times.

**15** Type **Catherine Turner**, and then press [Enter].

**16** Type **Owner**, and then press [Enter].

**17** Type **The Garden Company**.

Stop Recording

**18** On the Macro toolbar, click the **Stop Recording** button.

The macro stops recording, and the **Stop Recording** toolbar closes.

**19** On the **Tools** menu, point to **Macro**, and then click **Macros**.

The **Macros** dialog box appears.

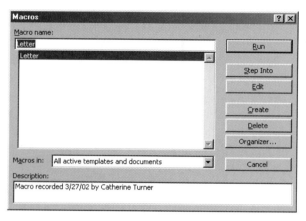

**20** In the list of macros, click **Letter**, and then click **Run**.

A second letter template is inserted in the document.

**21** On the Standard toolbar, click the **Save** button to save the document.

Close Window

**22** Click the **Close Window** button in the document window.

The RecordMacro document closes.

## Customizing Macro Tasks

W2002e-5-1

Sometimes a macro does not work as you expect, so you need to modify it. You can rerecord the macro to correct the problem or you can directly edit and change the macro in the Visual Basic Editor program using Microsoft Visual Basic, a programming language contained in Word in an abbreviated form. Macros are stored as a **module** within a Visual Basic project. **Projects** are executable programs that can be stored in a Word document or template. To edit the macro, on the **Tools** menu, point to **Macro**, and then click **Macros**. A list of all existing macros will appear in the **Macros** dialog box. Click the macro you want to edit, and then click **Edit**. The Visual Basic Editor program appears, where you can select a module within a project and make changes.

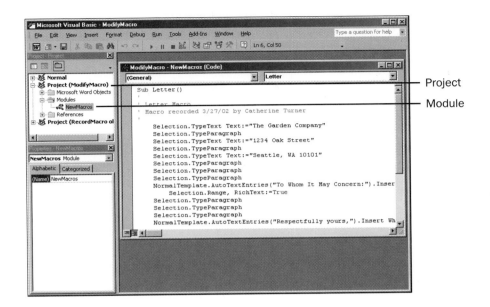

Project

Module

**Important**

A macro virus is a type of computer virus that is stored in a macro within a file, template, or add-in. For the best protection against macro viruses, you should purchase and install specialized antivirus software. To further reduce the risk of macro infection in Word files, set the macro security level to **High** or **Medium**, and use digital signatures. To set the macro security level, on the **Tools** menu, click **Options**, click the **Security** tab, click **Macro Security**, click the **Security Level** tab, and then select the security level that you want to use.

When you no longer need a macro, or if you want to remove a poorly functioning macro to rerecord it with the same name, you can delete it. Deleting a macro from a template or document is straightforward. After you delete a macro from the list of available macros in a document or template, you also need to delete its associated toolbar button or menu command (if you created one). Delete a macro button from a toolbar or menu by holding down [Alt] and dragging the macro button into any blank space in the document.

After creating and running a macro to format a letter, the owner of The Garden Company wants to fine-tune the macro so that it reformats some of the text to bold. Then she will use the edited macro to create a new letter.

ModifyMacro

In this exercise, you edit an existing macro to add character formatting, and then you delete a macro.

Open

**1** On the Standard toolbar, click the **Open** button.

The **Open** dialog box appears.

**2** Navigate to the **SBS** folder on your hard disk, double-click the **Word** folder, double-click the **Customizing** folder, and then double-click the **ModifyMacro** file.

The ModifyMacro document opens.

**3** On the **Tools** menu, point to **Macro**, and then click **Macros** to open the **Macros** dialog box.

**4** In the list of macros, click **Letter**, and then click **Edit**.

The macro instructions are displayed in the Visual Basic Editor code window.

**5** Click the ModifyMacro - NewMacros (Code) window, if necessary, and then scroll to the bottom of the window.

**6** Click to the left of the text *Selection.TypeText Text:="Catherine Turner"*, and then click [Enter] to insert a blank line before the instruction.

**7** Press the [↑] key, and then type **Selection.Font.Bold = wdToggle**.

As you type, the Visual Basic Editor opens a menu of possible commands. You can select a command from the menu instead of typing the entire command.

The new instruction appears in the code. The new instruction tells the program to display in bold all of the text that follows.

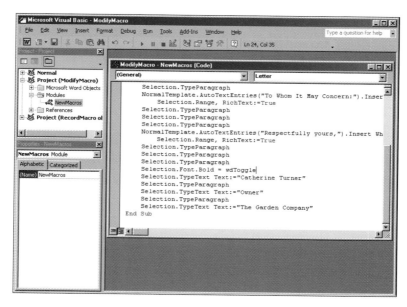

## Important

For additional information on inserting and editing macro commands in the Visual Basic Editor, or even creating macros that perform complicated tasks that cannot be recorded, use the **Help** menu in the Visual Basic Editor window.

**8** On the **File** menu, click **Close and Return to Microsoft Word**.

The Visual Basic Editor closes, and the macro is saved with the change.

**9** Press Ctrl+End to place the insertion point at the end of the document.

**10** On the **Tools** menu, point to **Macro**, and then click **Macros** to open the **Macros** dialog box.

## Tip

You can also press Alt+L, a keyboard shortcut already set to run the Letter macro.

**11** In the **Macros** dialog box, click the **Macros in** down arrow, and then click **ModifyMacro (document)**, if necessary.

**12** In the list of macros, click **Letter**, and then click **Run**.

The letter text at the end of the document appears in bold.

**13** On the **Tools** menu, point to **Macro**, and then click **Macros** to open the **Macros** dialog box.

**14** In the **Macros** dialog box, click the **Macros in** down arrow, click **Modify-Macro (document)**, if necessary, click **Letter**, and then click **Delete**.

An alert box appears, asking if you want to delete the macro Letter.

**15** Click **Yes**.

The alert box closes, and Word deletes the Letter macro.

**16** In the **Macros** dialog box, click the **Close** button.

The **Macros** dialog box closes.

**17** On the Standard toolbar, click the **Save** button to save the document.

Close Window

**18** Click the **Close Window** button in the document window.

The ModifyMacro document closes.

## Chapter Wrap-Up

To finish this chapter:

Close

● On the **File** menu, click **Exit**, or click the **Close** button in the Word window.

Word closes.

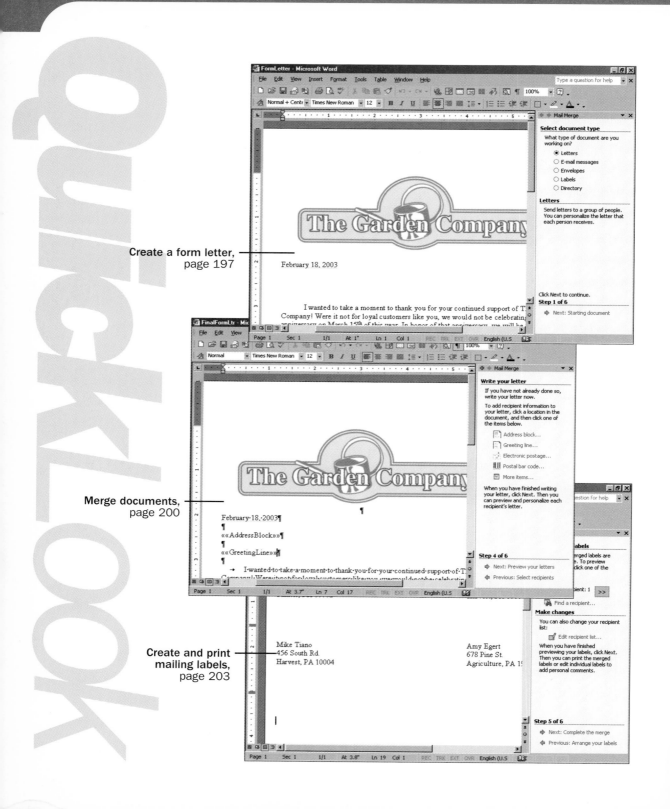

**Create a form letter,**
page 197

**Merge documents,**
page 200

**Create and print**
**mailing labels,**
page 203

# Chapter 11
# Creating Form Letters and Labels

**After completing this chapter, you will be able to:**

✔ Understand mail merge.
✔ Prepare data for a form letter.
✔ Select data for a form letter.
✔ Create a form letter.
✔ Merge data with a form letter.
✔ Create and print labels.

One of the frequent tasks of running a business is to create direct mail pieces and send them to customers. Most people don't have time to create a personalized letter for each recipient, but they don't want to send a generic "Dear Customer" letter either. The solution is to use Microsoft Word's Mail Merge Wizard to set up and create form letters and matching labels.

In this chapter, you produce a personalized mass mailing for The Garden Company. The marketing manager has already created the body of the form letter in one document and a mailing list in another Word document. You use the Mail Merge Wizard to add a name and address to the mailing list in the data document. Then you sort the list by zip code and filter it to select only certain customers. After preparing the data document, you prepare the form letter by inserting merge codes for the inside address and greeting line. Then you complete the mail merge by previewing the letters and saving the personalized copies in a new document. Finally, you create and print mailing labels for each customer.

This chapter uses the practice files FormLetter, NewFormLtr, FinalFormLtr, MergeLtr, Data, Data2, and Data3 that you installed from this book's CD-ROM. For details about installing the practice files, see "Using the Book's CD-ROM" at the beginning of this book.

## Understanding Mail Merge

The mail merge process involves taking information from one document, known as the **data source**, and combining it with another document, known as the **main document**. The data source is a document, spreadsheet, database, or file that contains the personalized information (such as names, addresses, and phone numbers) that ends up in the main document. The main document contains text that does not change as well as **merge fields**, which are placeholders that indicate where Word inserts the personalized information from the data source. When you insert a merge field into the main document, Word retrieves the information from the data source and merges it into the main document.

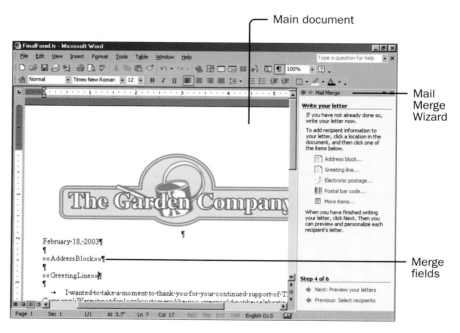

You can use the Mail Merge Wizard to merge a data source, such as a database or contacts list, and a main document, such as a form letter or labels, in six easy steps. To start the Mail Merge Wizard, you point to **Letters and Mailings** on the **Tools** menu, and then click **Mail Merge Wizard**. The **Mail Merge** task pane appears, showing the first step in the mail merge process. The first step is to select a document type, such as a letter, e-mail message, envelope, label, or directory list. The document type determines the steps the Mail Merge Wizard will take to complete the process. Each document type takes slightly different steps.

For the letter document type, the second step is to select a starting document. The third step is to select or create a data source. You can use existing data that you created in Word or in another program, such as Microsoft Outlook, or you can create the data as you work through the Mail Merge Wizard. After you select the data document and create the form letter with merge fields, you can **filter** the recipient list to send letters only to certain people. For example, if your mailing list includes customers from across the United States, you can select only those customers from Pennsylvania to target the mailing to that area. You can set up a simple **query**—or set selection criteria—to indicate how to filter the recipients. You can also sort the list, such as in alphabetical or zip code order, so that the letters can be organized for a bulk mailing.

The fourth step is to create a letter (the main document) and to insert merge fields. The fifth step is to preview the letter with the merged data. You can exclude data that you don't want to include in the mail merge at this step. The final step is to personalize and print the individual letters. To create the personalized letters, you **merge** them into a new document or to the printer. If you merge to a new document, Word inserts all the letters into a single document so that you can review them before printing or save a permanent copy. For example, if your main document is a one-page letter and your data source contains 15 names, the Mail Merge Wizard creates a new document with 15 pages that contain one-page letters with the merged information. If you merge to the printer, Word prints one personalized letter for each name and address retrieved from the mailing list. In addition to printing form letters, you can use the mail merge process to print mailing labels.

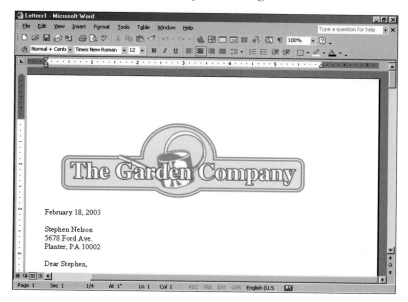

**Important**

Instead of using the Mail Merge Wizard in the **Mail Merge** task pane, you also can use the Mail Merge toolbar to create and merge documents such as personalized letters, labels, envelopes, and directories. To open the Merge toolbar, on the **View** menu, point to **Toolbars**, and then click **Mail Merge**.

# Preparing Data for a Form Letter

W2002e-7-1

Before you create a form letter, you need to either select or create a list of names and addresses. If your list is short and you don't plan to update it frequently, you can create a list in Word. You can enter the names and addresses in a table or in a list where each part of the address is separated by a comma or a tab, as in *Fine, Suzan, 4567 Main St., Buffalo, NY, 98052*. The information is organized into sets, or data records, for each entry in the data source. A single name and address is called a **record**.

If your mailing list is long and frequently updated, you can create or use a list from another program, such as Microsoft Access, Microsoft Excel, Microsoft Visual FoxPro, or the Contacts list in Microsoft Outlook or Microsoft Outlook Express. When you use information from another program, all the data in the source file is inserted into the mail merge, so you will probably need to exclude any unwanted information during the mail merge process.

**Important**

> If you are creating your own list in Word, make sure that the field names do not include spaces. For example, *ItemsPurchased* is an acceptable merge field name, but *Items Purchased* is not.

The owner of The Garden Company is preparing a mass mailing and wants to select a Word document as the mailing list for the form letter and then add a new recipient to the mailing list.

FormLetter
Data

In this exercise, you will start the Mail Merge Wizard, open a form letter (the main document), select a data document containing a mailing list, and then add a new name and address record to it.

**1**   Start Word, if necessary.

Open

**2**   On the Standard toolbar, click the **Open** button.

The **Open** dialog box appears.

**3**   Navigate to the **SBS** folder on your hard disk, double-click the **Word** folder, double-click the **MergingData** folder, and then double-click the **FormLetter** file.

The FormLetter document opens.

Mail Merge
task pane
new for
**Office**XP

**4**   On the **Tools** menu, point to **Letters and Mailings**, and then click **Mail Merge Wizard** to open the **Mail Merge** task pane showing Step 1 of 6 in the wizard.

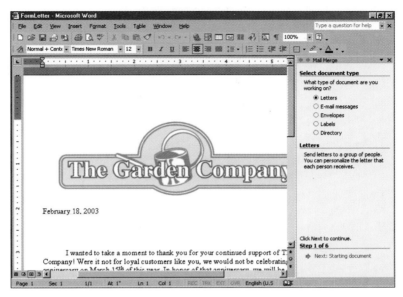

5   In the **Mail Merge** task pane, click the **Letters** option, if necessary, and then click **Next: Starting document** at the bottom of the pane.

Step 2 of 6 in the wizard appears in the **Mail Merge** task pane.

6   In the **Mail Merge** task pane, click the **Use the current document** option, if necessary, and then click **Next: Select recipients** at the bottom of the pane.

Step 3 of 6 in the wizard appears.

7   In the **Mail Merge** task pane, click the **Use an existing list** option, if necessary, and then click **Browse** in the **Use an existing list** section to open the **Select Data Source** dialog box.

**Important**

In the **Select Data Source** dialog box, you can select a Word document, Excel spreadsheet, or Access database as the data source in the mail merge.

8   Navigate to the **SBS** folder on your hard disk, double-click the **Word** folder, double-click the **MergingData** folder, and then double-click the **Data** file.

The **Mail Merge Recipients** dialog box appears, displaying the records contained in the Data file.

Customer name and address records from the data document

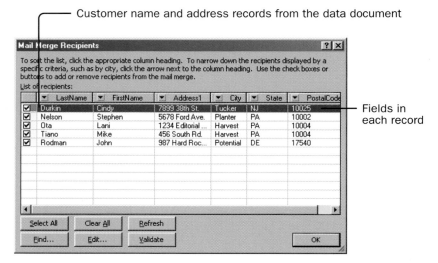

Fields in
each record

**9** In the **Mail Merge Recipients** dialog box, click any field, and then click **Edit** to open the **Data Form** dialog box.

**10** Click **Add New**, if necessary, to clear the data fields so that you can add a new record.

**11** In the **FirstName** box, type **Amy**, and then press the ⎯Tab⎯ key.

**12** In the **LastName** box, type **Egert**, and then press ⎯Tab⎯.

**13** In the **Address1** box, type **678 Pine St.**, and then press ⎯Tab⎯.

**14** In the **City** box, type **Agriculture**, and then press ⎯Tab⎯.

**15** In the **State** box, type **PA**, and then press ⎯Tab⎯.

**16** In the **PostalCode** box, type **19003**.

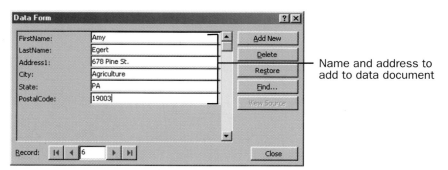

Name and address to
add to data document

**17**  Click **Close** to close the **Data Form** dialog box.

A new record appears at the end of the **Mail Merge Recipients** dialog box, indicating that you have added a name and address record to the data document.

### Important

To add a series of new records in the **Data Form** dialog box, leave the box open and click **Add New** after you enter each record.

**18**  Click **OK** to close the **Mail Merge Recipients** dialog box.

**19**  On the Standard toolbar, click the **Save** button to save the document.

### Important

If you need to exit the Mail Merge Wizard before you finish the process, you can save the main document. Word retains the data source and merge field information and keeps your place in the Mail Merge Wizard.

Close Window

❌

**20**  Click the **Close Window** button in the document window, and then click **Yes** to save the Data document, if necessary.

The FormLetter document closes.

## Using Outlook Data in a Form Letter

W2002e-7-3

When you use the Mail Merge Wizard, you can use information from your contacts list in Microsoft Outlook. Selecting Outlook contacts as the data source takes a few simple steps with the Mail Merge Wizard. When you use Outlook information as the data source in a mail merge, all the information in your contacts list is gathered into the mail merge, so you will probably need to exclude some contacts from the list that you don't want to be included in the mail merge.

*To complete the following procedure, you need Microsoft Outlook installed on your computer.*

To use Outlook data in a form letter.

**1**  On the **Tools** menu, point to **Letters and Mailings**, and then click **Mail Merge Wizard** to open the **Mail Merge** task pane showing Step 1 of 6 in the wizard.

**2**  In the **Mail Merge** task pane, click the **Letters** option, if necessary, and then click **Next: Starting document** at the bottom of the pane.

Step 2 of 6 in the wizard appears in the **Mail Merge** task pane.

3    In the **Mail Merge** task pane, click the **Use the current document** option, if necessary, and then click **Next: Select recipients** at the bottom of the pane.

Step 3 of 6 in the wizard appears.

4    In the **Mail Merge** task pane, click the **Select from Outlook contacts** option, and then click **Next: Write your letter** at the bottom of the pane.

5    Click **OK**, if necessary, to select your Outlook profile.

The **Select Contact List folder** dialog box appears.

6    Click a contact list, and then click **OK**.

The **Mail Merge Recipients** dialog box appears, displaying all the contacts from your Outlook Contacts folder.

7    Clear the check boxes in the left column to exclude contacts from the mail merge.

8    Click **OK** to close the **Mail Merge Recipients** dialog box.

9    In the **Mail Merge** task pane, click **Next: Write your letter** at the bottom of the pane.

Step 4 of 6 in the wizard appears. You continue to use the Mail Merge Wizard to write and preview a form letter and complete the mail merge.

# Selecting Data for a Form Letter

W2002e-7-1

After you set up a data document, you can sort the information that it contains. Sorted data is easier to organize and track. If you are sending a large mass mailing, for example, you might need to sort the mailing pieces by zip code to comply with U.S. Postal Service regulations for bulk mailings.

You can also filter, or exclude, the data in the data document to target the form letter recipients. For example, you can target only those customers who live in a particular state or work for a particular company. When you filter data, all the data remains in the data source; only the data you include appears in the mail merge list. A query is the process of setting criteria to extract specific data from a list or database.

The owner of The Garden Company wants to send the form letter only to customers in Pennsylvania and sort them by zip code for bulk mailing purposes.

NewFormLtr
Data2

In this exercise, you edit a recipient list to sort the name and address records by zip code. Then you create a simple query to filter the records and select only those for customers living in Pennsylvania.

Open

**1** On the Standard toolbar, click the **Open** button.

The **Open** dialog box appears.

**2** Navigate to the **SBS** folder on your hard disk, double-click the **Word** folder, double-click the **MergingData** folder, and then double-click the **NewFormLtr** file.

The NewFormLtr document opens.

**3** On the **Tools** menu, point to **Letters and Mailings**, and then click **Mail Merge Wizard**.

The **Mail Merge** task pane appears.

**4** In the **Mail Merge** task pane, click the **Next** link until Step 3 of 6 appears in the wizard, if necessary.

**5** Click **Select a different list** in the **Use an existing list** section to open the **Select Data Source** dialog box.

**6** Navigate to the **SBS** folder on your hard disk, double-click the **Word** folder, double-click the **MergingData** folder, and then double-click the **Data2** file.

The **Mail Merge Recipients** dialog box appears.

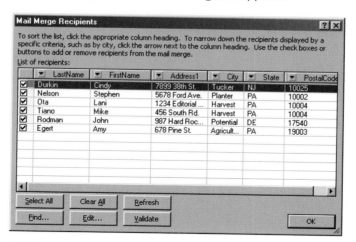

**7** Click the **PostalCode** down arrow, and then click **Advanced**.

The **Query Options** dialog box appears, showing the **Filter Records** tab.

**8** Click the **Sort Records** tab to display the sorting options.

**9** Click the **Sort by** down arrow, and then click **PostalCode**.

**10** Click **Ascending**, if necessary, and then click **OK** to close the **Query Options** dialog box.

The data is sorted in ascending zip code order.

**11** In the **Mail Merge Recipients** dialog box, click the **State** down arrow, and then click **Advanced**.

The **Query Options** dialog box appears, displaying the **Filter Records** tab.

**12** Click the **Field** down arrow, and then click **State**.

Several other query options become available.

**13** Click the **Comparison** down arrow, and then click **Equal to**, if necessary.

**14** In the **Compare to** box, type **PA**.

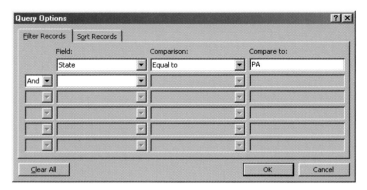

**15** Click **OK**.

The **Query Options** dialog box closes, and the **Mail Merge Recipients** dialog box is updated to reflect only Pennsylvania residents in ascending zip code order.

Addresses of customers in
Pennsylvania, sorted by zip code

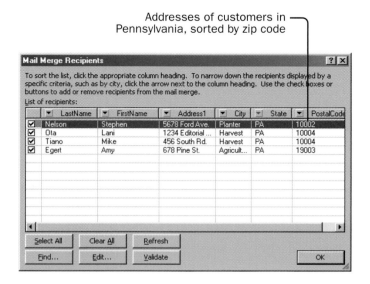

## Important

Only four records appear now because they are the only customers of The Garden Company that fit the specified sort criteria. The other records are still in the database; they have just been excluded from this mailing according to the filter settings.

**16** Click **OK** to close the **Mail Merge Recipients** dialog box.

**17** On the Standard toolbar, click the **Save** button to save the document.

Close Window

**18** Click the **Close Window** button in the document window.

The NewFormLtr document closes.

# Creating a Form Letter

W2002e-7-1

A form letter is the main document in the mail merge process. The form letter contains boilerplate text that is the same for each recipient. The form letter is merged with the contents of the data source to create an individualized letter for each recipient. You can create a form letter in two ways: by using an existing letter and inserting merge fields into it; or by creating a new main document as you work through the mail merge process, entering the boilerplate text of the letter, and then inserting the merge fields that you want to use. Each merge field corresponds to a piece of information in the data source and appears in the main document with the greater than and less than characters around it. For example the <<Address Block>> merge field corresponds to name and address information in the data source.

The owner of The Garden Company wants to finish a form letter by adding merge fields for the name, address, and greeting line to the main document.

FinalFormLtr
Data3

In this exercise, you modify a form letter by adding merge fields for a standard inside address and informal greeting line.

**1** On the Standard toolbar, click the **Open** button.

Open

The **Open** dialog box appears.

**2** Navigate to the **SBS** folder on your hard disk, double-click the **Word** folder, double-click the **MergingData** folder, and then double-click the **FinalFormLtr** file.

The FinalFormLtr document opens.

**3** On the **Tools** menu, point to **Letters and Mailings**, and then click **Mail Merge Wizard**.

The **Mail Merge** task pane appears.

**4** In the **Mail Merge** task pane, click the **Next** link until Step 3 of 6 appears in the wizard, if necessary.

**5** Click **Select a different list** in the **Use an existing list** section to open the **Select Data Source** dialog box.

**6** Navigate to the **SBS** folder on your hard disk, double-click the **Word** folder, double-click the **MergingData** folder, and then double-click the **Data3** file.

The **Mail Merge Recipients** dialog box appears.

**7** Click **OK** to close the **Mail Merge Recipients** dialog box.

**8** In the **Mail Merge** task pane, click **Next: Write your letter** at the bottom of the pane.

Step 4 of 6 in the wizard appears in the **Mail Merge** task pane.

Show/Hide ¶

**9** On the Standard toolbar, click the **Show/Hide ¶** button to show formatting marks, if necessary.

**10** In the document window, click the second blank line under the date, and then in the **Mail Merge** task pane, click **Address block**.

The **Insert Address Block** dialog box appears, showing the options that you have for setting address elements in the Address Block merge fields.

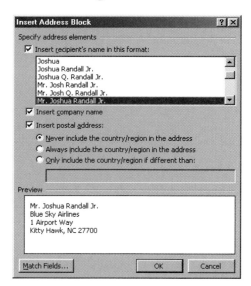

**11** Click **OK** to accept the default settings.

The Address Block merge field is inserted into the document. When you merge the document with data, a name and address will be inserted into the Address Block merge field.

**12** In the document window, click the second blank line after the Address Block merge field, and then in the **Mail Merge** task pane, click **Greeting line**.

The **Greeting Line** dialog box appears, showing options for setting up the greeting line.

13 Under **Greeting line format**, click the second down arrow, and then click **Joshua**.

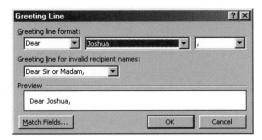

14 Click **OK** to close the **Greeting Line** dialog box.

The Greeting Line merge field appears in the document. When you merge the document with data, a name will get inserted in the Greeting Line merge field.

The letter is ready to merge with the data fields provided in the data document.

Greeting Line merge field

Address Block merge field

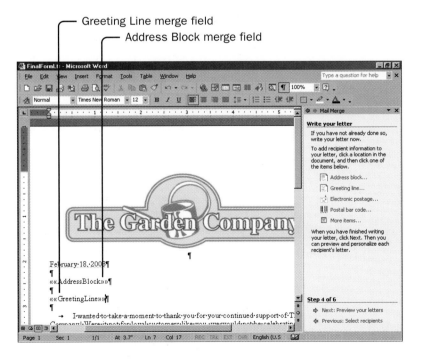

## Tip

Insert
Greeting Line

The **Insert Greeting Line** button on the Mail Merge toolbar is another way to customize your salutation if you are working on a form letter outside the Mail Merge Wizard. You can use the down arrows on the Mail Merge toolbar to select formal or informal styles of greetings and personal or businesslike forms of address.

**15** On the Standard toolbar, click the **Show/Hide ¶** button to hide formatting marks, if necessary.

**16** On the Standard toolbar, click the **Save** button to save the document.

Close Window

**17** Click the **Close Window** button in the document window.

The FinalFormLtr document closes.

# Merging Data with a Form Letter

W2002e-7-1

After you set up a data document and enter merge fields into a main document, you are ready to merge the documents to create personalized form letters. The process combines the main document with the data source and creates a new document with all the merged information. The new document contains individualized copies of the main document for each record in the data source. The length of the new document depends on the number of records in the data source and the length of the main document. If your main document is two pages long and your data source contains ten names, the new document will be 20 pages long. You can edit the new document to personalize individual copies of the main document.

Now that the owner of The Garden Company has added merge fields for the name, address, and greeting line to the form letter that she will send to customers in Pennsylvania, she is ready to merge the main document with the names and addresses to create personalized copies of the letter for each recipient.

MergeLtr
Data3

In this exercise, you review merged data, add a merge field to personalize a sentence in the body of a letter, and then merge letters into a new document containing one personalized copy of the letter for each recipient.

**1** On the Standard toolbar, click the **Open** button.

The **Open** dialog box appears.

Open

**2** Navigate to the **SBS** folder on your hard disk, double-click the **Word** folder, double-click the **MergingData** folder, and then double-click the **MergeLtr** file.

The MergeLtr document opens.

**3** On the **Tools** menu, point to **Letters and Mailings**, and then click **Mail Merge Wizard**.

The **Mail Merge** task pane appears.

**4** In the **Mail Merge** task pane, click the **Next** link until Step 3 of 6 appears in the wizard, if necessary.

**5** Click **Select a different list** in the **Use an existing list** section to open the **Select Data Source** dialog box.

**6** Navigate to the **SBS** folder on your hard disk, double-click the **Word** folder, double-click the **MergingData** folder, and then double-click the **Data3** file.

The **Mail Merge Recipients** dialog box appears.

**7** Click **OK** to close the **Mail Merge Recipients** dialog box.

**8** In the **Mail Merge** task pane, click the **Next** link until Step 5 of 6 appears in the wizard.

The data merges with the form letter.

Right arrow

>>

**9** In the **Mail Merge** task pane, click the **Right arrow** button to display the next data recipient in the merged letter.

## Tip

You can exclude recipients from the mail merge. In the **Mail Merge** task pane in Step 5 of 6, click the **Left** arrow button or **Right** arrow button to display the recipient you want to exclude, and then click **Exclude this recipient**.

**10** In the **Mail Merge** task pane, click **Previous: Write your letter** to return to Step 4 of 6.

**11** In the document window, scroll down to the second paragraph, and then click just before the comma at the beginning of the paragraph.

**12** In the **Mail Merge** task pane, click **More items** in the **Write your letter** section.

The **Insert Merge Field** dialog box appears.

**13** Click the **Database Fields** option, and then in the **Fields** box, click the **First-Name** field, if necessary.

**14** Click **Insert**, and then click **Close** to close the **Insert Merge Field** dialog box.

<<*FirstName*>> appears at the beginning of the second paragraph.

**15** In the **Mail Merge** task pane, click **Next: Preview your letters**.

The form letter shows a recipient's name at the beginning of the second paragraph.

**16** In the **Mail Merge** task pane, click **Next: Complete the merge** to proceed to Step 6 of 6.

**17** In the **Mail Merge** task pane, click **Edit individual letters** in the **Merge** section.

The **Merge to New Document** dialog box appears.

**18** Click the **All** option, if necessary, and then click **OK**.

Word creates a new document called Letters1 that contains personalized copies of the form letters, one for each person in the name and address list in the data document.

Save

**19** On the Standard toolbar, click the **Save** button.

The **Save As** dialog box appears.

**20** Navigate to the **MergingData** folder, type **LetterMrg** in the **File name** box, and then click **Save**.

Word saves the new document called Letters1 with the name LetterMrg.

Close Window

**21** Click the **Close Window** button in the document window.

The LetterMrg document closes and the MergeLtr document appears.

**22** On the Standard toolbar, click the **Save** button to save the MergeLtr document.

**23** Click the **Close Window** button in the document window.

The MergeLtr document closes.

# Creating and Printing Labels

W2002e-7-2

You can use a data document to create more than one kind of merge document. For example, you can use a data document to print mailing labels or envelopes to use with your mailing. The process for creating mailing labels is similar to the mail merge process for form letters, except that you insert merge fields into a main document that contains a table with cells in a specific size for labels. During the process for creating mailing labels, you can select brand-name labels in a specific size, such as Avery standard 5159. After you merge the data into the main document with the labels, you can print the labels on a printer.

After creating personalized copies of a form letter for The Garden Company customers, the owner now wants to print mailing labels for the same customers.

Data3

In this exercise, you use the Mail Merge Wizard to create mailing labels and then print the labels on standard paper to proofread them.

## Tip

To complete this exercise, you need a printer connected to your computer and the printer software installed.

New Blank Document

**1** On the Standard toolbar, click the **New Blank Document** button.

A new blank document window opens.

**2** On the **Tools** menu, point to **Letters and Mailings**, and then click **Mail Merge Wizard** to open the **Mail Merge** task pane showing Step 1 of 6 in the wizard.

**3** In the **Mail Merge** task pane, click the **Labels** option, and then click **Next: Starting document** to proceed to Step 2 of 6.

**4** In the **Mail Merge** task pane, click the **Change document layout** option, if necessary, and then click **Label options** in the **Change document layout** section.

The **Label Options** dialog box appears.

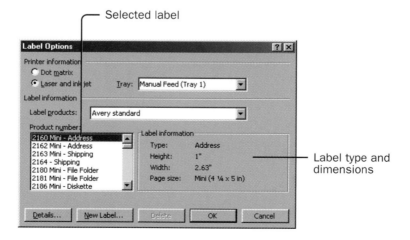

204

**5** In the **Product number** list, scroll down, click **5159-Address**, and then click **OK**.

The document window is divided into label-sized rectangles.

## Important

The document window might appear blank. The table appears without a shaded border with label-size rectangles.

**6** In the **Mail Merge** task pane, click **Next: Select recipients** to proceed to Step 3 of 6.

**7** In the **Mail Merge** task pane, click **Use an existing list**, if necessary, and then click **Browse** to open the **Select Data Source** dialog box.

The **Select Data Source** dialog box appears.

**8** Navigate to the **SBS** folder on your hard disk, double-click the **Word** folder, double-click the **MergingData** folder, and then double-click the **Data3** file.

The **Mail Merge Recipients** dialog box appears.

**9** Make sure that all the recipient check boxes are selected in the first column, and then click **OK**.

The **Mail Merge Recipients** dialog box closes and the *<<Next Record>>* merge field appears in all of the labels in the main document window.

**10** In the **Mail Merge** task pane, click **Next: Arrange your labels** to proceed to Step 4 of 6.

**11** With the insertion point positioned in the upper-left address label in the main document window, click **Address block** to open the **Insert Address Block** dialog box.

**12** Click **OK** to accept the default settings and to close the **Insert Address Block** dialog box.

The *<<AddressBlock>>* merge field appears in the upper-left address label in the main document window.

**13** In the **Mail Merge** task pane, click the **Update all labels** button in the **Replicate labels** section.

The *<<AddressBlock>>* merge field appears in all of the labels in the main document window.

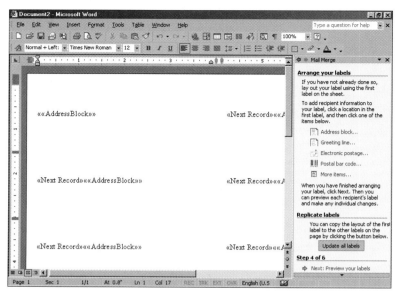

**14** In the **Mail Merge** task pane, click **Next: Preview your labels** to proceed to Step 5 of 6.

Names and addresses from the recipient list appear in the mailing labels.

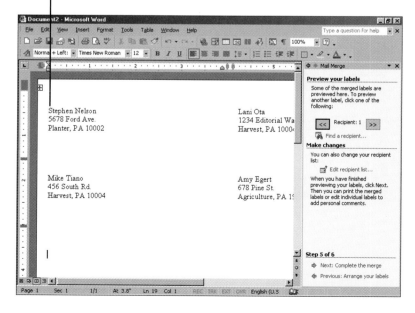

**15** In the **Mail Merge** task pane, click **Next: Complete the merge**.

The mail merge recipients appear in the mailing label document.

## Tip

If you change your mind during the mail merge process and decide to save the document as a normal document, on the **Tools** menu, point to **Letters and Mailings**, and then click **Show Mail Merge Toolbar**. On the Mail Merge toolbar, click the **Main document setup** button, click **Normal Word document**, and then click **OK**. You can now save the document without any mail merge information.

**16** In the **Mail Merge** task pane, click **Print**.

The **Merge to Printer** dialog box appears with the **All** option selected.

**17** Click **OK** to open the **Print** dialog box.

**18** Select a printer, if necessary, and then click **OK** to print the labels.

The labels are printed on regular paper on the printer that you chose.

**19** On the **File** menu, click **Save As**, navigate to the **SBS** folder on your hard disk, double-click the **Word** folder, double-click the **MergingData** folder, enter MailLabels as the file name, and then click **Save** to save the mailing labels document.

Close Window

**20** Click the **Close Window** button in the document window.

The MailLabels document closes.

## Chapter Wrap-Up

To finish this chapter:

Close

● On the **File** menu, click **Exit**, or click the **Close** button in the Word window.

Word closes.

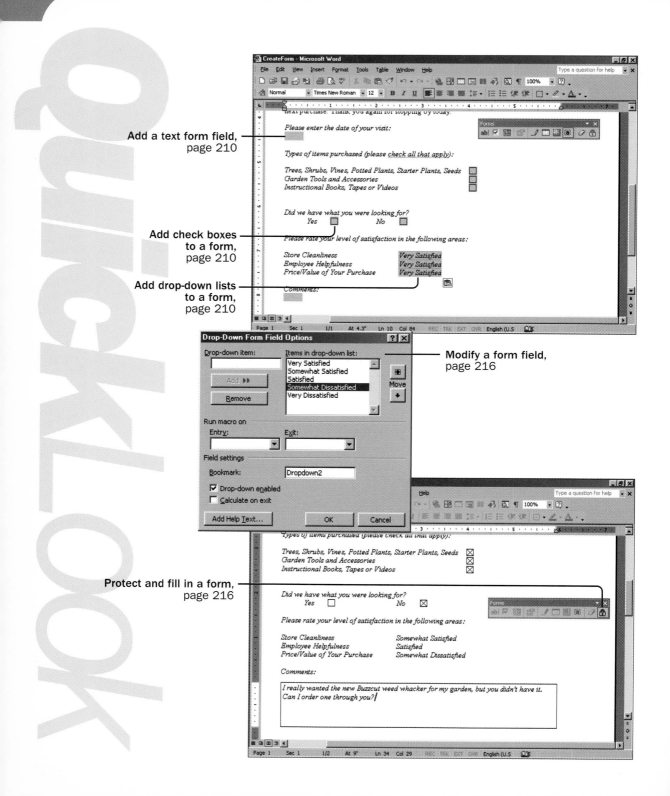

**Add a text form field,**
page 210

**Add check boxes to a form,**
page 210

**Add drop-down lists to a form,**
page 210

**Modify a form field,**
page 216

**Protect and fill in a form,**
page 216

# Chapter 12
# Creating Forms

## After completing this chapter, you will be able to:
✔ **Create a form document.**
✔ **Modify and use a form document.**

Forms are an easy way to collect information in a consistent manner, such as a survey, invoice, or order form. With a form, you can ask specific questions and get the response in the format that you want, such as yes/no or a brief comment. **Forms** can be either printed or online documents with instructions, questions, and fields (blanks) where users can enter their responses.

You can transform any document into a form by associating form fields with the questions in the document. **Form fields** are predefined places where users enter their answers to the questions on the form. Word includes many different types of form fields: text boxes for typed entries, date fields, time fields, fields that perform calculations, and check boxes, where users can click the box that represents their answer.

You can print Word forms so that users can respond on paper when it is most convenient for them to do so (as in a store customer satisfaction card). You can also distribute the form electronically and let users complete the form online. In this case, Word lets you protect the form document so that users cannot change the layout of the form while completing it.

In this chapter, you'll create a customer satisfaction survey. You will insert various form fields, including text fields, check boxes, and drop-down lists; you will also add a password to protect the form against inadvertent changes to the layout. Finally, you'll test the form that you created.

 This chapter uses the practice files CreateForm and UseForm that you installed from this book's CD-ROM. For details about installing the practice files, see "Using the Book's CD-ROM" at the beginning of this book.

# Creating a Form Document

W2002e-2-8

To create a form, you insert form fields into a document. In Word, you can insert several types of form fields: a text box for typed text, a check box for yes or no responses, and a drop-down list for predefined choices.

**Text form fields** are divided into six types: Regular text, Number, Date, Current date, Current time, and Calculation. **Regular text** fields can accept any combination of keyboard characters, including letters, numbers, or symbols. This text field is useful for comments and short text answers. **Number** fields accept only numeric values, making them appropriate for a quantity or price field on an order form. A **Date** field lets a user type a date in any standard date format that you specify when you create the date field, such as *12/21/2003*. You insert a **Current date** field when you want Word to complete the field by entering the current date set in your computer. You insert a **Current time** field when you want Word to complete the field by entering the current system time. You use a **Calculation** field to perform a calculation based on the formula and values that you supply, such as when you want to display a total order amount.

Another type of form field is the **Check box form field**, which lets you provide several options so that users can click one or more to indicate their choices. For example, suppose the marketing manager of The Garden Company wanted to know which brands of seeds were most favored by customers. One solution would be to poll customers in the store with a brief survey card listing all of the major seed manufacturers with check boxes next to each one and instructions to "choose your favorite." Check boxes are also good for true/false and yes/no responses.

In addition to text and check box form fields, you can insert a drop-down form field. Use a **Drop-down form field** when you want to limit users to several possible predefined answers. You specify all the possible options, and users choose one. In this way, drop-down form fields ensure that users will enter consistent and accurate information. For example, if you use a text box for users to respond to a question such as "How was our service?" you would have to read and tally the responses by hand. However, if you use a drop-down list and limit the user's responses to *excellent, very good, good, fair,* and *poor*, the responses are easier to gather and interpret.

After you insert a form field into a document, you can click the **Form Field Options** button on the Forms toolbar to specify form field properties, such as field type and length, in the **Form Field Options** dialog box. The choices in the **Form Field Options** dialog box change based on the selected form field type.

The marketing manager at The Garden Company is creating a survey form that customers can complete online to provide information about their visit. The form will use text fields to gather general comments, check boxes to gather responses to yes/no questions, and drop-down fields to find out about the quality of customer service.

**CreateForm**

In this exercise, you insert text form fields, check box form fields, and drop-down form fields to create a form.

**1**   Start Word, if necessary.

**Open**

**2**   On the Standard toolbar, click the **Open** button.

The **Open** dialog box appears.

**3**   Navigate to the **SBS** folder on your hard disk, double-click the **Word** folder, double-click the **CreatingForms** folder, and then double-click the **CreateForm** file.

The CreateForm document opens.

**4**   On the **View** menu, point to **Toolbars**, and then click **Forms**.

The Forms toolbar appears.

**5**   Scroll down the document, click the blank line below the text *Please enter the date of your visit* to position the insertion point at the beginning of the line.

**Text Form Field**

ab|

**6**   On the Forms toolbar, click the **Text Form Field** button.

A text form field is inserted. By default, the Regular text format is applied to the text form field.

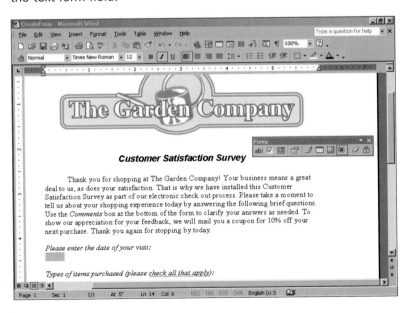

**Form Field Options**

**7**   On the Forms toolbar, click the **Form Field Options** button.

The **Text Form Field Options** dialog box appears.

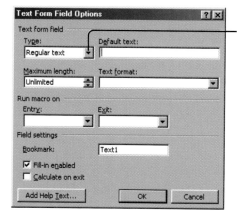

Click to choose a field type.

**8** In the **Text Form Field Options** dialog box, click the **Type** down arrow, and then click **Date**.

**9** Click the **Date format** down arrow, click **MMMM d, yyyy**, and then click **OK**.

The **Text Form Field Options** dialog box closes. When the users fill out this field, the date will be styled the way that you specified, such as July 22, 2003.

## Tip

Form Field Shading

New fields are shaded by default to make it obvious where users should enter their responses. To remove shading, click the **Form Field Shading** button on the Forms toolbar.

**10** Press `Ctrl`+`End` to position the insertion point at the end of the document below the word *Comments*.

Text Form Field

**ab|**

**11** On the Forms toolbar, click the **Text Form Field** button.

A text form field is inserted.

**12** Scroll up, click to the right of the phrase *Trees, Shrubs, Vines, Potted Plants, Starter Plants, Seeds*, and then press `Tab`.

Check Box Form Field

**13** On the Forms toolbar, click the **Check Box Form Field** button.

A check box is added to the right of the word *Seeds*.

Form Field Options

**14** On the Forms toolbar, click the **Form Fields Options** button.

The **Check Box Form Field Options** dialog box appears.

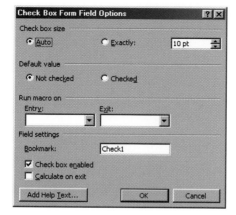

## Tip

You can add help text to form fields to provide instructions for filling out the field. In any **Form Field Options** dialog box, click **Add Help Text**, click the **Type your own** option, type your help text in the box, and then click **OK**.

**15** In the **Check box size** area, click the **Exactly** option, and then click the up arrow until **12 pt** appears.

**16** Click **OK**.

The check box is resized to show 12-point text and is unchecked by default.

Copy

**17** Drag to select the check box, if necessary, and then click the **Copy** button on the Standard toolbar.

The check box is copied to the Office Clipboard.

## Tip

To save time, you can copy and paste one type of form field and then revise it as necessary instead of setting up a new form field for each response.

Paste

**18** Click the next line, to the right of the text *Garden Tools and Accessories*, press ⌨Tab, and then click the **Paste** button on the Standard toolbar.

The check box is pasted to the right of the word *Accessories*, directly below the other check box, and the **Paste Options** button appears.

**19** Click the next line, to the right of the text *Instructional Books, Tapes or Videos*, press ⌨Tab, and then click the **Paste** button on the Standard toolbar.

The check box is pasted to the right of the word *Videos*, directly below the other check boxes, and the **Paste Options** button appears.

**20** Hold down Ctrl, and then drag the selected check box to the right (one tab) of the word *Yes*.

The check box is pasted to the right of the word *Yes*, and the **Paste Options** button appears.

**21** Hold down Ctrl, and then drag the selected check box to the right (one tab) of the word *No*.

The check box is pasted to the right of the word *No*, and the **Paste Options** button appears.

Inserted check boxes

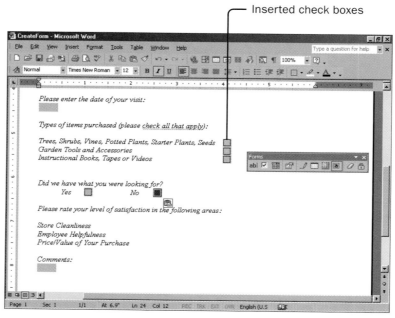

**22** Scroll down the document, click to the right of the words *Store Cleanliness*, and then press Tab.

Drop-Down Form Field

**23** On the Forms toolbar, click the **Drop-Down Form Field** button.

A drop-down form field is inserted to the right of the words *Store Cleanliness*.

Form Field Options

**24** On the Forms toolbar, click the **Form Field Options** button to open the **Drop-Down Form Field Options** dialog box.

**25** In the **Drop-down item** box, type **Very Satisfied**, and then click **Add**.

The words *Very Satisfied* are shown in the **Items in drop-down list** box.

**26** In the **Drop-down item** box, type **Somewhat Satisfied**, and then click **Add**.

The entry appears in the **Items in drop-down list** box.

**27** In the **Drop-down item** box, type Satisfied, and then click **Add**.

The entry is added to the **Items in drop-down list** box.

**28** In the **Drop-down item** box, type Very Dissatisfied, and then click **Add**.

The entry is added to the **Items in drop-down list** box.

**29** In the **Drop-down item** box, type Mildly Dissatisfied, and then click **Add**.

The entry is added to the **Items in drop-down list** box.

Move Up

**30** Click the **Move Up** button.

The *Mildly Dissatisfied* entry moves up in the list.

**31** Click **OK**.

The **Drop-Down Form Field Options** dialog box closes, and the drop-down form field appears, showing the first entry—*Very Satisfied*.

Copy

**32** Drag to select the drop-down box, if necessary, and then click the **Copy** button on the Standard toolbar.

The drop-down box is copied to the Office Clipboard.

**33** Click the next line, to the right of the text *Employee Helpfulness*, press ⎚Tab⎚, and then press ⎚Ctrl⎚+⎚V⎚.

The drop-down box is pasted to the right of the text.

**34** Click the next line, to the right of the text *Price/Value of Your Purchase*, press ⎚Tab⎚, and then press ⎚Ctrl⎚+⎚V⎚.

The drop-down box is pasted to the right of the text.

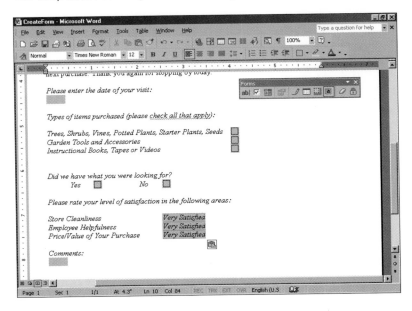

**Close Window**

**35** On the Standard toolbar, click the **Save** button to save the document.

**36** Click the **Close Window** button in the document window.

The CreateForm document closes.

# Modifying and Using a Form Document

W2002e-2-9
W2002e-2-8

You can enhance the look of a form by changing formatting, adding graphics, and changing **form field properties** in the document. To customize a field, form field properties allow you to change attributes, such as text field length or the check box default setting. You can format fields in a form in the same way that you format other text in Word.

When you are finished working with the form, you can print the form or distribute the form electronically and let users complete the form online. If you distribute the form electronically, you need to save the form as a template so that each user creates a separate document with his or her responses. You can send the form in an e-mail message or store the form in a central location where others can access the file. If you have a network, you can make the electronic forms available for others to fill out online. If you have a Web site, you can save the form as a Web page and publish it to the Internet.

**Protect Form**

Before you distribute the form to users, you need to protect the form so that users can interact only with the fields, not change the form itself. In fact, you cannot use a form to gather responses until you protect it. If you need to change the layout or content, you need to unprotect the form. You use the **Protect Form** button on the **Forms** toolbar to turn protection on and off. You can add further protection to a form by adding password protection, which ensures that only password holders can unlock, unprotect, and edit the form.

The marketing manager is ready to distribute The Garden Company's customer survey form online. He plans to fine-tune the form, protect it from user modification, test the form by responding to all the questions and by typing a comment, and then lock the form.

**UseForm**

In this exercise, you format a text field, change the default value of a check box, change an item in a drop-down list form field, insert a frame, remove the shading from all form fields on a form, and then protect the form. You also view and test the activated form fields of a form and then protect the form using a password.

Open

**1** On the Standard toolbar, click the **Open** button.

The **Open** dialog box appears.

**2** Navigate to the **SBS** folder on your hard disk, double-click the **Word** folder, double-click the **CreatingForms** folder, and then double-click the **UseForm** file.

The UseForm document opens.

**3** On the **View** menu, point to **Toolbars**, and then click **Forms**, if necessary, to display the Forms toolbar.

**4** Scroll down the document, and then click the shaded area text form field below the text *Please enter the date of your visit* to select the text field.

Outside Border

**5** On the Formatting toolbar, click the **Outside Border** down arrow, click **Outside Border**, and then click a blank area of the document to deselect the text form field.

A border appears around the text form field.

**6** Scroll down the document, and then double-click the check box next to the word *Yes*.

The **Check Box Form Field Options** dialog box appears.

**7** In the **Default value** area, click the **Checked** option, and then click **OK**.

An X mark is placed in the check box as the default value.

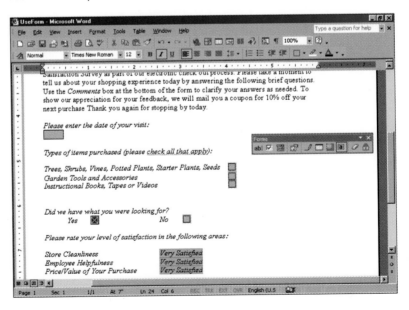

**8** Scroll down the document, if necessary, to the line that contains the text *Store Cleanliness*, and then double-click the first drop-down form field.

The **Drop-Down Form Field Options** dialog box appears.

**9** In the **Items in drop-down list** box, click **Mildly Dissatisfied**, and then click **Remove**.

The text *Mildly Dissatisfied* is removed from the **Items in drop-down list** box.

Move Up

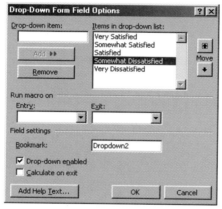

**10** In the **Drop-down item** box, type **Somewhat Dissatisfied**, click **Add**, and then click the **Move Up** button.

The text *Somewhat* Dissatisfied appears second from the end.

**11** Click **OK** to close the **Drop-Down Form Field Options** dialog box.

**12** Repeat steps 8 through 11 for the next two drop-down form fields.

**13** Scroll down, and then click the text form field below the *Comments* heading.

Insert Frame

**14** On the Forms toolbar, click the **Insert Frame** button.

The text is shifted to the left margin, a frame is inserted around the text box, and black selection handles appear around the frame.

**15** Drag the text box field down about a quarter-inch to provide space between the text *Comments* and the text box.

**16** Drag the lower-right selection handle down and to the right until the box is about six inches wide and an inch and a half high.

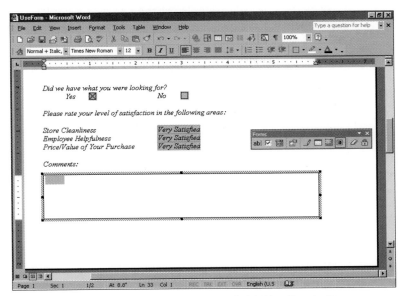

**Form Field Shading**

**17** On the Forms toolbar, click the **Form Field Shading** button.

The shading is removed from all form fields.

**18** On the Forms toolbar, click the **Protect Form** button.

**Protect Form**

The form is protected, and the form fields are ready to be filled out.

**19** Scroll to the top of the document, click the date text form field, type **6/25/03**, and then press `Tab`.

The date *June 25, 2003* appears in the field, and the focus changes to the first check box on the form.

**20** Click each of the check boxes below the *Types of items purchased* heading.

X's appear in each box.

## Tip

When filling out a form, you can also press    to insert an X in a check box.

**21** Under the *Did we have what you were looking for?* heading, select the **No** check box, and then clear the **Yes** check box.

The **Yes** box is empty, and the **No** box is selected.

## Important

In a Word form, check boxes are independent of each other. You need to manually select or clear each check box. One check is not cleared automatically when another box is checked.

**22** Click the drop-down box next to the text *Store Cleanliness*, and then click **Somewhat Satisfied**.

The text *Somewhat Satisfied* appears in the drop-down field.

**23** Click the drop-down box next to the text *Employee Helpfulness*, and then click **Satisfied**.

The text *Satisfied* appears in the drop-down field.

**24** Click the drop-down box next to the text *Price/Value of Your Purchase*, and then click **Somewhat Dissatisfied**.

The text *Somewhat Dissatisfied* appears in the drop-down field.

**25** Click the text form field below the *Comments* heading to select the text field, and then type **I really wanted the new Buzzcut weed whacker for my garden, but you didn't have it. Can I order one through you?**

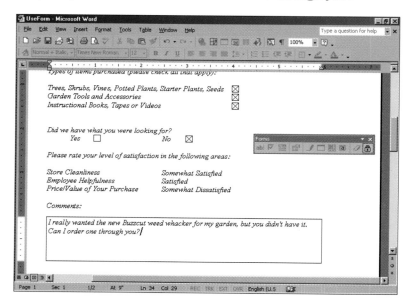

Protect Form

**26** On the Forms toolbar, click the **Protect Form** button.

The form is unprotected.

**27** On the **Tools** menu, click **Protect Document**.

The **Protect Document** dialog box appears.

**28** In the **Protect Document** dialog box, click the **Forms** options, if necessary.

**29** In the **Password** box, type the password Garden.

As you type the password, asterisks appear instead of the characters that you type to keep your password confidential.

**30** Click **OK**.

The **Confirm Password** dialog box appears.

**31** In the **Reenter password to open** box, type the password Garden again, and then click **OK**.

Word protects the form, and both dialog boxes close.

Protect Form

**32** On the Forms toolbar, click the **Protect Form** button to display the **Unprotect Document** dialog box, type the password Garden, and then click **OK**.

Word accepts the password and unprotects the document. The password protection for the form is removed. You can now make changes to the form.

**33** On the **File** menu, click **Save As**.

The **Save As** dialog box appears.

**34** In the **File name** box, type SendForm.

**35** Click the **Save as type** down arrow, and then click **Document Template**.

**36** Navigate to the **SBS** folder on your hard disk, double-click the **Word** folder, double-click the **CreatingForms** folder, and then click **Save**.

Word saves the form as a template.

Close Window

**37** Click the **Close Window** button in the document window.

The UseForm document closes.

## Chapter Wrap-Up

To finish this chapter:

Close

● On the **File** menu, click **Exit**, or click the **Close** button in the Word window.

Word closes.

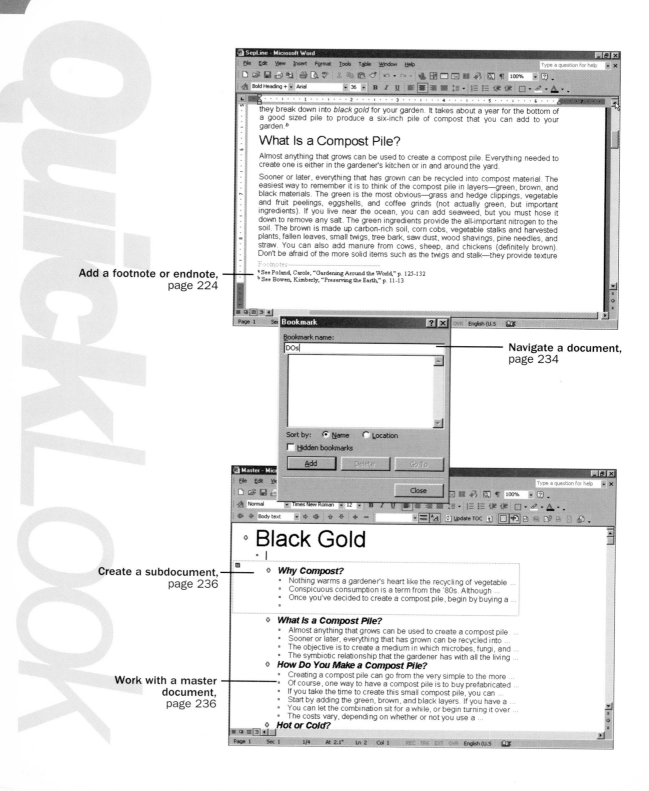

# Chapter 13
# Working with Footnotes and Bookmarks

**After completing this chapter, you will be able to:**

✔ Add and revise footnotes and endnotes.

✔ Change the note separator.

✔ Navigate a document.

✔ Manage master documents and subdocuments.

When you are stating facts to support your position, you can insert notes—either footnotes or endnotes—to cite your references. **Footnotes** appear at the end of each page that contains cited sources. Footnotes are numbered sequentially from start to finish within a page or in the document. **Endnotes** are just like footnotes except that they appear on a separate page at the end of the document. If you change the pagination of the document, or if you insert or delete a footnote or endnote, Word updates the reference numbers so that they remain consecutive.

Instead of scrolling through a long document to find a specific word, phrase or section, you can use bookmarks. **Bookmarks** are used to mark text so that you, or your reader, can return to it quickly. Using bookmarks as a destination lets you navigate a long document quickly. You can also navigate documents with bookmarks by selecting a bookmark as a destination in the **Go To** dialog box.

Bookmarks are just one way that Word can help you manage long or complex documents. Another way is with the **master document**, a document that contains a set of related documents called **subdocuments.** When a group is collaborating on a long document, such as an annual report, it might be more efficient to split the document into subdocuments. Then each member of the group can work on a subdocument simultaneously. They can make changes to a subdocument independently of the master document and then recombine the subdocuments with the master.

In this chapter, you'll insert footnotes and endnotes, edit reference marks and notes, change the appearance of the separator line between body text and notes, add and use bookmarks, and work with master documents and subdocuments.

 This chapter uses the practice files Footnote, ReviseNotes, SepLine, Bookmark, and Master that you installed from this book's CD-ROM. For details about installing the practice files, see "Using the Book's CD-ROM" at the beginning of this book.

# Adding Footnotes and Endnotes

W2002e-2-5

Footnotes and endnotes serve the same purpose—they explain, comment on, or provide references for text in a printed document. A footnote appears at the bottom of the page containing the associated text, while an endnote appears at the end of a document or at the end of a section in that document. You can include both footnotes and endnotes in the same document. For example, you could use footnotes to provide additional detail and define terms, and endnotes to cite sources. Most documents use either footnotes or endnotes. If you create a footnote or endnote and later decide that you need the other type, you can convert one to the other at any time.

Footnotes and endnotes consist of a reference mark and note text. A **reference mark** is a number or character in the main text of the document that indicates additional information is included in a footnote or endnote. By default, Word uses numbers as reference marks although you can create your own custom marks. The **note text** is the content of the footnote or endnote. You can add note text of any length and format note text just as you would any other text.

To insert a note, you click where you want the reference mark to appear—by convention, this is at the end of the text associated with the note—and then you use the **Reference** command on the **Insert** menu to add your note. Word inserts the same reference mark in the body text and at the bottom of the page for footnotes or the end of the document for endnotes. The insertion point then appears in the notes area so that you can enter the note text.

The master gardener for The Garden Company has been compiling research on composting and wants to cite sources to support the information.

Footnote

In this exercise, you insert footnotes and endnotes into a long document and then convert endnotes to footnotes for consistency.

**1**   Start Word, if necessary.

Open

**2**   On the **Standard** toolbar, click the **Open** button.

The **Open** dialog box appears.

**3**   Navigate to the **SBS** folder on your hard disk, double-click the **Word** folder, double-click the **CreatingNotes** folder, and then double-click the **Footnote** file.

The Footnote document opens in Normal view.

**4**   Click at the end of the first paragraph (which ends with the word *Ireland*) to place the insertion point after the period.

**5**   On the **Insert** menu, point to **Reference**, and then click **Footnote**.

The **Footnote and Endnote** dialog box appears.

**6**   In the **Location** area, click the **Footnotes** option, if necessary.

**7** In the **Format** area, click the **Number format** down arrow, and then click **1,2,3...**, if necessary, to select a new number format.

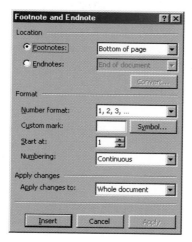

**8** Click **Insert**.

The Notes pane appears. Word inserts the reference mark *1* in the text and moves the insertion point next to the note's reference mark at the end of the page.

**9** Type **See Poland, Carole, "Gardening Around the World," p. 125-132** to enter the footnote.

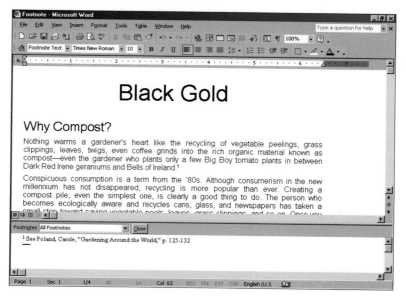

**10** In the Notes pane, click **Close** to close the Notes pane.

**11** Click the **Print Layout View** button to switch to Print Layout view.

**12** Scroll down to the third paragraph on page 1, and then click at the end of the paragraph (which ends with the word *garden*) to place the insertion point after the period.

**13** On the **Insert** menu, point to **Reference**, and then click **Footnote**.

The **Footnote and Endnote** dialog box appears.

**14** In the **Location** area, click the **Footnotes** option, if necessary, and then click **Insert**.

Word inserts the reference mark *2* in the text and moves the insertion point next to the note's reference mark at the end of the page.

**15** Type **See Bowen, Kimberly, "Preserving the Earth," p. 11-13** to enter the footnote.

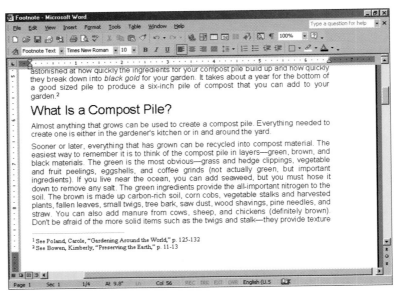

**16** Scroll down to the third paragraph below the heading *What Is a Compost Pile?*, and then click at the end of the paragraph (which ends with the word *delphiniums*) to place the insertion point after the period.

**17** On the **Insert** menu, point to **Reference**, and then click **Footnote**.

The **Footnote and Endnote** dialog box appears.

**18** In the **Location** area, click the **Endnotes** option to create an endnote.

**19** Click **Number format** down arrow, click **I, II, III, …**, and then click **Insert**.

Word inserts the reference mark *I* in the text and moves the insertion point next to the note's reference mark at the end of the document.

**20** Type **See Sutton, Brad, "Microbiology in Everyday Life," p. 75-98** to enter the endnote.

The endnote appears at the end of the document.

**21** Right-click anywhere in the endnote to open a shortcut menu.

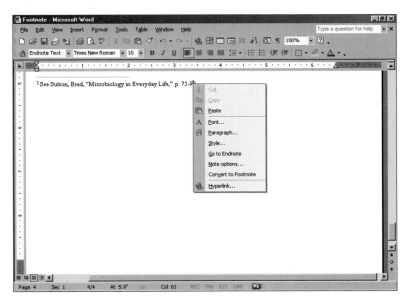

**22** Click **Convert to Footnote.**

The shortcut menu closes. The endnote is converted to footnote 3 and appears at the bottom of page 2.

**23** On the Standard toolbar, click the **Save** button to save the document.

Close Window

**24** Click the **Close Window** button in the document window.

The Footnote document closes.

# Revising Footnotes and Endnotes

W2002e-2-5

After you insert a footnote or endnote into a document, you can revise the footnote or endnote text or the reference mark at any time. Adding or deleting text can change the position of your notes. Fortunately, as you change the body text in a document, Word repositions your notes. When your edits affect footnoted sentences, or when you move, copy, or delete notes in your document, Word renumbers the reference marks for you. If you place the reference mark in the wrong location, you can cut and paste or drag to move a reference mark to a new location. If you need to refer to the same footnote or endnote in more than one place in the document, you can copy and paste to copy a note. When you move, copy, or delete a note, you work with the reference mark in the document window.

The document view that you use determines the kind of work that you can do with notes. Use Print Layout view to see both footnotes and endnotes as they appear in the document. Use Web Layout view to see only endnotes. In Web Layout view, if you double-click a reference mark, you see the endnotes at the end of the document. Although footnotes and endnotes do not appear in Normal and Outline views, you can double-click a reference mark to open the Notes pane to view footnotes and endnotes. As you scroll through a document, you can select and point to a reference mark to display a ScreenTip with text from the footnote or endnote.

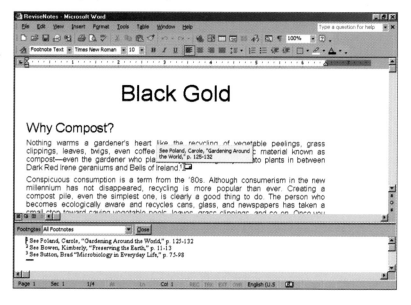

Browse by
Footnote

Word provides tools to help you find specific footnotes or endnotes quickly or to browse through them in sequence. You can use the **Go To** tab in the **Find and Replace** dialog box to find and display a specific reference mark for a footnote or endnote. If you don't know where to locate a footnote in a document, you can use the **Browse by Footnote** icon on the **Select Browse Object** menu to display each footnote reference mark.

Word applies default styles to the reference marks for footnotes and endnotes. By default, footnote reference marks use the 1, 2, 3 format, and endnote reference marks use the i, ii, iii style. You can use the **Footnote and Endnote** dialog box to specify other styles—such as the I, II, III, or A, B, C format—as well.

The master gardener for The Garden Company wants to find, review, and revise the footnotes in an article about composting and then modify the document with an alphabetic style for reference marks.

ReviseNotes

In this exercise, you browse for and view footnotes and then move, copy, and delete notes. You also modify the style of reference marks.

Open

**1**  On the Standard toolbar, click the **Open** button.

The **Open** dialog box appears.

**2**  Navigate to the **SBS** folder on your hard disk, double-click the **Word** folder, double-click the **CreatingNotes** folder, and then double-click the **Revise-Notes** file.

The ReviseNotes document opens.

Normal View

**3**  Click the **Normal View** button, if necessary, to switch to Normal view.

**4**  Double-click the reference mark for footnote 1.

The Notes pane opens.

## Tip

You can also click the **Footnotes** command on the **View** menu to open the Notes pane.

**5**  In the Notes pane, click anywhere in footnote 3 to place the insertion point in the footnote.

The reference mark 3 appears in the document window.

**6**  Press the ⬆ key twice to move the insertion point up to footnote 2 and footnote 1.

The reference mark 1 appears in the document window.

**7**  In the Notes pane, click **Close**.

The Notes pane closes.

Print Layout View

**8**  Click the **Print Layout View** button.

The document appears in Print Layout view.

Select Browse Object

**9**  Click the **Select Browse Object** button at the bottom of the vertical scroll bar to display a menu of browsing options.

**10**  On the **Select Browse Object** menu, click the **Browse by Footnote** icon (column 3, row 2).

The insertion point moves to reference mark 2.

Next Footnote

**11**  Click the **Next Footnote** button at the bottom of the vertical scroll bar.

The insertion point moves to reference mark 3.

**12**  In the main document window, select the reference mark 3, and then scroll up to display the entire paragraph with the reference mark 3.

**13**  Hold down the Ctrl key, and then drag the reference mark 3 to the end of the first sentence in the same paragraph (which ends with *grow and feed*).

A copy of the reference mark appears at the end of the first sentence along with the **Paste Options** button, and the original footnote remains at the bottom of the page. The reference marks are renumbered.

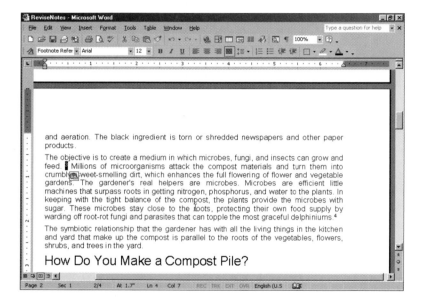

## Tip

To move a footnote instead of copying it, select the reference mark, and then drag it to a new location.

**14**  Select the reference mark 4 for the footnote, and then press the Del key to delete the footnote.

**15**  On the **Edit** menu, click **Go To**.

The **Find and Replace** dialog box appears, showing the **Go To** tab.

**16**  In the **Go to what** list, click **Footnote**.

**17**  In the **Enter footnote number** box, type 1.

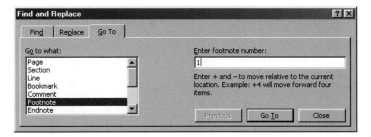

**18**  Click **Go To**.

The insertion point moves to the left of the first footnote's reference mark.

**19**  In the **Find and Replace** dialog box, click **Close** to close the dialog box.

**20**  On the **Insert** menu, point to **Reference**, and then click **Footnote**.

The **Footnote and Endnote** dialog box appears.

**21**  Click the **Footnotes** option, if necessary.

**22**  In the **Format** area, click the **Number format** down arrow, and then click **a,b,c …**

**23**  Verify that *Whole document* appears in the **Apply changes to** box, and then click **Apply**.

All footnotes change to lowercase letters in alphabetical order.

**24**  Select the reference mark *a* for the first footnote.

Italic
*I*

**25**  On the Formatting toolbar, click the **Italic** button.

The reference mark for this footnote only changes to italics.

**26**  Scroll down, if necessary, and then select the reference mark *b*.

**27** On the **Format** menu, click **Styles and Formatting**.

The **Styles and Formatting** task pane appears.

**28** Click the **Select All** button to select all the footnotes in the document, and then under **Pick formatting to apply**, click **Footnote Reference**.

All the footnotes now appear with italic reference marks.

Close

**29** In the **Styles and Formatting** task pane, click the **Close** button to close the task pane.

**30** On the Standard toolbar, click the **Save** button to save the document.

Close Window

**31** Click the **Close Window** button in the document window.

The ReviseNotes document closes.

# Changing the Note Separator

The **note separator** line divides the notes from the body of the document. By default, Word displays the note separator as a solid black line. In Normal view, you can customize separators by adding borders, text, or graphics.

The master gardener for The Garden Company wants to edit the note separator line to include the word *Footnotes*.

SepLine

In this exercise, you modify the note separator line and then change it back to the default style.

**1** On the Standard toolbar, click the **Open** button.

The **Open** dialog box appears.

**2** Navigate to the **SBS** folder on your hard disk, double-click the **Word** folder, double-click the **CreatingNotes** folder, and then double-click the **SepLine** file.

The SepLine document opens.

Normal View

**3** Click the **Normal View** button to switch to Normal view, if necessary.

**4** On the **View** menu, click **Footnotes** to open the Notes pane.

**5** In the Notes pane, click the **Footnotes** down arrow, and then click **Footnote Separator**.

A horizontal line appears in the Notes pane, and the insertion point moves to the beginning of the line.

**6** In the Notes pane, type *Footnotes*, and then click **Close** to close the Notes pane.

Print Layout View

**7** Click the **Print Layout View** button to switch to Print Layout view, and then scroll down the pages to view the footnotes and the new note separator.

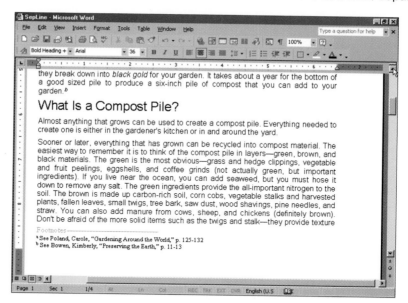

The word *Footnotes* appears with the horizontal separator in gray.

Normal View

**8** Click the **Normal View** button to switch to Normal view.

**9** On the **View** menu, click **Footnotes** to open the Notes pane.

**10** In the Notes pane, click the **Footnotes** down arrow, and then click **Footnote Separator**.

**11** On the Notes pane toolbar, click **Reset** to restore the default separator line, and then click **Close** to close the Notes pane.

**12** On the Standard toolbar, click the **Save** button to save the document.

**13** Click the **Close Window** button in the document window.

The SepLine document closes.

# Navigating a Document

WW2002e-2-7

You can quickly navigate to specific user-designated points in a document using bookmarks and the Document Map. You can use bookmarks for your own convenience or the convenience of your readers. They mark locations in a document that you identify and name for future reference. Like a physical paper bookmark, a Word bookmark helps you find your place in a document. You can also use bookmarks to create cross-references, mark page ranges for index entries, create hyperlinks for Web pages, or highlight glossary terms in the text and connect them to definitions that appear elsewhere in the document. To add a bookmark, you select text or an item in a document and assign it a bookmark name.

As you work with long documents, you can use the Document Map to help you navigate headings in your document. Document Map splits the view of a document into two panes. Heading titles appear in the left pane, and the document appears in the right pane. When you click a heading in the left pane, the corresponding heading in the document appears in the right pane. You can right-click an item in the left pane to choose the level of detail to display in the Document Map. For example, you can display all headings or only level one headings, or you can expand or collapse the text below individual headings.

The master gardener for The Garden Company is expecting additional research on composting do's and don'ts and wants to insert a bookmark into the document as a reminder about where to add this research when it arrives.

Bookmark

In this exercise, you insert and navigate to a bookmark in a document and then jump to a heading in a document with the Document Map.

**1** On the Standard toolbar, click the **Open** button.

Open

The **Open** dialog box appears.

**2** Navigate to the **SBS** folder on your hard disk, double-click the **Word** folder, double-click the **CreatingNotes** folder, and then double-click the **Bookmark** file.

The Bookmark document opens.

**3** Scroll down to the last page in the document, and then click before the text *COMPOSTING DO's and DON'Ts.*

**4** On the **Insert** menu, click **Bookmark** to open the **Bookmark** dialog box.

**5**    In the **Bookmark name** box, type **DOs**.

**6**    Click **Add**.

The **Bookmark** dialog box closes, and the bookmark named *DOs* is inserted into the document. The bookmark doesn't visually appear in the document.

**7**    Press Ctrl+Home to place the insertion point at the beginning of the document.

**8**    On the **Insert** menu, click **Bookmark**.

The **Bookmark** dialog box appears, and the document's only bookmark, *DOs*, is selected in the **Bookmark name** list.

**9**    In the **Bookmark** dialog box, click **Go To**.

The insertion point moves to the location of the bookmark, and the **Bookmark** dialog box remains open.

**10**   In the **Bookmark** dialog box, verify that *DOs* is selected, and click **Delete**.

The *DOs* bookmark is deleted.

**11**   Click **Close** to close the **Bookmark** dialog box.

**12**   On the **View** menu, click **Document Map**.

The Document Map for the current document appears.

**13**   In the left pane, click **What Is a Compost Pile?**.

The heading *What Is a Compost Pile?* appears at the top of the right pane with the insertion point to the left of the heading.

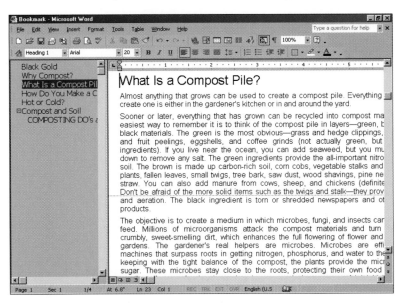

**14**   On the **View** menu, click **Document Map** to display Normal view.

**15** On the Standard toolbar, click the **Save** button to save the document.

**16** Click the **Close Window** button in the document window.

The Bookmark document closes.

# Managing Master Documents and Subdocuments

W2002e-2-6

When you must manage a lengthy project, such as a book, business plan, or major report that involves multiple sections, you can use the master document and subdocument features built into Word to help you collaborate on the project with others. For example, you could create a book as a master document, with each chapter a subdocument. The master document contains all the subdocuments, which are linked to the master. You can work on the subdocuments separately. After you merge the subdocuments back into the master, you can use the master to create a table of contents, an index, cross-references, and headers and footers in the whole document.

To create a master document, you create an outline in **Outline view**. You use the Outlining toolbar to assign headings and subheadings in the outline. For example, you could create headings for Chapter 1, Chapter 2, and so on. Then you select a section of the document and use the **Create Subdocument** button on the Outlining toolbar to divide that part of the master document into a subdocument. You can also use the **Insert Subdocument** button on the Outlining toolbar to add existing documents to a master document to make them subdocuments.

As you work on a master document and its subdocuments, you can use the buttons on the Outlining toolbar to change your view of the documents. For example, you can click the **Collapse Subdocuments** button on the Outlining toolbar to hide the contents of subdocuments and display them only as hyperlinks. This makes it easier to navigate, arrange, and organize a master document. When the subdocuments are collapsed, you can click a hyperlink to open a subdocument and edit it, or you can drag subdocument titles to reorder them. If you want to work with the master document as a whole, such as to check its spelling, click the **Expand Subdocuments** button to show the contents of all subdocuments.

The master gardener for The Garden Company wants to create a master document for the composting project and then ask other employees to contribute information in a series of subdocuments.

Master

In this exercise, you create a master document in Outline view, create subdocuments, and then open and modify a subdocument.

**1** On the Standard toolbar, click the **Open** button.

Open

The **Open** dialog box appears.

**2** Navigate to the **SBS** folder on your hard disk, double-click the **Word** folder, double-click the **CreatingNotes** folder, and then double-click the **Master** file.

The Master document opens.

Outline View

**3**    Click the **Outline View** button.

Word switches to Outline view and displays the Outlining toolbar. The insertion point appears to the left of the first heading.

Show First Line Only

**4**    On the Outlining toolbar, click the **Show First Line Only** button.

The first line of each paragraph appears in the outline.

**5**    Click the plus sign next to the heading *Why Compost?* to select the heading and all its associated body text.

**6**    Scroll down to the end of the document, hold down `Shift`, and then click the plus sign next to the heading *Compost and Soil* to select all the text between the headings.

Demote

**7**    On the Outlining toolbar, click the **Demote** button, scroll up to the top of the document, and then click to the right of the heading *Why Compost?*.

The *Compost and Soil* heading is designated a level two heading, and the text below it is indented accordingly.

**8**    Scroll up, and then click the plus sign next to the heading *Why Compost?* to select the heading and all its associated body text.

Create Subdocument

**9**    On the Outlining toolbar, click the **Create Subdocument** button.

The Subdocument icon appears in the left margin of the document, a light border surrounds the selected text, and the heading becomes a subdocument within the master document.

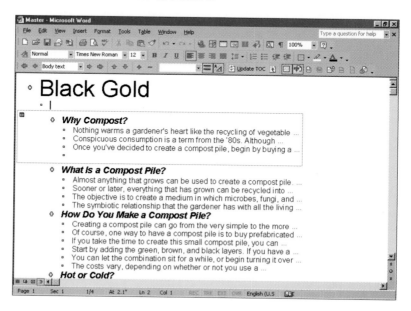

**10** Repeat steps 8 and 9, selecting the plus sign for each of the following headings: *What Is a Compost Pile?, How Do You Make a Compost Pile?, Hot or Cold?,* and *Compost and Soil.*

Collapse
Subdocuments

**11** On the Outlining toolbar, click the **Collapse Subdocuments** button.

A message appears, asking if you want to save changes to the master document first.

**12** Click **OK**.

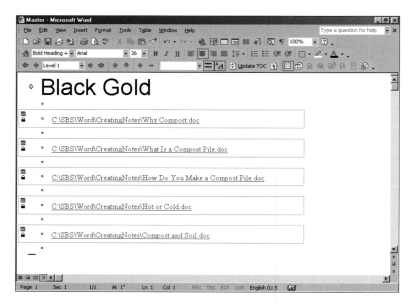

The subdocuments appear as hyperlinks. Each hyperlink displays the path to the subdocument. The path defaults to the same folder as the master document, and the subdocument is named with the heading title.

**13** Hold down ⌃, and then click the first hyperlink (the one associated with the *Why Compost?* heading).

The subdocument opens in its own document window.

Bold
**B**

**14** Scroll to the end of the document, and then select the text *black gold* (near the end of the third paragraph). On the Formatting toolbar, click the **Bold** button to format the text to stand out.

Save

**15** On the Standard toolbar, click the **Save** button, and then click the **Close Window** button to save and close the subdocument.

Word saves and closes the subdocument, and the master document appears.

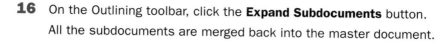

Expand
Subdocuments

**16** On the Outlining toolbar, click the **Expand Subdocuments** button.

All the subdocuments are merged back into the master document.

Show First Line
Only

**17** On the Outlining toolbar, click the **Show First Line Only** button.

The headings expand to show all the text in the outline. The change to the Why Compost subdocument is reflected in the master document.

## Tip

Word count
new for
**Office**XP

If you are working on a book or other project where you need to know how many characters, words, paragraphs, or pages are in the document, Word can perform a count for you. On the **Tools** menu, click **Word Count** to open the **Word Count** dialog box with the count information. If you want to include footnotes and endnotes in the count, select the **Include footnotes and endnotes** check box in the **Word Count** dialog box. As you add or delete text, you can click **Recount** on the Word Count toolbar to quickly perform a recount. To show the Word Count toolbar, click **Show Toolbar** in the **Word Count** dialog box or on the **View** menu, point to **Toolbars**, and then click **Word Count**.

**18** On the Standard toolbar, click the **Save** button to save the document.

Close Window

**19** Click the **Close Window** button in the document window.

The Master document closes.

# Chapter Wrap-Up

To finish this chapter:

Close

● On the **File** menu, click **Exit**, or click the **Close** button in the Word window.

Word closes.

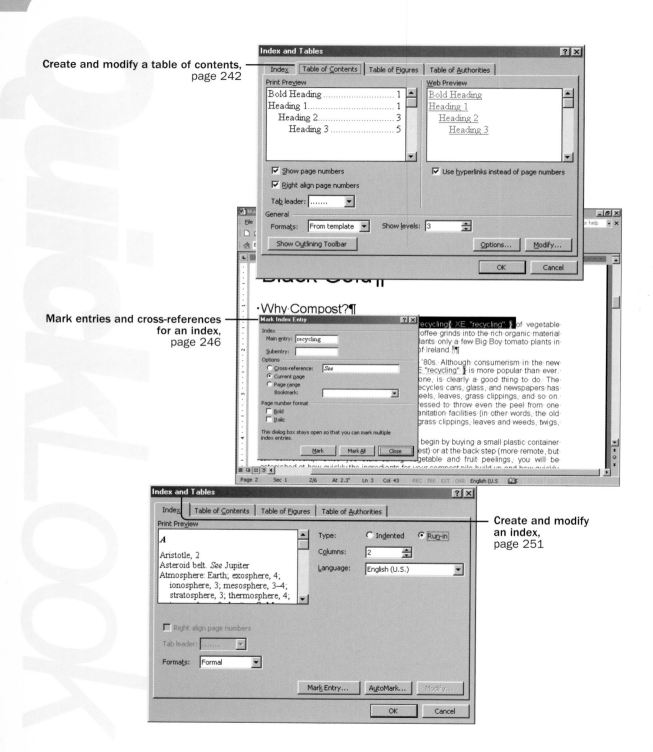

# Chapter 14
# Working with Tables of Contents and Indexes

**After completing this chapter, you will be able to:**

✔  **Create and modify a table of contents.**

✔  **Mark entries for an index.**

✔  **Create and modify an index.**

You can include tables of contents and indexes in your long documents to help readers locate information. A **table of contents** typically appears at the beginning of a document and lists the main headings and subheadings in the document along with corresponding page numbers. You can use a table of contents to provide an overview of the topics covered in a document and to let readers quickly navigate to a topic. For example, The Garden Company Guide to Garden & Yard Power Tools has the following sections in its table of contents:

An **index** typically appears at the end of a document and alphabetically lists the main topics, names, and terms used in a document along with the corresponding page numbers. Each index listing is called an **entry**. You can create an index entry for a word, phrase, or symbol for a topic that spans one or more pages or one that refers to another entry, called a **cross-reference**. If you have many index entries for a specific topic area, you might want to use a multilevel index. A multilevel index contains topics with related subtopics. Each subtopic index listing is called a **subentry**. For example, if you have a main index entry *Lawn Equipment*, you could then group the subentries *mower* and *weed trimmer* below it.

The Garden Company Guide to Garden & Yard Power Tools includes information in several places about adjusting the fuel-air mixture on a four-cycle engine and has the following entries in its index:

*L*

Lawn

     Types, 59-60
     maintaining, 61-62
     mowing. *See* Mowers
     fertilizing, 62-64

*M*

Mowers

     accessories, 90
     designs of, 91
     features of, 94
     maintaining, 97
     types, 92

Before you create an index in Word, you must mark each entry and subentry that you want to include in the index. You must also mark appropriate cross-references. After you finish marking entries, subentries, and cross-references, you use the **Index and Tables** command on the **Reference** submenu on the **Insert** menu to create an index. Later, when you edit the document and add or delete sections that change the page numbering of the document, Word tracks those changes and applies them when you update the index.

In this chapter, you'll create and modify a table of contents, mark entries and cross-references for an index, and then create and modify an index.

This chapter uses the practice files TabContents, MarkEntry, and CreateIndex that you installed from this book's CD-ROM. For details about installing the practice files, see" "Using the Book's CD-ROM" at the beginning of this book.

# Creating and Modifying a Table of Contents

W2002e-2-3

Word uses heading styles in a document to identify table of contents entries. When you create a table of contents, level one headings appear with level two headings indented below them. Lower level headings appear indented sequentially after that in outline form. To create and format a table of contents, you designate headings and subheadings in **Outline view** and then click the **Index and Tables** command on the **Reference** submenu on the **Insert** menu. Word provides several predefined table of contents formats, including **Classic**, **Formal**, and **Simple**. The default setting is **From template**, which integrates the table of contents with the current document template that you are using (Normal.dot or any other). The **From template** design creates a table of contents with uppercase letters for level one headings and title case for level two headings.

You can also customize the format of your table of contents by changing individual styles for the table of contents. To modify table styles, you use the **Modify** command on the **Table of Contents** tab in the **Index and Tables** dialog box. This opens the **Style** dialog box and displays the nine styles for table of contents entries. You can set the styles for table of contents entries the same way that you set the style for any other text in Word.

Suppose you create a table of contents but later change the document and its pagination. You can use Word to update only the page numbers or the entire table of contents. The table of contents is shaded to indicate that Word treats it as a single field. Each entry in the table of contents is hyperlinked to the heading it references. When you point to a table of contents entry, a ScreenTip appears, displaying the text *Current Document Ctrl+click to follow link.* You hold down the Ctrl key and then click the entry to go to the corresponding section.

You can format a table of contents as you would any other text in Word—you select text and then apply formatting attributes or a style. To edit the text in a table of contents, you edit the corresponding headings. Then you can click in the table of contents and press the F9 key to update it. Although you can directly edit the text in a table of contents, you should edit the headings and then update the table of contents using F9 so that the entries and heading text match exactly.

TabContents

In this exercise, you open a document that uses heading styles and then you create a table of contents. You also change a document by inserting page breaks and then updating the table of contents.

**1** Start Word, if necessary.

Open

**2** On the Standard toolbar, click the **Open** button.

The **Open** dialog box appears.

**3** Navigate to the **SBS** folder on your hard disk, double-click the **Word** folder, double-click the **CreatingTOC** folder, and then double-click the **TabContents** file.

The TabContents document opens.

Print Layout View

**4** Click the **Print Layout View** button, if necessary, to switch to Print Layout view to see and verify page numbers.

**5** On the **Insert** menu, click **Break** to open the **Break** dialog box, and then click **OK** to start a new page at the beginning of the document.

**6** Press Ctrl+Home to place the insertion point at the beginning of the document.

**7** Type **Table of Contents**, and then press the Enter key.

The insertion point moves down a line on the page.

**8** On the **Insert** menu, point to **Reference**, and then click **Index and Tables**.

The **Index and Tables** dialog box appears.

**9** Click the **Table of Contents** tab to display table of contents settings.

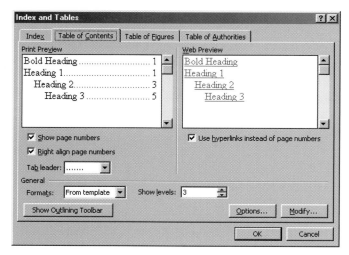

10    Click the **Formats** down arrow, and then click **Distinctive**.

The Distinctive table of contents format appears in the preview box.

11    Click the **Tab leader** down arrow, and then click the dashed line (third item in the list) to display the dashed tab leader in the preview box.

12    Click **Show Outlining Toolbar** to display the Outlining toolbar under the Formatting toolbar in the document window.

13    Click **OK**.

Word inserts a table of contents with the modified Distinctive format.

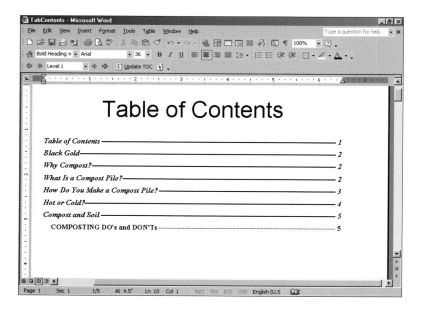

## Tip

If you are working with pictures in your document, you can also use the **Index and Tables** dialog box to create a table of figures. The captions that you associate with each picture are used to create the table of figures, just as headings are used to create the table of contents.

**14** Scroll down to page 2, and then click to the left of the heading *What Is a Compost Pile?*.

**15** On the **Insert** menu, click **Break** to open the **Break** dialog box, and then click **OK** to start a new page.

The heading *What Is a Compost Pile?* is moved to page 3.

**16** Scroll down the page, click to the left of the heading *How Do You Make a Compost Pile?*, and then press ⌨Ctrl+⌨Enter to start a new page.

The heading *How Do You Make a Compost Pile?* is moved to page 4.

**17** Scroll down to page 5, and then select the line *What's the Cost?*.

**18** On the Formatting toolbar, click the **Style** down arrow, and then click **Heading 1**.

The text is changed to the Heading 1 style.

Go to TOC

**19** On the Outlining toolbar, click the **Go to TOC** button to select the table of contents on page 1, and then scroll up to display the entire table.

The entries in the table of contents appear shaded in gray.

Update TOC

**20** On the Outlining toolbar, click the **Update TOC** button.

The **Update Table of Contents** dialog box appears with the **Update page numbers only** option selected.

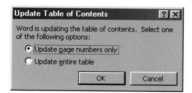

**21** Click the **Update entire table** option, and then click **OK** to update the table of contents with new page numbers and headings.

## Tip

You can also update the table of contents by pressing ⌨F9 or reopening the **Index and Tables** dialog box from the **Insert** menu and then clicking **OK**.

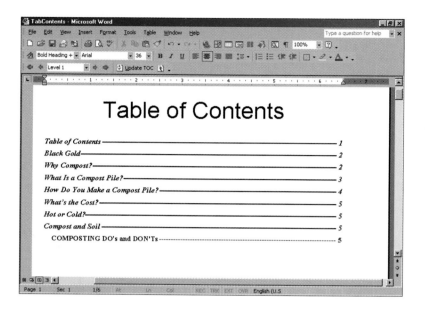

## Tip

If you are working with legal references in a legal document, such as regulations, cases, statutes, and constitutional provisions, you can also use the **Index and Tables** dialog box to create a table of authorities. The legal references that you mark are used to create the table of authorities, just as headings are used to create a table of contents.

**22** On the Standard toolbar, click the **Save** button to save the document.

Close Window

**23** Click the **Close Window** button in the document window.

The TabContents document closes.

# Marking Entries for an Index

W2002e-2-3
W2002e-2-4

Before you can create an index in Word, you must first mark the entries that you want to include in the index. For example, mark names, terms, headings, and other text related to the subject of the document. Choose text that will help readers find every topic in the document. To mark an entry, you select the text and then enter or accept an index entry name. Word then inserts an **XE** (index entry) field code that defines the text and page number for an index entry and other options, such as a subentry text. An XE field code appears as a formatting mark in the document. You need to click the **Show/Hide ¶** button on the Standard toolbar to display or hide the formatting marks.

You can use the **Mark Index Entry** dialog box to mark each index entry individually or to mark each occurrence of the index entry text. After you mark an entry, the **Mark Index Entry** dialog box stays open so that you can select and mark more index entries. You can also format index entries as you mark them; for example, you can underline book titles or make page numbers bold so that they'll appear that way in the index.

In an index, a **cross-reference** indicates another index entry that is related to the current entry. For example, if you look up *narcissus* in an index, it might include a cross-reference such as *See daffodils*. As you create an index, you must anticipate the readers' needs and associate related terms for them. For example, if you were indexing The Garden Company Guide to Lawn & Garden Tools, you might want to cross-reference information about the fuel-air mixture under the index heading about carburetors.

When you mark entries for an index, setting a cross-reference is one option in the **Mark Index Entry** dialog box. By default, the cross-reference text is *See*, but you can type any text, such as *See also*. After the cross-reference text, you type the index entry to which you want to refer readers.

MarkEntry

In this exercise, you format and mark entries, subentries, and cross-references for an index.

**1**  On the Standard toolbar, click the **Open** button.

The **Open** dialog box appears.

Open

**2**  Navigate to the **SBS** folder on your hard disk, double-click the **Word** folder, double-click the **CreatingTOC** folder, and then double-click the **MarkEntry** file.

The MarkEntry document opens.

**3**  In the table of contents, hold down ⌃, and then click the entry *Why Compost?*.

Page 2 appears in the document window.

**4**  In the first sentence below the heading *Why Compost?*, select the word *recycling*.

**5**  On the **Insert** menu, point to **Reference**, and then click **Index and Tables**.

The **Index and Tables** dialog box appears.

**6**  Click the **Index** tab.

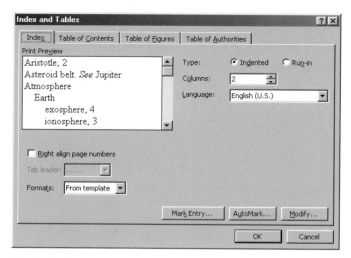

**7** Click **Mark Entry**.

The **Mark Index Entry** dialog box appears, with the word *recycling* in the **Main entry** box.

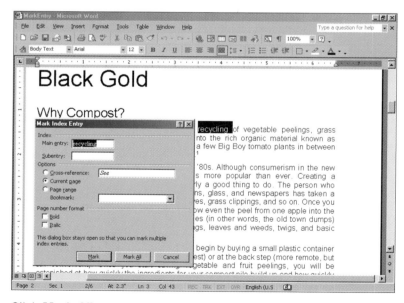

**8** Click **Mark All**.

Formatting marks appear, and all occurrences of the word *recycling* are marked with index entry field codes.

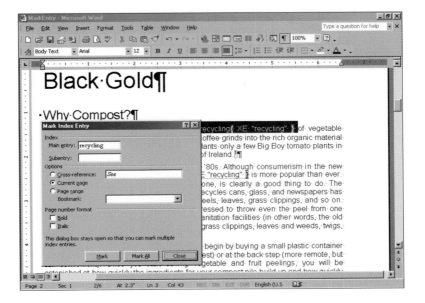

## Tip

**Mark All** is appropriate when you want to index important terms that appear throughout the document. Choose **Mark** when you want to index a single instance of a concept or subtopic.

**9** Click **Close** to close the **Mark Index Entry** dialog box.

Show/Hide ¶

**10** On the Standard toolbar, click the **Show/Hide ¶** button to turn formatting marks off.

**11** Click at the end of the second paragraph (which ends with the word *material*) on page 1 to place the insertion point after the period.

**12** Press <kbd>Alt</kbd>+<kbd>Shift</kbd>+<kbd>X</kbd> to open the **Mark Index Entry** dialog box.

**13** In the **Main entry** box, type **Compost**.

**14** Press the <kbd>Tab</kbd> key to place the insertion point in the **Subentry** box, and then type **Creating**.

**15** Drag the title bar of the **Mark Index Entry** dialog box to the lower-right corner of your screen.

**16** Select the word *ingredients* in the third paragraph (fourth line) on page 2.

**17** Click the title bar in the **Mark Index Entry** dialog box to activate it.

The word *ingredients* appears in the **Main entry** box.

**18** In the **Page number format** area, select the **Bold** check box, and then click **Mark All**.

When Word creates the index, it will show the page number for the *ingredients* entry in bold.

**19** Scroll up, and then select the word *recycles* in the second paragraph (fourth line) on page 2.

**20** Click the title bar in the **Mark Index Entry** dialog box to activate it, and then clear the **Bold** check box in the **Page number format** area to turn off the page number format.

**21** In the **Options** area, click the **Cross-reference** option.

The insertion point moves to the space after the word *See* in the **Cross-reference** box.

**22** Type **recycling**, and then click **Mark**.

A cross-reference to the *recycling* entry appears for the *recycles* index entry. When Word creates the index, it will show *recycles. See recycling*.

**23** Click **Close** to close the **Mark Index Entry** dialog box.

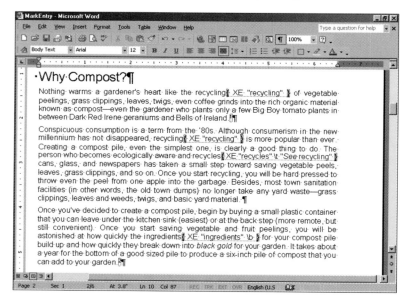

Show/Hide ¶

¶

**24** On the Standard toolbar, click the **Show/Hide ¶** button to turn formatting marks off.

**25** On the Standard toolbar, click the **Save** button to save the document.

Close Window

✕

**26** Click the **Close Window** button in the document window.

The MarkEntry document closes.

# Creating and Modifying an Index

W2002e-2-3

When you finish marking entries, subentries, and cross-references for an index, you're ready to create the index. To create an index, you position the insertion point where you want the index to appear (typically at the end of the document) and then use the **Indexes and Tables** dialog box to format and insert the index. Word creates all the entries, subentries, and cross-references previously marked in the document and displays them in the specified format.

## Tip

To make sure that the document is paginated correctly before you create an index, hide field codes and hidden text. If the XE (index entry) fields are visible, click **Show/ Hide ¶** on the Standard toolbar. To hide field codes, on the **Tools** menu, click **Options**, click the **View** tab, and then clear the **Field codes** check box.

Word provides a number of preset formatting options for indexes, just as it does for tables of contents. You can choose **Classic**, **Fancy**, **Modern**, **Bulleted**, **Formal**, or **Simple**, each of which is visible in the preview box when you select the format. You also determine the format of the **tab leader**, which separates the entry from the page number associated with it. Tab leaders can be dotted, dashed, or solid lines. Finally, you determine whether to use a run-in index or an indented index. An **indented index** lists subentries on separate lines below main entries. A **run-in index** lists subentries on the same line as the main entries.

After you create and insert an index, it is shaded to indicate that it is a single field in Word. To format an index after you create it, you click anywhere in the shaded index area and then format text as you would any other text. You can also use the **Index and Tables** dialog box to apply one of the index formats. To edit the index text, you click in an XE field code to place the insertion point and edit the text as you would other text. To delete an index entry, you can select the XE field code and press the ⌫ key and then recreate the index. You can update the index by clicking in the index and then pressing ⌑ or by opening the **Index and Tables** dialog box and then clicking **OK**.

CreateIndex

In this exercise, you create and format an index, add an entry to the index, and then update the index.

Open

**1**   On the Standard toolbar, click the **Open** button.

The **Open** dialog box appears.

**2**  Navigate to the **SBS** folder on your hard disk, double-click the **Word** folder, double-click the **CreatingTOC** folder, and then double-click the **CreateIndex** file.

The CreateIndex document opens.

**3**  Press ⌷Ctrl⌷+⌷End⌷ to place the insertion point at the end of the document, and then press ⌷Ctrl⌷+⌷Shift⌷+⌷Enter⌷ to insert a new page.

The insertion point moves to the top of the new page.

**4**  Type **Index**, press ⌷Enter⌷ twice, and then select the word *Index*.

Bold

**B**

**5**  On the Formatting toolbar, click the **Bold** button, click the **Font Size** down arrow, and then click **18** to format the word *Index*.

**6**  Press the ⌷↓⌷ key twice.

The insertion point moves down to line 3 on the page.

**7**  On the **Insert** menu, point to **Reference**, and then click **Index and Tables**.

The **Index and Tables** dialog box appears.

**8**  Click the **Index** tab, if necessary, to display index settings.

**9**  Click the **Formats** down arrow, and then click **Formal** to select the pre-defined index format.

**10**  Clear the **Right Align Page Numbers** check box to move the page number alignment to the left near the index entry.

**11**  In the **Type** area, click the **Run-in** option to wrap subentry text in the index.

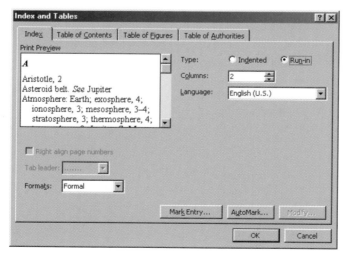

The preview box displays a sample of the format.

**12**  Click the **Columns** down arrow until **1** appears in the box.

**13** In the **Type** area, click the **Indented** option.

The preview box displays a sample of the format.

**14** Click **OK**.

The index appears in one column.

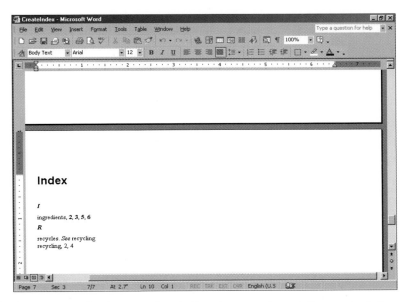

**15** Scroll up to the last section in the document, and then select the word *compost* (third line from the end).

**16** On the **Insert** menu, point to **Reference**, and click **Index and Tables**.

The **Index and Tables** dialog box appears.

**17** Click the **Index** tab, if necessary, and then click **Mark Entry**.

The **Mark Index Entry** dialog box appears, with the word *compost* in the **Main entry** box.

**18** Click **Mark All**, and then click **Close** to close the **Mark Index Entry** dialog box.

All occurrences of the word *compost* are marked for the index.

**19** Press [Ctrl]+[End] to place the insertion point at the end of the document.

**20** Click anywhere in the index, press [F9], and then click in a blank area of the screen to deselect the index.

The index is updated with the new entry for *compost*.

Show/Hide ¶

¶

**21** On the Standard toolbar, click the **Show/Hide ¶** button to turn formatting marks off.

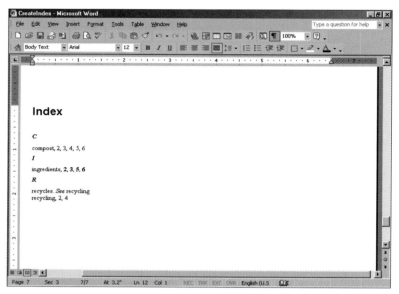

**22** On the Standard toolbar, click the **Save** button to save the document.

Close Window
☒

**23** Click the **Close Window** button in the document window.

The CreateIndex document closes.

# Chapter Wrap-Up

To finish this chapter:

Close
☒

● On the **File** menu, click **Exit**, or click the **Close** button in the Word window.

Word closes.

# Quick Reference

**14    To edit text**

**1**    Select the text or click to place the insertion point where you want to edit.

**2**    Press <kbd>Del</kbd> or <kbd>Backspace</kbd> to delete text, and then retype the text.

**14    To close a document**

Close Window
<kbd>X</kbd>

●    On the **File** menu, click **Close**, or click the **Close Window** button in the document window

**19    To find and replace text**

**1**    On the **Edit** menu, click **Replace** to open the **Find and Replace** dialog box.

**2**    In the **Find what** box, type the text you want to find.

**3**    Press <kbd>Tab</kbd> to move the insertion point to the **Replace with** box, type the text you want to use instead, if desired, and then click **Find Next**.

**4**    Click **Replace** or **Replace All** to replace text or **Find Next** to find text.

**5**    Click **OK**, and then click the **Close** button.

**Chapter    2    Changing the Look of Text in a Document**

Page    **23    To change the appearance of text**

**1**    Select the text you want to change.

**2**    On the Formatting toolbar, click a formatting button, or on the **Format** menu, click **Reveal Formatting** to open the **Reveal Formatting** task pane, and then use the links to open dialog boxes and make changes.

**28    To insert an AutoText entry**

●    On the **Insert** menu, point to **AutoText**, point to a category, and then click an entry.

**33    To format a paragraph**

**1**    Click in the paragraph or select any part of it.

**2**    Apply the formats that you want from the toolbars, or on the **Format** menu, click **Paragraph** to open the **Paragraph** dialog box, and then make changes.

**41    To create a bulleted or numbered list**

**1**    Select the text.

**2**    On the Formatting toolbar, click the **Numbering** button or the **Bullets** button, or on the **Format** menu, click **Bullets and Numbering** to display the **Bullets and Numbering** dialog box, click a tab, and then click a bullet or numbering style.

**Chapter 3 Changing the Look of a Document**

Page 46 **To create a new template based on an existing Word template**

**1** On the **View** menu, click **Task Pane**, if necessary, to display the **New Document** task pane.

**2** In the **New Document** task pane, click **General Templates** in the **New from template** section.

**3** Click a tab, click a template icon, and then click **OK**.

**4** Enter information in the document placeholders.

**5** On the **File** menu, click **Save As.**

**6** In the **File name** box, type a new name, and then click **Save**.

50 **To change line and page break options**

**1** On the **Format** menu, click **Paragraph** to display the **Paragraph** dialog box, and then click the **Line and Page Breaks** tab, if necessary.

**2** Select the **Widow/Orphan control** check box, if desired, select the **Keep lines together** check box, if desired, and then click **OK**.

**3** On the **Insert** menu, click **Break** to open the **Break** dialog box.

**4** Select the option(s) you want, and then click **OK**.

50 **To add a header or footer to a document**

**1** On the **View** menu, click **Header and Footer**.

**2** Using the Header and Footer toolbar to move around and make selections, type header and/or footer text.

**3** Use the Header and Footer toolbar to format and change the header and/or footer text.

**4** On the Header and Footer toolbar, click the **Close** button.

56 **To open and use the Styles and Formatting task pane to change styles**

**1** Select the text you want to style.

**2** On the **Format** menu, click **Styles and Formatting** to open the **Styles and Formatting** task pane.

**3** In the **Styles and Formatting** task pane, point to the preview box in the **Formatting of selected text** section to display information about the current style.

**4** In the **Styles and Formatting** task pane, click an option from the **Pick formatting to apply** section, or click **New Style**, and then define a new style with the options in the **New Style** dialog box.

60  **To apply a theme to an existing document**

**1**  On the **Format** menu, click **Theme**.

**2**  In the **Choose a Theme** list, click a theme.

**3**  Select the **Vivid Colors** check box, if desired, to brighten the colors in the theme.

**4**  Click **OK**.

**Chapter  4  Proofreading and Printing a Document**

Page  63  **To check the spelling and grammar in a document**

Spelling and Grammar

ABC✓

**1**  On the Standard toolbar, click the **Spelling and Grammar** button.

**2**  Use the **Spelling and Grammar** dialog box to respond to text that is flagged.

**3**  Click **OK** to close the alert message that Word has finished checking the spelling and grammar in the document.

69  **To preview a document**

Print Preview

●  On the Standard toolbar, click the **Print Preview** button.

69  **To print a document**

**1**  On the **File** menu, click **Print**.

**2**  In the **Print** dialog box, select a printer, and then choose the print options you want to use.

**3**  Click **OK**.

69  **To print an envelope or label to accompany a letter document**

**1**  Select the inside address at the top of the document.

**2**  On the **Tools** menu, point to **Letters and Mailings**, and then click **Envelopes and Labels**.

**3**  In the **Envelopes and Labels** dialog box, click the **Envelopes** tab or **Labels** tab, select the options you want to use, and then click **Print**.

**Chapter  5  Presenting Information in Tables and Columns**

Page  76  **To create a new table**

**1**  Click in the document to place the insertion point where you want to create a table.

**2**  On the **Table** menu, point to **Insert**, and then click **Table**.

**3**  Type the number of columns and rows you want to use, and then click **OK**.

**4**    Click in a cell and type your text. Use the ⌨ key to navigate from cell to cell.

**5**    Use buttons on the Tables and Borders toolbar (such as **Merge Cells**, **Split Cells**, **Align**, or **Distribute**) to format and modify the table or individual cells.

76  **To convert existing plain text to a table**

**1**    Select the block of text that you want to convert to a table.

**2**    On the **Table** menu, point to **Convert**, and then click **Text to Table**.

**3**    Type the number of columns you want to use, and then click **OK**.

76  **To sort information in a table**

**1**    Click in the table to place the insertion point in the column where you want to the sort information.

**2**    On the **Table** menu, click **Sort**.

**3**    In the **Sort** dialog box, select the options you want to use, and then click **OK**.

82  **To format text in a table**

**1**    In Print Layout view, select the table text that you want to format.

**2**    Use the Formatting toolbar, the Tables and Borders toolbar, and the **Format** menu to make changes to the text and the table.

85  **To calculate data in a table**

**1**    Click in the table to place the insertion point.

**2**    On the **Table** menu, click **Formula** to display the **Formula** dialog box.

**3**    In the **Formula** dialog box, use the current formula or select another one, and then click **OK**.

85  **To embed an Excel worksheet in a Word document**

**1**    Click in the document to place the insertion point where you want to embed the Excel worksheet.

**2**    On the **Insert** menu, click **Object** to open the **Object** dialog box, and then click the **Create from File** tab.

**3**    Click **Browse**, navigate to the Excel worksheet you want to embed, click the file, and then click **OK**.

89  **To format text into columns**

**1**    On the **Format** menu, click **Columns**.

**2**    In the **Columns** dialog box, type the number of columns you want to use, and then click **OK**.

**Chapter  6  Working with Graphics**

Page  93  **To insert and modify an organization chart**

1    Click in the document to place the insertion point where you want to insert the organization chart.

Insert Diagram
or Organiza-
tion Chart

2    On the Drawing toolbar, click the **Insert Diagram or Organization Chart** button.

3    Click the organization chart icon, and then click **OK**.

4    For each entry on the chart, click a text box, and then type text.

5    Use the Organization Chart toolbar to modify the organization chart.

96  **To search for, insert, and modify clip art**

Insert Clip Art

1    On the Drawing toolbar, click the **Insert Clip Art** button.

2    In the **Insert Clip Art** task pane, type a word in the **Search text** box, and then click **Search**.

3    In the **Results** list, click a picture, and then click the **Close** button to close the **Insert Clip Art** task pane.

4    Drag the sizing handles to resize the picture, if necessary.

5    Use the Picture toolbar to modify the clip art.

96  **To insert and modify a picture**

1    Click in the document to place the insertion point where you want to insert the picture.

2    On the **Insert** menu, point to **Picture**, and then click **From File**.

3    Navigate to the file you want to insert, and then double-click the picture to insert it.

4    Drag the sizing handles to resize the picture, if necessary.

5    Use the Picture toolbar to modify the picture.

101  **To modify the placement and text wrapping attributes of a picture**

1    Click the picture you want to modify.

2    On the **Format** menu, click **Picture**.

3    In the **Format Picture** dialog box, click the **Layout** tab, and then click **Advanced**.

4    In the **Advanced Layout** dialog box, on the **Text Wrapping** tab, select the placement and text wrapping options you want to use, and then click **OK**.

5    Click **OK** to close the **Format Picture** dialog box.

**To insert and modify WordArt**

Insert WordArt

**1** On the Drawing toolbar, click the **Insert WordArt** button.

**2** In the **WordArt Gallery** dialog box, click a WordArt style, and then click **OK**.

**3** In the **Edit WordArt Text** dialog box, type your text, and then select the formatting options you want.

**4** Click **OK**.

**5** Use the WordArt toolbar to modify the object.

**To open a drawing canvas and draw a shape**

**1** On the Drawing toolbar, click a shape button.

**2** Drag to draw a shape.

**To modify a shape**

**1** Click the shape to select it.

**2** Use the Drawing toolbar and the Drawing Canvas toolbar to modify the shape.

**Chapter 7 Working with Charts**

**To add a chart to a document**

**1** Click in the document to place the insertion point where you want to add the chart.

**2** On the **Insert** menu, point to **Picture**, and then click **Chart**.

**3** Drag the title bar of the datasheet window so that it is positioned below the sample chart, if necessary.

**4** Click the **Select All** button on the datasheet (the upper-left button), and then press ⎣Del⎦.

**5** Click in the cells and type your text, using the ⎣Enter⎦ and ⎣Tab⎦ keys to move from cell to cell.

**To modify the appearance of a chart**

**1** Double-click the chart in the document to activate it.

Chart Type

**2** On the Standard toolbar, click the **Chart Type** down arrow, and then click a chart type.

**3** Use the resize handles on the borders of the chart to modify the size of the chart.

**4** Click to select various chart areas and use Graph's Formatting toolbar and menus to modify color, fills effects, gridlines, legend, and other chart items.

**124**   **To import data into a chart**

1   Double-click the chart in the document to activate it.

2   If necessary, drag the datasheet to position it below the chart.

3   Drag to select the area in the datasheet where you want to import the data.

Import File

4   On the Standard toolbar, click the **Import File** button.

5   Navigate to the file you want to import, and then double-click the file.

6   If necessary, choose the data that you want to import from the **Import Data Options** dialog box.

7   Clear the **Overwrite existing cells** check box to prevent the incoming data from overwriting the existing chart data, if desired.

8   Click **OK**.

**Chapter   8**   **Collaborating with Others**

**Page   130**   **To track changes**

1   On the **View** menu, point to **Toolbars**, and then click **Reviewing**.

Track Changes

2   On the Reviewing toolbar, click the **Track Changes** button.

**130**   **To accept or reject tracked changes**

1   On the **View** menu, point to **Toolbars**, and then click **Reviewing**.

2   On the Reviewing toolbar, click the **Next** button to select the next change in the document.

Reject
Change/Delete
Comment

3   To accept or reject individual changes, on the Reviewing toolbar, click the **Accept Change** button to accept the change or the **Reject Change/Delete Comment** button to reject the change and delete any accompanying comment.

4   To accept all changes at once, on the Reviewing toolbar, click the **Accept Change** down arrow, and then click **Accept All Changes in Document**.

**136**   **To merge a document with other versions of the document**

1   Open the original document.

2   On the **Tools** menu, click **Compare and Merge Documents**.

3   In the **Compare and Merge Documents** dialog box, navigate to the folder containing other versions of the document.

4   Click the file for another version of the document, click the **Merge** down arrow, and then click **Merge into current document**.

**136**  **To compare merged documents**

**1**  On the Reviewing toolbar, click the **Show** down arrow, point to **Reviewers**, and then click one of the reviewers to hide their revisions, click **All Reviewers** to view revisions made by all reviewers, or click **Formatting** to view only insertions and deletions, not formatting changes.

**2**  Use the Reviewing toolbar to accept or reject tracked changes.

**3**  On the Reviewing toolbar, click the **Display for Review** down arrow, and then click **Final Showing Markup** to view the document with all the revision marks or click **Final** to view the document with all the current changes and without the revision marks.

**139**  **To show and review comments**

Web Layout View

**1**  Click the **Web Layout View** button to switch to Web Layout view.

**2**  On the **View** menu, click **Markup** to show comments and changes and to display the Reviewing toolbar.

Next

**3**  On the Reviewing toolbar, click the **Next** button to display the next comment in the document.

Reviewing Pane

**4**  On the Reviewing toolbar, click the **Reviewing Pane** button to open the **Reviewing Pane**.

**5**  Make changes to comments directly in the **Reviewing Pane**.

**6**  On the Reviewing toolbar, click the **Reviewing Pane** button to close the **Reviewing Pane**.

**139**  **To add or delete a comment**

New Comment

**1**  On the Reviewing toolbar, click the **New Comment** button.

**2**  In the comment balloon, type your text.

**3**  Click a blank area of the document to deselect the comment.

**4**  To delete a comment, right-click anywhere on text with a comment, and then click **Delete Comment**.

**144**  **To set a password for a document**

**1**  On the **Tools** menu, click **Options**.

**2**  In the **Options** dialog box, click the **Security** tab to display security options.

**3**  In the **Password to modify** box or **Password to open** box, type a password.

**4**  Click **OK** to close the **Options** dialog box.

**5**  In the **Confirm Password** dialog box, retype your password, and then click **OK**.

147 **To send a document for review via e-mail**

**1** Open the document you want to send out for review.

**2** On the **File** menu, point to **Send To**, and then click **Mail Recipient (for Review).**

**3** Click **OK** if the **Choose Profile** dialog box opens.

**4** Click in the **To** box, if necessary, and then type an e-mail address.

**5** Click anywhere in the message pane, and then type a message.

**6** On the Message toolbar, click the **Send** button.

Chapter 9 **Working with Documents on the Web**

Page 152 **To change Web browser options**

**1** On the **Tools** menu, click **Options**.

**2** Click the **General** tab, and then click **Web Options**.

**3** Click the **Browser** tab, if necessary, click the **People who view this Web page will be using** down arrow, and then click a browser.

**4** In the **Options** list, verify that the **Disable features not supported by these browsers** check box is selected, and then click **OK** to close the **Web Options** dialog box.

**5** Click **OK** to close the **Options** dialog box.

152 **To save a document as a Web page**

**1** On the **File** menu, click **Save as Web Page**.

**2** Navigate to the folder in which you want to save the Web page, and then type the file name in the **File name** box.

**3** Click the **Save as type** down arrow, and then click **Web Page**.

**4** Click **Save**, and then click **Continue** when the message box appears.

152 **To insert a hyperlink into a document**

**1** Select the text or object to which you want to add a hyperlink.

Insert
Hyperlink

**2** On the Standard toolbar, click the **Insert Hyperlink** button.

**3** In the **Insert Hyperlink** dialog box, click a file in the list of folders and file names, and then click **Target Frame**.

**4** Click **OK** to accept the default settings in the **Set Target Frame** dialog box, and then click **OK** to close the **Insert Hyperlink** dialog box.

162 **To open a Web document in Word and modify it**

Open

1 On the Standard toolbar, click the **Open** button.
2 Navigate to the Web document file, and then double-click the file.
3 Add, delete, or modify the existing text.
4 On the Standard toolbar, click the **Save** button to save the Web document.
5 Click the **Close Window** button in the document window.

163 **To assign a digital signature to a Web document**

1 Install and run the **Sertcert.exe** file.
2 Open the Web document to which you want to add a signature.
3 On the **Tools** menu, point to **Macro**, and then click **Visual Basic Editor**.
4 In the Project window, under **Project (WebSignature)**, click **ThisDocument**, if necessary, to select the current document in Word.
5 If a window is open in the right pane of the Visual Basic Editor window, click its **Close** button to close it.
6 On the **Tools** menu in the Visual Basic Editor window, click **Digital Signature**.
7 In the **Digital Signature** dialog box, click **Choose**, select a certificate in the list, and then click **View Certificate**.
8 Click **OK** to close the **Certificate** dialog box, and then click **OK** to close the **Select Certificate** dialog box.
9 Click **OK** to close the **Digital Signature** dialog box, and then click the **Close** button in the Visual Basic Editor window.

163 **To assign a digital signature to a document**

1 Install and run the **Sertcert.exe** file.
2 Open the document to which you want to add a signature.
3 On the **Tools** menu, click **Options**, and then click the **Security** tab.
4 In the **Options** dialog box, click **Digital Signatures**.
5 In the **Digital Signatures** dialog box, click **Add**.
6 In the **Select Certificate** dialog box, select a certificate in the list, and then click **OK** to close the **Select Certificate** dialog box.
7 Click **OK** to close the **Digital Signature** dialog box, and then click **OK** to close the **Options** dialog box.

**Chapter 10**   **Customizing Word for the Way You Work**

Page    169    **To customize menus**

**1**    On the **Tools** menu, click **Customize** to open the **Customize** dialog box, and then click the **Options** tab, if necessary.

**2**    Click **Reset my usage data**, and then click **Yes** to reset Word menus and toolbars to their default settings, if necessary.

**3**    Click the **Commands** tab, and then click an option in the **Categories** list.

**4**    In the **Commands** list, click a command, and then drag it to a menu and place it in the list of menu commands before releasing the mouse button.

**5**    Drag any menu command to a blank area of the screen to remove it.

**6**    Click **Close** to close the **Customize** dialog box.

169    **To create a custom menu**

**1**    On the **Tools** menu, click **Customize** to open the **Customize** dialog box.

**2**    Click the **Commands** tab, scroll down to the end of the **Categories** list, and then click **New Menu**.

**3**    Drag **New Menu** from the **Commands** list to the right end of the Word menu bar next to the **Help** menu.

**4**    On the menu bar, right-click **New Menu**.

**5**    In the **Name** box on the shortcut menu, select the text *New Menu*, type the new menu name, and press ⏎ Enter .

**6**    On the menu bar, click the new menu.

**7**    In the **Categories** list of the **Customize** dialog box, click a category.

**8**    In the **Commands** list, drag commands onto the new empty menu.

**9**    Click **Close** to close the **Customize** dialog box.

174    **To customize a toolbar**

Toolbar Options

**1**    On the right edge of a toolbar, click the **Toolbar Options** button.

**2**    Point to **Add or Remove Buttons**, and then point to a toolbar to see all the possible buttons that you can assign to that toolbar.

**3**    Click a button to add it to or remove it from the toolbar.

174 **To create a custom toolbar**

**1** Right-click any toolbar, and then click **Customize** to open the **Customize** dialog box.

**2** Click the **Toolbars** tab, and then click **New** to open the **New Toolbar** dialog box.

**3** In the **Toolbar name** box, type a new name.

**4** Click the **Make toolbar available to** down arrow, click **CustomToolbar** to make the new toolbar available only to this document, and then click **OK**.

**5** In the **Customize** dialog box, click the **Commands** tab.

**6** In the **Categories** list of the **Customize** dialog box, click a category.

**7** In the **Commands** list, drag commands onto the new blank toolbar.

**8** Click **Close** to close the **Customize** dialog box.

179 **To create a macro**

**1** Click in the document to place the insertion point where you want to add the macro in the document.

**2** On the **Tools** menu, point to **Macro**, and then click **Record New Macro** to open the **Record Macro** dialog box.

**3** In the **Macro name** box, type a name.

**4** Click the **Store macro in** down arrow, and then click the current document name.

**5** Click the **Keyboard** button to open the **Customize Keyboard** dialog box, press any key combination to place the key combination in the **Press new shortcut key** box, click **Assign**, and then click **Close**.

**6** Perform the actions that you want to record as a macro.

Stop Recording

**7** On the Macro toolbar, click the **Stop Recording** button.

182 **To run a macro**

**1** On the **Tools** menu, point to **Macro**, and then click **Macros**.

**2** In the list of macros, click the name of a macro, and then click **Run**.

182  **To edit an existing macro**

**1**   On the **Tools** menu, point to **Macro**, and then click **Macros** to open the **Macros** dialog box.

**2**   Select a macro from the list of macros, and then click **Edit**.

**3**   Click the NewMacros (Code) window, if necessary, to activate the window.

**4**   Add, delete, or modify macro language text.

**5**   On the **File** menu, click **Close and Return to Microsoft Word**.

**Chapter 11**   **Creating Form Letters and Labels**

Page   187   **To start the Mail Merge Wizard**

**1**   On the **Tools** menu, point to **Letters and Mailings**, and then click **Mail Merge Wizard**.

**2**   The **Mail Merge** task pane appears, showing the first step in the mail merge process. Follow the steps in the task pane to complete the mail merge.

190   **To select and edit a data document for a merge**

**1**   In the **Mail Merge** task pane, click a document type option, and then click **Next: Starting document** at the bottom of the pane to move to Step 2.

**2**   In the **Mail Merge** task pane, click the **Use the current document** option, if necessary, and then click **Next: Select recipients** at the bottom of the pane to move to Step 3.

**3**   In the **Mail Merge** task pane, click the **Use an existing list** option, if necessary, and then click **Browse** in the **Use an existing list** section to open the **Select Data Source** dialog box.

**4**   Navigate to the folder that contains the data source, and then double-click the file.

**5**   In the **Mail Merge Recipients** dialog box, click a field, and then click **Edit** to open the **Data Form** dialog box.

**6**   Click **Add New**, if necessary, to clear the data field so that you can add a new record, and then type in the information.

**7**   Add, delete, or modify the current records in the **Data Form** dialog box.

**8**   Click **Close** to close the **Data Form** dialog box.

**9**   Click **OK** to close the **Mail Merge Recipients** dialog box.

Save

**10**   On the Standard toolbar, click the **Save** button to save the document.

**11**   Click the **Close Window** button in the document window, and then click **Yes** to save the data document, if necessary.

**194** **To select and sort data for a form letter**

**1** In the **Mail Merge** task pane, click the **Next** link until Step 3 of 6 appears in the wizard.

**2** In the **Use an existing list** section, click **Select a different list** to open the **Select Data Source** dialog box and double-click the new data file, or select **Edit recipient list**.

**3** In the **Mail Merge Recipients** dialog box, click one of the down arrows, and then click **Advanced** to open the **Query Options** dialog box.

**4** Click the **Sort Records** tab, and then define sorting criteria.

**5** Click the **Filter Records** tab, and then define filtering criteria.

**6** Click **OK** to close the **Query Options** dialog box.

**197** **To modify a form letter**

**1** In the **Mail Merge** task pane, click the **Next** link until Step 4 of 6 appears in the wizard.

Show/Hide ¶

**2** On the Standard toolbar, click the **Show/Hide ¶** button to show formatting marks, if necessary.

**3** In the document window, click a location in the document, and then click one of the options in the task pane under **Write your letter**.

**4** Click **OK** to accept the default settings.

**5** Continue to select locations in the document and insert merge fields from the options in the task pane.

**6** On the Standard toolbar, click the **Show/Hide ¶** button to hide formatting marks, if necessary.

**200** **To merge data with a form letter**

**1** In the **Mail Merge** task pane, click **Next** until Step 5 of 6 appears in the wizard.

Right arrow

**2** In the **Mail Merge** task pane, click the **Right arrow** button to display and review the next data recipient in the merged letter.

**3** In the **Mail Merge** task pane, click **Next: Complete the merge** to proceed to Step 6 of 6.

**4** In the **Mail Merge** task pane, click **Edit individual letters** in the merge section.

**5** In the **Merge to New Document** dialog box, click the **All** option, and then click **OK**.

**203** **To create and print labels**

**1** In the **Mail Merge** task pane, click the **Labels** option, and then click **Next: Starting document** to proceed to Step 2 of 6.

**2** In the **Mail Merge** task pane, click the **Change document layout** option, if necessary, and then click the **Labels** options in the **Change document layout** section.

**3** In the **Label Options** dialog box, click an option in the **Product number** list, and then click **OK**.

**4** In the **Mail Merge** task pane, click **Next: Select recipients** to proceed to Step 3 of 6.

**5** In the **Mail Merge** task pane, click **Use an exisiting list**, if necessary, and then click **Browse** to open the **Select Data Source** dialog box.

**6** Double-click the data source file you want to use.

**7** In the **Mail Merge Recipients** dialog box, select the recipient check boxes you want in the first column, if necessary, and then click **OK**.

**8** In the **Mail Merge** task pane, click **Next: Arrange your labels** to proceed to Step 4 of 6.

**9** With the insertion point positioned in the upper-left address label in the main document window, click **Address block** to open the **Insert Address Block** dialog box.

**10** Click **OK** to accept the default settings and to close the **Insert Address Block** dialog box.

**11** In the **Mail Merge** task pane, click the **Update all labels** button in the **Replicate labels** section.

**12** In the **Mail Merge** task pane, click **Next: Preview your labels** to proceed to Step 5 of 6.

**13** In the **Mail Merge** task pane, click **Next: Complete the merge**.

**14** In the **Mail Merge** task pane, click **Print**.

**15** Click **OK** to open the **Print** dialog box, select a printer, and then click **OK**.

**Chapter 12** **Creating Forms**

**Page 210** **To create a text form field in a form document**

**1** On the **View** menu, point to **Toolbars**, and then click **Forms**.

**2** Click in the document to place the insertion point where you want to add a form field.

Text Form Field  **3** On the Forms toolbar, click the **Text Form Field** button.

Form Field
Options

**4** On the Forms toolbar, click the **Form Field Options** button.

**5** In the **Text Form Field Options** dialog box, click the **Type** down arrow, and then click a type.

**6** Click **OK**.

Page   210   **To create a check box form field in a form document**

**1** On the **View** menu, point to **Toolbars**, and then click **Forms**.

**2** Click in the document to place the insertion point where you want to add a check box form field.

Check Box
Form Field

**ab|**

**3** On the Forms toolbar, click the **Check Box Form Field** button.

**4** On the Forms toolbar, click the **Form Field Options** button.

**5** In the **Check box size** area, click an option, and then click the up or down arrow until the point size you want appears.

**6** Click **OK**.

Page   210   **To create a drop-down form field in a form document**

**1** On the **View** menu, point to **Toolbars**, and then click **Forms**.

**2** Click in the document to place the insertion point where you want to add a drop-down form field.

Drop-Down
Form Field

**3** On the Forms toolbar, click the **Drop-Down Form Field** button.

**4** On the Forms toolbar, click the **Form Field Options** button.

**5** In the **Drop-down** item box, type your text, and then click **Add**.

**6** Continue to add text to the drop-down item box, and then click **OK**.

216   **To modify a form document**

**1** On the **View** menu, point to **Toolbars**, and then click **Forms**.

**2** Select the form field you want to modify.

**3** On the Forms toolbar, click the **Form Field Options** button.

**4** In the **Form Field Options** dialog box, select form field options, and then click **OK**.

**5** Use the Formatting toolbar to change the formatting of the form field.

216   **To protect a form document**

**1** On the **View** menu, point to **Toolbars**, and then click **Forms**.

Protect Form

**2** On the Forms toolbar, click the **Protect Form** button.

**Chapter 13**   **Working with Footnotes and Bookmarks**

**Page**   **224**   **To add a footnote**

**1**   Click in the document to place the insertion point where you want to add a footnote.

**2**   On the **Insert** menu, point to **Reference**, and then click **Footnote**.

**3**   In the **Footnote and Endnote** dialog box, click the **Footnotes** option in the **Location** area, if necessary.

**4**   In the **Format** area, click the **Number format** down arrow, and then click an option to select a new number format.

**5**   Click **Insert**, and then type the footnote text.

**6**   In the Notes pane, click **Close**.

224   **To add an endnote**

**1**   Click in the document to place the insertion point where you want to add an endnote.

**2**   On the **Insert** menu, point to **Reference**, and then click **Footnote**.

**3**   In the **Footnote and Endnote** dialog box, click the **Endnotes** option in the **Location** area, if necessary.

**4**   In the **Format** area, click the **Number format** down arrow, click an option, and then click **Insert**.

**5**   Type the endnote text.

224   **To convert an endnote to a footnote**

**1**   Right-click anywhere in the endnote to open a shortcut menu.

**2**   Click **Convert to Footnote**.

227   **To browse for footnotes**

**1**   Click the **Print Layout View** button.

Select Browse
Object

**2**   Click the **Select Browse Object** button at the bottom of the vertical scroll bar to display a menu of browsing options.

**3**   On the **Select Browse Object** menu, click the **Browse by Footnote** icon.

**4**   Click the **Next Footnote** button at the bottom of the vertical scroll bar.

227   **To view a specific footnote or endnote**

**1**   On the **Edit** menu, click **Go To**.

**2**   In the **Find and Replace** dialog box, click **Footnote** or **Endnote** in the **Go to what** list.

**3** In the **Enter footnote number** box or **Enter endnote number** box, type the note number that you want to go to.

**4** Click **Go To**.

**5** In the **Find and Replace** dialog box, click **Close**.

227 **To format footnotes and endnotes**

**1** On the **Insert** menu, point to **Reference**, and then click **Footnote or Endnote**.

**2** In the **Footnote and Endnote** dialog box, make changes in the **Format** area, and then select where you want to apply the changes in the **Apply changes** area.

**3** Click **Apply** to close the **Footnote and Endnote** dialog box.

**4** On the **Format** menu, click **Styles and Formatting** to open the **Styles and Formatting** task pane. Use this task pane to make changes to one or all of the notes in the document.

227 **To revise footnotes and endnotes**

● To move a note, in the main document window, select the reference mark, and then drag it to a new location.

● To copy a note, select a reference mark, hold down the Ctrl key, and then drag the copied reference mark to a new location.

● To delete a note, select a reference mark, and then press Del.

232 **To modify the note separator**

Normal View

**1** Click the **Normal View** button, if necessary, to switch to Normal view.

**2** On the **View** menu, click **Footnotes** to open the Notes pane.

**3** In the Notes pane, click the **Footnotes** down arrow, and then click **Footnote Separator**.

**4** In the Notes pane, type to add text to the note separator.

**5** Click **Close** to close the Notes pane.

234 **To insert to a bookmark**

**1** On the **Insert**, menu, click **Bookmark**.

**2** In the **Bookmark name** box, type bookmark text.

**3** Click **Add**.

### 234   **To navigate to a bookmark**

**1**    Press <kbd>Ctrl</kbd>+<kbd>Home</kbd> to place the insertion point at the beginning of the document.

**2**    On the **Insert** menu, click **Bookmark**.

**3**    In the **Bookmark** dialog box, select the boomark to which you want to navigate, and then click **Go To**.

**4**    Click **Close** to close the **Bookmark** dialog box.

### 234   **To jump to a heading in a document with the Document Map**

**1**    On the **View** menu, click **Document Map**.

**2**    In the left pane of the **Document Map**, click a heading.

**3**    On the **View** menu, click **Document Map** to return to the previous view.

### 236   **To create a master document with subdocuments**

Outline View

**1**    Click the **Outline View** button.

**2**    On the Outlining toolbar, use the **Promote** button or **Demote** button to designate a heading, such as level one or level two.

**3**    Click the plus sign next to the heading in which you want to create a subdocument to select the heading and all its associated body text.

Create Subdocument

**4**    On the Outlining toolbar, click the **Create Subdocument** button.

**5**    Repeat steps 3 and 4 to create more subdocuments.

Collapse Subdocuments

**6**    On the Outlining toolbar, click the **Collapse Subdocuments** button, and then click **OK**. The subdocuments appear as hyperlinks.

### 236   **To open and modify subdocuments**

**1**    Open a master document, hold down <kbd>Ctrl</kbd>, and then click a subdocument hyperlink to open the subdocument in its own document window.

**2**    Select text in the document, and then use the toolbars to modify the text.

Save

**3**    On the Standard toolbar, click the **Save** button, and then click the **Close Window** button to save and close the subdocument.

Expand Subdocuments

**4**    On the Outlining toolbar, click the **Expand Subdocuments** button to merge the subdocuments back into the master document.

**5**    On the Standard toolbar, click the **Save** button to save the document, and then click the **Close Window** button in the document window.

**Chapter 14**   **Working with Tables of Contents and Indexes**

**Page    242**   **To create a table of contents**

    **1**    Open a document that uses heading styles.

Print Layout
View

□

    **2**    Click the **Print Layout View** button.

    **3**    On the **Insert** menu, point to **Reference**, and then click **Index and Tables**.

    **4**    Click the **Table of Contents** tab to display table of contents settings.

    **5**    Click the **Formats** down arrow, and then click a format option.

    **6**    Click the **Tab leader** down arrow, and then select a tab leader option.

    **7**    Click **OK**.

**246**   **To mark entries for an index**

    **1**    Select a word within the document you want to mark.

    **2**    On the **Insert** menu, point to **Reference**, and then click **Index and Tables** to open the **Index and Tables** dialog box.

    **3**    Click the **Index** tab, and then click **Mark Entry**.

    **4**    In the **Mark Index Entry** dialog box, click **Mark All**.

    **5**    Click **Close** to close the **Mark Index Entry** dialog box.

**246**   **To mark entries and subentries for an index**

    **1**    Select a word within the document you want to mark.

    **2**    On the **Insert** menu, point to **Reference**, and then click **Index and Tables** to open the **Index and Tables** dialog box.

    **3**    Click the **Index** tab, and then click **Mark Entry**.

    **4**    Press ⇥ to place the insertion point in the **Subentry** box, and then type a word related to the word in the **Main entry** box.

    **5**    In the **Mark Index Entry** dialog box, click **Mark All**.

    **6**    Click **Close** to close the **Mark Index Entry** dialog box.

**246**   **To mark a cross-reference for an index**

    **1**    Select a word within the document that you want to cross-reference.

    **2**    On the **Insert** menu, point to **Reference**, and then click **Index and Tables** to open the **Index and Tables** dialog box.

    **3**    Click the **Index** tab, and then click **Mark Entry**.

    **4**    In the **Options** area, click the **Cross-reference** option, type the cross-reference word, and then click **Mark**.

    **5**    Click **Close** to close the **Mark Index Entry** dialog box.

246 **To format entires, subentries, or cross-references for an index**

1 Select the entry, subentry, or cross-reference within the document you want to format.

2 Press [Ctrl]+[Shift]+[X] to open the **Mark Index Entry** dialog box.

3 In the **Page number format** area, select the **Bold** check box or the **Italic** check box, and then click **Mark All**.

4 Click **Close** to close the **Mark Index Entry** dialog box.

251 **To create and format an index**

1 Click in the document to place the insertion point where you want the index to start.

2 On the **Insert** menu, point to **Reference**, and then click **Index and Tables**.

3 In the **Index and Tables** dialog box, click the **Index** tab, if necessary, to display index settings.

4 Click the **Formats** down arrow, and then select a predefined index format.

5 In the **Type** area, click the **Run-in** or the **Indented** option.

6 Continue to select options in the **Index and Tables** dialog box to format the index.

7 Click **OK**.

# Glossary

**absolute**   The position of a picture that is determined by measurements you set.

**attributes**   The characteristics that change the appearance of text. You can change the appearance of text by making it bold, italic, or colored.

**AutoCorrect**   A feature that corrects commonly misspelled words as you type.

**bookmark**   A location in a document that is used to mark text so that you, or your reader, can return to it quickly.

**bullet**   A small graphic, such as a large dot, that sets off an item in a list.

**cell**   The intersection of a row and a column in a datasheet.

**character style**   A style for selected words and lines of text within a paragraph.

**charts**   Graphics that use lines, bars, columns, pie slices, or other markers to represent numbers and other values.

**check box form field**   A form field that lets you provide several options so that users can click one or more to indicate their choices.

**column headings**   Gray buttons across the top of a datasheet.

**comments**   Electronic notes about text or other parts of a document.

**cross-reference**   An entry that refers the reader to another entry.

**data marker**   A graphical element, such as a bar or area, in a chart that represents a value in a datasheet.

**data series**   A group of related data points in a datasheet.

**datasheet**   A numerical representation of data in cells that form rows and columns.

**data source**   A document that is combined with the main document in the mail merge process.

**data table**   A grid attached to a chart that shows the data used to create the chart.

**desktop publishing**   A process that combines text and graphics in an appealing and easy to read format, such as a report, newsletter, or book.

**destination file**   The file into which you are inserting information.

**diagram**   A visual and relational representation of information, such as an organization chart.

**digital signature**   A secure electronic stamp of authentication on a document.

**docked toolbar**   A toolbar that is attached to the edge of the Word window.

**drawing canvas**    An area that contains drawing shapes and pictures.

**drop-down form field**    A form field that lets you provide predefined answers so that users are limited to specified choices.

**embedded object**    An object that becomes part of the destination file and is no longer a part of the source file.

**endnotes**    References or citations that appear at the end of a document.

**entry**    An index listing.

**file**    Information, such as a document, that a program saves with a unique name.

**file format**    The way that a program stores a file so that the program can open it.

**fill effect**    The pattern, color, or texture in a chart element.

**filter**    To exclude records from a data list in a mail merge.

**filtered Web page**    An optimized Web page.

**floating toolbar**    A toolbar that is not attached to an edge of the Word window.

**font**    *See* font typeface.

**font effects**    A way to emphasize text using formatting options, such as bold type, italics, all capital letters, or shadows.

**font size**    The size of text, usually expressed in points.

**font typeface**    A complete set of characters that uses the same design.

**footer**    The text that is printed at the bottom of each page.

**footnotes**    References or citations that appear at the end of each page.

**form field properties**    Settings that allow you to change form field attributes, such as text field length or the check box default setting.

**form fields**    Predefined places where users enter their answers to the questions on a form.

**forms**    Printed or online documents with instructions, questions, and fields (blanks) where users can enter their responses.

**formula**    A mathematical expression that performs calculations, such as adding or averaging values.

**frame**    A window region on a Web page.

**graphic**    A picture or a drawing object.

**gridlines**    Lines that appear in a chart to make it easier to view the data.

**header**    The text that is printed at the top of each page.

**HTML**   *See* Hypertext Markup Language.

**hyperlinks**   Links to a location in the same file, another file, or an HTML page that are represented by colored and underlined text or by a graphic.

**Hypertext Markup Language (HTML)**   The markup language of tags that creates Web pages.

**indent markers**   Markers along the ruler that you use to control how text wraps on the left or right side of a document.

**indented index**   An index that uses subentries on separate lines below the main entries.

**index**   A list of the topics, names, and terms used in a document along with the corresponding page numbers, which typically appears at the end of a document.

**key combination**   Two or more keys pressed at the same time that perform an action.

**landscape**   Horizontal orientation in which the page is wider than it is tall.

**legend**   A chart element that identifies the patterns or colors assigned to the data.

**link bar**   A collection of graphic or text buttons representing hyperlinks to pages in a Web site and external Web sites.

**linked object**   An object that maintains a direct link to the source file.

**links**   *See* hyperlinks.

**macro**   A recorded series of commands (keystrokes and instructions) that are treated as a single command.

**mail merge**   The process of combining a data source document and a main document to create a single merged document.

**main document**   The document that is combined with the data source in the mail merge process.

**manual page break**   A page break that you insert in a document. A manual page break appears as a dotted line across the page with the label *Page Break*.

**master document**   A document that contains a set of subdocuments.

**merge**   The process of combining a data source document and a main document to create a single merged document.

**merge fields**   Placeholders that indicate where Word inserts personalized information from a data source.

**module**   A location within a Visual Basic project where a macro is stored.

**Normal view**   The default editing view, which you use to write and edit documents.

**note separator**   The line that divides the notes from the body of the document.

**note text**   The content of the footnote or endnote.

**Object Linking and Embedding (OLE)**   A feature that allows you to insert a file created in one program into a document that was created in another program.

**Office Assistant**   A help system that answers questions, offers tips, and provides help for Microsoft Office XP program features.

**Office Clipboard**   A storage area shared by all Office programs where multiple pieces of information from several different sources are stored.

**orphan**   The first line of a paragraph printed by itself at the bottom of a page.

**Outline view**   A view that shows the structure of a document, which consists of headings and body text.

**page orientation**   The way in which a page is laid out in a printed document.

**paragraph**   Any amount of text that ends when you press the ⎡Enter⎤ key.

**paragraph styles**   Styles for entire paragraphs, including their indents, alignment, and tabs.

**Personalized menus**   Menus that adjust so that only the commands that you use most often appear on the short menus.

**picture**   A photograph, a scanned picture, a bitmap, or clip art that was created outside of Word.

**plot area**   The area that includes the data markers and the category (x) and value (y) axes in a chart.

**point**   A measurement for the size of text. A point is equal to about 1/72 of an inch.

**portrait**   Vertical orientation in which the page is taller than it is wide.

**Print Layout view**   A view that shows a document as it appears on the printed page.

**project**   An executable program that is stored in a Word document or template.

**publishing**   The process of saving a file as a Web page or Web site on a Web server for viewing on the World Wide Web or on a network.

**query**   A set of selection criteria that indicate how to filter recipients in a mail merge.

**read-only**   A setting that lets a user read or copy the file, but not change or save it.

**record**   A single set of items in a data source.

**reference mark**   A number or character in the main text of a document that indicates additional information is included in a footnote or endnote.

**relative**   The position of a picture that is determined by its relation to other specified parts of the document, such as the margin, the page, a column, or a character.

**Reviewing Pane**   A pane that shows information related to the changes and comments in a document.

**Reviewing toolbar**   A toolbar that contains buttons that let you accept and reject changes and comments.

**row headings**   Gray buttons along the left side of a datasheet.

**run-in index**   An index that lists subentries on the same line as the main entries in an index.

**section break**   A portion of a document that you can format with unique page settings, such as different margins. A section break appears as a double-dotted line across the page with the words *Section Break* and the type of section break in the middle.

**selection area**   A blank area to the left of a document's left margin that you can click to select parts of the document.

**Smart Tag**   A button that helps you control the result of certain actions, such as automatic text correction, automatic layout behavior, or copy and paste.

**soft page break**   A page break that Word inserts in a document. A soft page break appears as a dotted line across the page.

**sort**   To arrange information in a logical order.

**source file**   The original document created in the source program.

**source program**   The program that created a document that is a linked object in Word.

**spelling and grammar**   A feature that corrects errors and maintains professional writing standards.

**style**   A collection of text and paragraph formatting choices that you can apply to text throughout a document.

**Style area**   An area along the left side of a document that displays style names.

**subdocuments**   Sets of related documents that are used in master documents.

**subentry**   A subtopic index listing.

**tab leader**   An index format that separates the entry from the page number associated with it. Tab leaders can be dotted, dashed, or solid lines.

**tab stop**   A location along the ruler that you use to align text.

**Table AutoFormat**   A set of 18 predesigned table formats that include a variety of borders, colors, and attributes that will give a table a professional look.

**table of contents**   A list of the main headings and subheadings in a document along with corresponding page numbers, which typically appears at the beginning of a document.

**task pane**   A pane that allows you to access commands related to a specific task quickly without having to use menus and toolbars.

**template**   A special document that stores text, styles, formatting, macros, and page information for use in other documents.

**text form field**   A form field that lets you provide several types of text boxes so that users can enter text.

**theme**   A unified look in a document that incorporates heading and text styles.

**thesaurus**   A feature that looks up alternative words or synonyms for a word.

**Uniform Resource Locator (URL)**   A unique address for a page on the Web, such as *http://www.microsoft.com*.

**version**   A record of changes made to a document.

**watermarks**   Dimmed pictures or text that appears faintly in the background of a printed document.

**Web archive**   A Web site that saves all the elements, including text and graphics, into a single document.

**Web Layout view**   A view that shows a document as it appears as a Web page.

**Web page**   A special document in HTML designed to be viewed in a Web browser.

**Web server**   A storage location where you save a Web site or Web page for viewing on the World Wide Web or on a network.

**Web site**   A collection of Web pages with navigation tools and a designed theme.

**widow**   The last line of a paragraph printed by itself at the top of a page.

**WordArt**   A feature that allows you to change the shape and appearance of text in a document.

**word processing**   A process by which you create, edit, and produce text documents.

**word wrap**   The movement of text to the next line when typing goes beyond the right margin.

**workgroup templates**   Templates shared over a network.

**XE**   An index entry field code that defines the text and page number for an index entry and other options, such as a subentry text.

# Index

## Symbols

# D

**data**
copying, 86–87, 124
*See also* chart data; records (in data documents); table data
**data documents (data sources), 187–188, 277**
editing, 191–193, 268–269
field names, 190
filtering records, 188–189, 194, 196, 269
merging with main documents, 189, 200–203, 269–270
*See also* merge documents
selecting, 188, 191, 268
sorting records, 194, 195, 269
*See also* mailing lists
**Data Form dialog box, 192**
**data markers (in charts), 118, 277**
**data series (in charts), 119, 277**
formatting, 121
labeling, 122
**data series labels, creating, 122**
**data sources. See data documents**
**data tables (for charts), 119, 277**
inserting, 122–123
**datasheets, 113–114, 277**
and charts, 113
displaying, 114
editing text, 117
hiding, 123
moving the insertion point, 117
**Date fields, 210**
*See also* text form fields
**dates, inserting, 29, 32**
**decimal tab, 34**
**default file location, changing, 49**
**Del key, deleting characters, 15**
**deleting**
comments, 139, 141, 263
footnotes/endnotes, 228, 230
index entries, 251
macros, 183, 185
styles, 59
text, 15
*See also* removing
**demoting headings, 237**
**deselecting**
cells in tables, 80
charts, 123
objects, 110
text, 14

**desktop-publishing documents, 277**
**destination files, 87, 277**
**Diagram Gallery dialog box, 94**
**diagrams, 93, 277**
creating org charts, 94–96, 260
**dialog boxes, moving, 30**
**dictionaries**
custom, adding words to, 64, 67
online dictionary, 66
**Digital Signature dialog box, 165, 166–167**
**digital signatures, 151, 183, 277**
attaching, 163–167, 265
**docked toolbars, 174, 277**
**Document Map, navigating documents via headings, 234, 235, 274**
**Document Recovery task pane, 9**
**document window(s), 2**
closing, 13, 256
displaying, 13
information icon, 70
**documents**
adding to master documents, 236
attaching templates to, 46
blank, 4, 255
browsing, 11, 13
for footnotes, 228, 229–230, 272–273
changes in. *See* revisions
comparing reviewed versions, 136, 137, 263
creating, 6–9, 10
blank, 4, 255
from templates, 46, 48–49
current document indicator, 12
data sources. *See* data documents
displaying in browsers, 153–155
formatting. *See* formatting documents
information about, displaying, 10
linking, 153, 157–159
main. *See* main documents
master. *See* master documents
merging data documents with main documents, 189, 200–203, 269–270
*See also* merge documents
merging reviewed versions, 136–139, 262
moving the insertion point, 10–11, 12
naming, 9

navigating. *See* navigating documents
opening, 10, 12, 255
with passwords, 145–146
paginating, 50, 53–54, 251
passwords. *See* passwords (for documents)
previewing, 51, 69, 70–71, 258
merge documents, 189, 202
as Web pages, 152
printing, 69, 71–73, 258
merge documents, 189
program buttons, 11–12
proofreading, 63–71
protecting. *See* protecting documents
read-only setting, 144, 280
recovered versions, 9
repagination of, 50
repairing, 12
reviewing. *See* reviewing documents
saving, 6, 8–10, 255
to floppy disks, 8
in other file formats, 10, 255
reviewed versions, 132, 135
time interval, 9
as Web pages, 152, 155–156, 264
saving mailing labels in, 207
scrolling, 11, 12–13
selecting, 15
selection area, 14
sending via e-mail, 147–149, 264
signing, 163, 166–167, 266
Style area, 281
subdocuments. *See* subdocuments
switching between, 12
types, 188, 191
*See also* data documents; forms (form documents); main documents; master documents; merge documents; subdocuments
version information, 10
views. *See* views (of documents)
**dotted lines under words/phrases, 7, 29**
**double-line borders, creating, 28–29**
**dragging text, 16**
**drawing canvas, 107, 108, 278**
moving, 110
resizing, 111

## G

## H

# Perspection

*Microsoft Word 2002 Step by Step* has been created by the professional trainers and writers at Perspection, Inc. to the exacting standards you've come to expect from Microsoft Press. Together, we are pleased to present this training book.

Perspection, Inc. is a software training company committed to providing information and training to help people use software more effectively in order to communicate, make decisions, and solve problems. Perspection writes and produces software training books, and develops multimedia and Web-based training. This book incorporates Perspection's training expertise to ensure that you'll receive the maximum return on your time. With this straightforward, easy-to-read training tool, you'll get the information and training you need to get the job done. You'll focus on the skills that increase productivity while working at your own pace and convenience.

We invite you to visit the Perspection Web site at:

*www.perspection.com*

Microsoft Press, the book publishing division of Microsoft Corporation, is the leading publisher of information about Microsoft products and services. Microsoft Press is dedicated to providing the highest quality computer books and multimedia training and reference tools that make using Microsoft software easier, more enjoyable, and more productive.

## Acknowledgments

The task of creating any book requires the talents of many hard-working people pulling together to meet impossible deadlines and untold stresses. We'd like to thank the outstanding team responsible for making this book possible: the project manager, Marjorie Hunt; the writers, Jane Pedicini, Jill Batistick, and Ed Dille; the editor, Lisa Ruffolo; the technical editors, Kristy Thielen and Melinda Lankford; the production team, Tracy Teyler, Beth Teyler, and Virginia Felix-Simmons; and the indexer, Michael Brackney.

At Microsoft Press, we'd like to thank Kong Cheung for the opportunity to undertake this project, Jenny Benson for her editorial expertise and support during the writing and production of the book, and Barbara Norfleet and Paula Gorelick for their FrameMaker training and "tricks of the trade."

Perspection

# Self-paced
# *training*
## *that works*
## *as hard as you do!*

Information-packed STEP BY STEP courses are the most effective way to teach yourself how to complete tasks with Microsoft® Office XP. Numbered steps and scenario-based lessons with practice files on CD-ROM make it easy to find your way while learning tasks and procedures. Work through every lesson or choose your own starting point—with STEP BY STEP modular design and straightforward writing style, *you* drive the instruction. And the books are constructed with lay-flat binding so you can follow the text with both hands at the keyboard. Select STEP BY STEP titles also provide complete, cost-effective preparation for the Microsoft Office User Specialist (MOUS) credential. It's an excellent way for you or your organization to take a giant step toward workplace productivity.

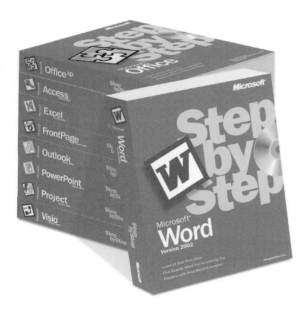

- **Microsoft Office XP Step by Step**
  ISBN 0-7356-1294-3

- **Microsoft Word Version 2002 Step by Step**
  ISBN 0-7356-1295-1

- **Microsoft Excel Version 2002 Step by Step**
  ISBN 0-7356-1296-X

- **Microsoft PowerPoint® Version 2002 Step by Step**
  ISBN 0-7356-1297-8

- **Microsoft Outlook® Version 2002 Step by Step**
  ISBN 0-7356-1298-6

- **Microsoft FrontPage® Version 2002 Step by Step**
  ISBN 0-7356-1300-1

- **Microsoft Access Version 2002 Step by Step**
  ISBN 0-7356-1299-4

- **Microsoft Project Version 2002 Step by Step**
  ISBN 0-7356-1301-X

- **Microsoft Visio® Version 2002 Step by Step**
  ISBN 0-7356-1302-8

*Microsoft*®

mspress.microsoft.com

# Target your
# *solution* *and fix it*
# *yourself—fast!*

**W**hen you're stuck with a computer problem, you need answers right now. *Troubleshooting* books can help. They'll guide you to the source of the problem and show you how to solve it right away. Use easy diagnostic flowcharts to identify problems. Get ready solutions with clear, step-by-step instructions. Go to quick-access charts with *Top 20 Problems* and *Prevention Tips*. Find even more solutions with handy *Tips* and *Quick Fixes*. Walk through the remedy with plenty of screen shots to keep you on track. Find what you need fast with the extensive, easy-reference index. And keep trouble at bay with the Troubleshooting Web site—updated every month with new FREE problem-solving information. Get the answers you need to get back to business fast with *Troubleshooting* books.

# Work smarter
## as you experience
# *Office XP*
## *inside out!*

**Y**ou know your way around the Office suite. Now dig into Microsoft Office XP applications and *really* put your PC to work! These supremely organized references pack hundreds of timesaving solutions, troubleshooting tips and tricks, and handy workarounds in concise, fast-answer format. All of this comprehensive information goes deep into the nooks and crannies of each Office application and accessory. Discover the best and fastest ways to perform everyday tasks, and challenge yourself to new levels of Office mastery with INSIDE OUT titles!

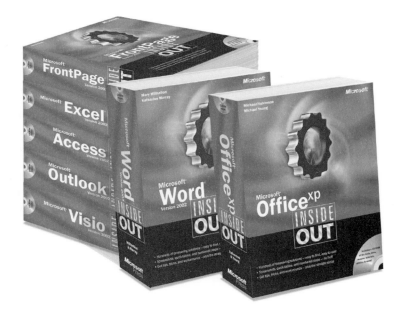

- MICROSOFT® OFFICE XP INSIDE OUT

- MICROSOFT WORD VERSION 2002 INSIDE OUT

- MICROSOFT EXCEL VERSION 2002 INSIDE OUT

- MICROSOFT OUTLOOK® VERSION 2002 INSIDE OUT

- MICROSOFT ACCESS VERSION 2002 INSIDE OUT

- MICROSOFT FRONTPAGE® VERSION 2002 INSIDE OUT

- MICROSOFT VISIO® VERSION 2002 INSIDE OUT

**mspress.microsoft.com**

Get a **Free**
e-mail newsletter, updates,
special offers, links to related books,
and more when you
## register on line!

**R**egister your Microsoft Press® title on our Web site and you'll get a FREE subscription to our e-mail newsletter, *Microsoft Press Book Connections.* You'll find out about newly released and upcoming books and learning tools, online events, software downloads, special offers and coupons for Microsoft Press customers, and information about major Microsoft® product releases. You can also read useful additional information about all the titles we publish, such as detailed book descriptions, tables of contents and indexes, sample chapters, links to related books and book series, author biographies, and reviews by other customers.

## Registration is easy. Just visit this Web page and fill in your information:

*http://mspress.microsoft.com/register*

**Microsoft**®

---

## Proof of Purchase

Use this page as proof of purchase if participating in a promotion or rebate offer on this title. Proof of purchase must be used in conjunction with other proof(s) of payment such as your dated sales receipt—see offer details.

### *Microsoft® Word Version 2002 Step by Step*
0-7356-1295-1

**CUSTOMER NAME**

Microsoft Press, PO Box 97017, Redmond, WA  98073-9830

# MICROSOFT LICENSE AGREEMENT

Book Companion CD

**IMPORTANT—READ CAREFULLY:** This Microsoft End-User License Agreement ("EULA") is a legal agreement between you (either an individual or an entity) and Microsoft Corporation for the Microsoft product identified above, which includes computer software and may include associated media, printed materials, and "online" or electronic documentation ("SOFTWARE PROD-UCT"). Any component included within the SOFTWARE PRODUCT that is accompanied by a separate End-User License Agreement shall be governed by such agreement and not the terms set forth below. By installing, copying, or otherwise using the SOFTWARE PRODUCT, you agree to be bound by the terms of this EULA. If you do not agree to the terms of this EULA, you are not authorized to install, copy, or otherwise use the SOFTWARE PRODUCT; you may, however, return the SOFTWARE PROD-UCT, along with all printed materials and other items that form a part of the Microsoft product that includes the SOFTWARE PRODUCT, to the place you obtained them for a full refund.

## SOFTWARE PRODUCT LICENSE

The SOFTWARE PRODUCT is protected by United States copyright laws and international copyright treaties, as well as other intellectual property laws and treaties. The SOFTWARE PRODUCT is licensed, not sold.

1. **GRANT OF LICENSE.** This EULA grants you the following rights:

   a. **Software Product.** You may install and use one copy of the SOFTWARE PRODUCT on a single computer. The primary user of the computer on which the SOFTWARE PRODUCT is installed may make a second copy for his or her exclusive use on a portable computer.

   b. **Storage/Network Use.** You may also store or install a copy of the SOFTWARE PRODUCT on a storage device, such as a network server, used only to install or run the SOFTWARE PRODUCT on your other computers over an internal network; however, you must acquire and dedicate a license for each separate computer on which the SOFTWARE PRODUCT is installed or run from the storage device. A license for the SOFTWARE PRODUCT may not be shared or used concurrently on different computers.

   c. **License Pak.** If you have acquired this EULA in a Microsoft License Pak, you may make the number of additional copies of the computer software portion of the SOFTWARE PRODUCT authorized on the printed copy of this EULA, and you may use each copy in the manner specified above. You are also entitled to make a corresponding number of secondary copies for portable computer use as specified above.

   d. **Sample Code.** Solely with respect to portions, if any, of the SOFTWARE PRODUCT that are identified within the SOFT-WARE PRODUCT as sample code (the "SAMPLE CODE"):

      i. **Use and Modification.** Microsoft grants you the right to use and modify the source code version of the SAMPLE CODE, *provided* you comply with subsection (d)(iii) below. You may not distribute the SAMPLE CODE, or any modified version of the SAMPLE CODE, in source code form.

      ii. **Redistributable Files.** Provided you comply with subsection (d)(iii) below, Microsoft grants you a nonexclusive, royalty-free right to reproduce and distribute the object code version of the SAMPLE CODE and of any modified SAMPLE CODE, other than SAMPLE CODE, or any modified version thereof, designated as not redistributable in the Readme file that forms a part of the SOFTWARE PRODUCT (the "Non-Redistributable Sample Code"). All SAMPLE CODE other than the Non-Redistributable Sample Code is collectively referred to as the "REDISTRIBUTABLES."

      iii. **Redistribution Requirements.** If you redistribute the REDISTRIBUTABLES, you agree to: (i) distribute the REDISTRIBUTABLES in object code form only in conjunction with and as a part of your software application product; (ii) not use Microsoft's name, logo, or trademarks to market your software application product; (iii) include a valid copyright notice on your software application product; (iv) indemnify, hold harmless, and defend Microsoft from and against any claims or lawsuits, including attorney's fees, that arise or result from the use or distribution of your software application product; and (v) not permit further distribution of the REDISTRIBUTABLES by your end user. Contact Microsoft for the applicable royalties due and other licensing terms for all other uses and/or distribution of the REDISTRIBUTABLES.

2. **DESCRIPTION OF OTHER RIGHTS AND LIMITATIONS.**

   • **Limitations on Reverse Engineering, Decompilation, and Disassembly.** You may not reverse engineer, decompile, or disassemble the SOFTWARE PRODUCT, except and only to the extent that such activity is expressly permitted by applicable law notwithstanding this limitation.

   • **Separation of Components.** The SOFTWARE PRODUCT is licensed as a single product. Its component parts may not be separated for use on more than one computer.

   • **Rental.** You may not rent, lease, or lend the SOFTWARE PRODUCT.

   • **Support Services.** Microsoft may, but is not obligated to, provide you with support services related to the SOFTWARE PRODUCT ("Support Services"). Use of Support Services is governed by the Microsoft policies and programs described in the user manual, in "online" documentation, and/or in other Microsoft-provided materials. Any supplemental software code provided to you as part of the Support Services shall be considered part of the SOFTWARE PRODUCT and subject to the terms and conditions of this EULA. With respect to technical information you provide to Microsoft as part of the Support Services, Microsoft may use such information for its business purposes, including for product support and development. Microsoft will not utilize such technical information in a form that personally identifies you.

- **Software Transfer.** You may permanently transfer all of your rights under this EULA, provided you retain no copies, you transfer all of the SOFTWARE PRODUCT (including all component parts, the media and printed materials, any upgrades, this EULA, and, if applicable, the Certificate of Authenticity), **and** the recipient agrees to the terms of this EULA.

- **Termination.** Without prejudice to any other rights, Microsoft may terminate this EULA if you fail to comply with the terms and conditions of this EULA. In such event, you must destroy all copies of the SOFTWARE PRODUCT and all of its component parts.

3. **COPYRIGHT.** All title and copyrights in and to the SOFTWARE PRODUCT (including but not limited to any images, photographs, animations, video, audio, music, text, SAMPLE CODE, REDISTRIBUTABLES, and "applets" incorporated into the SOFTWARE PRODUCT) and any copies of the SOFTWARE PRODUCT are owned by Microsoft or its suppliers. The SOFTWARE PRODUCT is protected by copyright laws and international treaty provisions. Therefore, you must treat the SOFTWARE PRODUCT like any other copyrighted material **except** that you may install the SOFTWARE PRODUCT on a single computer provided you keep the original solely for backup or archival purposes. You may not copy the printed materials accompanying the SOFTWARE PRODUCT.

4. **U.S. GOVERNMENT RESTRICTED RIGHTS.** The SOFTWARE PRODUCT and documentation are provided with RESTRICTED RIGHTS. Use, duplication, or disclosure by the Government is subject to restrictions as set forth in subparagraph (c)(1)(ii) of the Rights in Technical Data and Computer Software clause at DFARS 252.227-7013 or subparagraphs (c)(1) and (2) of the Commercial Computer Software—Restricted Rights at 48 CFR 52.227-19, as applicable. Manufacturer is Microsoft Corporation/One Microsoft Way/Redmond, WA 98052-6399.

5. **EXPORT RESTRICTIONS.** You agree that you will not export or re-export the SOFTWARE PRODUCT, any part thereof, or any process or service that is the direct product of the SOFTWARE PRODUCT (the foregoing collectively referred to as the "Restricted Components"), to any country, person, entity, or end user subject to U.S. export restrictions. You specifically agree not to export or re-export any of the Restricted Components (i) to any country to which the U.S. has embargoed or restricted the export of goods or services, which currently include, but are not necessarily limited to, Cuba, Iran, Iraq, Libya, North Korea, Sudan, and Syria, or to any national of any such country, wherever located, who intends to transmit or transport the Restricted Components back to such country; (ii) to any end user who you know or have reason to know will utilize the Restricted Components in the design, development, or production of nuclear, chemical, or biological weapons; or (iii) to any end user who has been prohibited from participating in U.S. export transactions by any federal agency of the U.S. government. You warrant and represent that neither the BXA nor any other U.S. federal agency has suspended, revoked, or denied your export privileges.

## DISCLAIMER OF WARRANTY

**NO WARRANTIES OR CONDITIONS.** MICROSOFT EXPRESSLY DISCLAIMS ANY WARRANTY OR CONDITION FOR THE SOFTWARE PRODUCT. THE SOFTWARE PRODUCT AND ANY RELATED DOCUMENTATION ARE PROVIDED "AS IS" WITHOUT WARRANTY OR CONDITION OF ANY KIND, EITHER EXPRESS OR IMPLIED, INCLUDING, WITHOUT LIMITATION, THE IMPLIED WARRANTIES OF MERCHANTABILITY, FITNESS FOR A PARTICULAR PURPOSE, OR NONINFRINGEMENT. THE ENTIRE RISK ARISING OUT OF USE OR PERFORMANCE OF THE SOFTWARE PRODUCT REMAINS WITH YOU.

**LIMITATION OF LIABILITY.** TO THE MAXIMUM EXTENT PERMITTED BY APPLICABLE LAW, IN NO EVENT SHALL MICROSOFT OR ITS SUPPLIERS BE LIABLE FOR ANY SPECIAL, INCIDENTAL, INDIRECT, OR CONSEQUENTIAL DAMAGES WHATSOEVER (INCLUDING, WITHOUT LIMITATION, DAMAGES FOR LOSS OF BUSINESS PROFITS, BUSINESS INTERRUPTION, LOSS OF BUSINESS INFORMATION, OR ANY OTHER PECUNIARY LOSS) ARISING OUT OF THE USE OF OR INABILITY TO USE THE SOFTWARE PRODUCT OR THE PROVISION OF OR FAILURE TO PROVIDE SUPPORT SERVICES, EVEN IF MICROSOFT HAS BEEN ADVISED OF THE POSSIBILITY OF SUCH DAMAGES. IN ANY CASE, MICROSOFT'S ENTIRE LIABILITY UNDER ANY PROVISION OF THIS EULA SHALL BE LIMITED TO THE GREATER OF THE AMOUNT ACTUALLY PAID BY YOU FOR THE SOFTWARE PRODUCT OR US$5.00; PROVIDED, HOWEVER, IF YOU HAVE ENTERED INTO A MICROSOFT SUPPORT SERVICES AGREEMENT, MICROSOFT'S ENTIRE LIABILITY REGARDING SUPPORT SERVICES SHALL BE GOVERNED BY THE TERMS OF THAT AGREEMENT. BECAUSE SOME STATES AND JURISDICTIONS DO NOT ALLOW THE EXCLUSION OR LIMITATION OF LIABILITY, THE ABOVE LIMITATION MAY NOT APPLY TO YOU.

## MISCELLANEOUS

This EULA is governed by the laws of the State of Washington USA, except and only to the extent that applicable law mandates governing law of a different jurisdiction.

Should you have any questions concerning this EULA, or if you desire to contact Microsoft for any reason, please contact the Microsoft subsidiary serving your country, or write: Microsoft Sales Information Center/One Microsoft Way/Redmond, WA 98052-6399.

# New Features in Word 2002

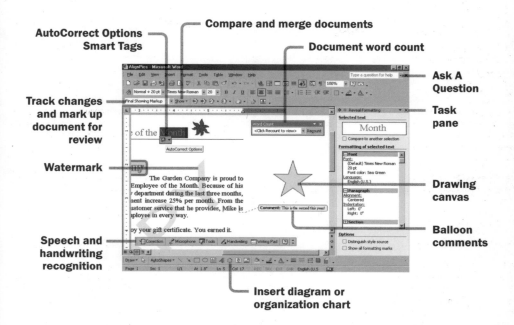

**AutoCorrect Options Smart Tags**

**Compare and merge documents**

**Document word count**

**Ask A Question**

**Track changes and mark up document for review**

**Task pane**

**Watermark**

**Drawing canvas**

**Speech and handwriting recognition**

**Balloon comments**

**Insert diagram or organization chart**

---

# Common Keyboard Shortcuts

| | |
|---|---|
| `Ctrl` + `Enter` | Create a new page |
| `Shift` + `Enter` | Insert a line break |
| `Ctrl` + `C` | Copy the selected text or object |
| `Ctrl` + `X` | Cut the selected text or object |
| `Ctrl` + `V` | Paste text or an object |
| `Ctrl` + `Z` | Undo the last action |
| `Ctrl` + `Y` | Redo the last action |
| `Ctrl` + `1` | Single-space lines |
| `Ctrl` + `2` | Double-space lines |
| `Ctrl` + `Shift` + `Space` | Create a nonbreaking space |
| `Ctrl` + `Shift` + `-` | Create a nonbreaking hyphen |
| `Ctrl` + `B` | Apply bold formatting |
| `Ctrl` + `I` | Apply italic formatting |
| `Ctrl` + `U` | Underline text |
| `F7` | Check spelling |

**To display and change formatting of selected text**

1  Select the text you want to format.
2  On the **Format** menu, click **Reveal Formatting**.
3  In the **Reveal Formatting** task pane, click a formatting option, and then change the text formatting settings.

**To create a bulleted or numbered list**

1  Select the lines of text you want to change to a bulleted or numbered list.
2  On the Formatting toolbar, click the **Bullets** button or the **Numbering** button.

**To create a document using a template**

1  On the **View** menu, click **Task Pane**.
2  In the **New Document** task pane, click **General Templates**.
3  Click a tab, click a template, and then click **OK**.

**To check spelling and grammar**

1  On the Standard toolbar, click the **Spelling and Grammar** button.
2  Use the buttons in the **Spelling and Grammar** dialog box to ignore or change selected text or to add new words to Word's dictionary, and then click **OK**.

**To print all or part of a document**

1  On the **File** menu, click **Print**.
2  In the **Print** dialog box, click the **Print what** down arrow, click the item you want to print, and then click OK.

**To print envelopes or labels**

1  On the **Tools** menu, point to **Letters and Mailings**, and then click **Envelopes and Labels**.
2  Click the **Envelopes** tab or the **Labels** tab.
3  Click **Options**, select the envelope or label type you want to use, click **OK**, and then click **Print**.

**To insert a table**

1  On the **Table** menu, point to **Insert**, and then click **Table**.
2  Type the number of columns and rows to use.
3  Select an AutoFit behavior or click **AutoFormat** to choose a table style, and then click **OK**.

**To add a border**

1  Select the text or table to which you want to add a border.
2  On the **Format** menu, click **Borders and Shading**, and then click the **Borders** tab.
3  In the **Setting** area, click a border style, and then click **OK**.

**To insert clip art**

1  On the **View** menu, point to **Toolbars**, and then click **Drawing**.
2  On the Drawing toolbar, click the **Insert Clip Art** button.
3  In the **Insert Clip Art** task pane, type a name in the **Search text** box, and then click **Search**.
4  In the Results area, click a clip art image.
5  Click the **Close** button in the task pane.

**To draw a shape**

1  On the Drawing toolbar, click a shape button (**Oval**, **Rectangle**, or one on the **AutoShapes** menu).
2  In the Drawing canvas, drag to draw a shape.

**To track changes**

1  On the **View** menu, point to **Toolbars**, and then click **Reviewing**.
2  On the Reviewing toolbar, click the **Track Changes** button.

**To review or insert a comment**

1  In **Web Layout** view or **Print Layout** view, on the **View** menu, click **Markup**.
2  On the Reviewing toolbar, click the **Next** button to review comments or click the **New Comment** button and type text to insert a comment.

**To save a document as a Web page**

1  On the **File** menu, click **Save as Web Page**.
2  In the **File name** box, type a name.
3  Click the **Save as type** down arrow, click a Web page type, and click **Save**.

**To create a form letter**

1  On the **Tools** menu, point to **Letters and Mailings**, and then click **Mail Merge Wizard**.
2  In the **Mail Merge** task pane, select a document type, and then click **Next**.
3  Follow the wizard's instructions to complete the process, and then click the **Close** button in the task pane.